D0646010

Another Quiet American

Allen and Bounheng,

Best wishes,

Brett

Another Quiet American

Stories of Life in Laos

Brett Dakin

ASIA BOOKS

Published and Distributed by
Asia Books Co. Ltd.,
5 Sukhumvit Road Soi 61,
PO Box 40,
Bangkok 10110,
Thailand.
Tel: (66) 0-2 715-9000 ext. 3202–4
Fax: (66)0-2 714-2799
E-mail: information@asiabooks.com
Website: asiabooks.com < http:asiabooks.com >

Typeset by COMSET Limited Partnership.
Printed by Darnsutha Press Ltd.

ISBN 974-8303-68-3

Contents

CONTENTS

Author's Note

This is a work of non-fiction. All events described within these pages took place, and each character you will meet is real. In order to protect their identities, however, I have changed most people's names. Open discussion of political issues—let alone direct criticism of the government—is prohibited in Laos, which has no free press. During my time there, I never revealed that I was writing about my life and the people in it. I apologize in advance to anyone who may feel betrayed by the publication of this book. The likelihood of any harm coming to those I knew in Laos is very small, but I have often reconsidered the wisdom of publishing this book. In the end, though, I felt that these stories of life in Laos needed to be told.

As for Lao words and phrases, I have not followed any rigid system of transliteration. The transcriptions simply reflect the way I hear and speak the language. On a related note, a disclaimer: while I do hope you will learn much about Laos and its history, politics, and culture from the book, it is not an academic work and should not be taken as such.

Thanks are due to all of my friends and colleagues who so graciously took the time to read and comment on the book. Thanks as well to Princeton-in-Asia for getting me to Laos in the first place. Above all, thanks to my parents, without whose steadfast support over the years this project—as with so much else—would not have been possible.

Part I

Remembering

I want to remember, but sometimes it's hard. Hard, even, to imagine I was ever there. It seems so far away, sometimes. So far from this life.

As I sit at my desk in Cambridge, Massachusetts, I try to remember. It is bitterly cold outside, and there are only a few more hours of sunlight left in the day. Relieved to be in my room, sheltered from the winds that whip against my windows, I let the steam from my tea rise and warm my lips. And I try to remember. I try to recall each detail of my life in Laos. The delicate bell of the fruit vendor, who pushed his cart of fresh pineapple and sugar cane down the street past my bedroom window each morning. The heat that at first I couldn't stand, but which eventually I came to welcome, even to need. The thick coating of dust from the city's roads that covered my body, and which at the end of the day I had to scrape off my eyelids and from behind my ears. The warm, fetid smell of mud

3

just beyond my doorstep after a welcome rain. I want to remember it all, to sense it once again, but I feel the details slipping away.

From inside this old brick building, I'm protected from the frost outside, but it still takes a bit of work. I am easily distracted. The cars on Massachusetts Avenue fight their way past each other, blowing their horns in frustration. No one in Laos used their horns, I remember now. In Vientiane, the traffic was so light, the vehicles so few, that the horn rarely struck me as necessary. The button on my Honda Dream never worked, but it never mattered. The frigid weather (and people) here, the rigid order of life, the relentless traffic on the streets: it all seems so far removed from my life in Laos.

And I often find myself wondering: was it real? Was I ever there?

Sometimes music helps to bring it back. I place a recording of traditional Lao music in my stereo, turn out the lights, put on the headphones, and listen. I let the insistent beat and soothing tone of the singer's voice wash over me. Soon, I lose myself in his poetic words. They recount a poor young man's failure to win the love he longs for:

I only ask you, beautiful young woman,
To help me construct the basis for love
Because I have never been able
To reveal words of love like this before.

It is New Year's Eve, he sings, the most joyful day of the year, and yet still she ignores him. The oak paneling and nineteenth-century plumbing that surround me fade away, and I once again feel the humidity of the night air in Vientiane. It is a humidity you can't escape, one you learn not to fight. You learn instead to let it embrace you, even to draw you in. And it soon becomes a source of comfort. I am walking from my house in Vientiane to the Lane Xang Hotel, near the banks of the Mekong, for a wedding reception, and I can hear the music already. I don't know the bride and groom well, but this isn't unusual. Weddings are grand, festive events in Laos, not intimate affairs limited to close friends. As I come closer, the canopy of Christmas lights that hangs above the dance floor near the hotel's swimming pool, one of only four in the city, comes into view.

There are days when, near dawn
I languish from love of you.
I'm nearly exploding with worry;
I've admired you emptily for a long time.

At the wedding reception now, I am dancing the *lamvong*, Laos' traditional dance, and it's real once again. Across from me, a Lao woman—a friend from work, perhaps, not a lover—dances with effortless grace. She scarcely moves, yet she leaves me breathless. She is at once impossibly beautiful and entirely beyond my reach. Her elegant yet tightly constrained movements put me and my clumsy attempts to shame. The music that fills my musty dormitory room lifts me up and away from Cambridge. I no longer need to resort to leafing through old photographs and imagining a past long gone. No longer a distant daydream that occasionally interrupts interminable lectures on administrative law, Laos is real. I am there.

Suddenly, a police siren outside pierces the music. I am jolted out of my thoughts, and transported back to this life. Laos is accessible, it seems, but never for very long. It remains, like my dance partner that night in Vientiane, just out of reach.

In 1997, I was a senior at Princeton, and graduation loomed on the horizon. Laos was the last thing on my mind. In a few months I would be released from the comfortable embrace of university, and would have to fend for myself. I had done well, and plenty of avenues were available to soothe my uncertainty about the future: the lucrative world of investment banking and management consulting; Internet start-ups which at that hopeful time still promised to be snapped up; an extended lease on student life at graduate school. But none of these options felt quite right. While my classmates marched off to interviews in suits and ties, I moved in the opposite direction. I felt the need to get away from a world of rankings and Top Ten lists—to escape the endless talk of first quartiles, second tiers, highest salaries, and lowest quality of life. After nearly two decades of uninterrupted formal education, I was ready for a break. I wanted to do some learning outside of the classroom—before someone sat me right back down in a conference room. What I wanted couldn't be ranked.

I was also looking for a challenge. Without having done a thing to deserve it, I had been born into a life of comfort and privilege. I had grown up in London, New York, and Washington, D.C., and had been educated in elite, private institutions just about every step of the way. I was grateful, of course, for all that I'd been given, and proud that I'd been able to succeed, but I felt trapped. From behind the ivy-covered gates of my university, I was searching for something new. And I needed to get out. As an East Asian Studies major at college, I had spent time living and working in Japan; one summer, I had even worked as an aide to a member of the Japanese parliament in Tokyo, which certainly had its moments. Sharing the microphone at a karaoke bar with a Japanese politician—a middle-aged woman who had once been a national entertainment sensation as a member of an all-female, all-drag singing group—had definitely been an experience. But I hadn't lived for more than a few months at a time in Asia, and I had never lived in a developing country.

My parents had served as Peace Corps volunteers as part of the first group ever to serve in Kenya, and their experience decades ago remained a central part of our family's history. My parents had hardly solved Kenya's woes back then—and, I felt, the Peace Corps had probably created more problems in the developing world than it had addressed during its thirty-year existence—but their awareness of what life was like in a place so different from their home had always struck me as integral to their approach to the world. I wanted to get away from my comfortable, sheltered life in the United States, it's true, but in a sense I was only emulating the choices my parents had made before me.

One morning that winter, I was strolling to class in Jones Hall, home to the East Asian Studies department. Jones was my favorite building at Princeton—and not simply because it was where I spent most of my time. A small, gothic gem in the center of the campus, it had once housed Princeton's famed Mathematics department. (Professor Einstein's office was in Room 112.) Mathematics had long since moved out of Jones and into a large, modern high-rise building to the west, leaving Jones to those of us who, by the time we were seniors in college, could barely complete our multiplication tables. I felt comfortable in the dimly lit halls and classrooms, surrounded by my Japanese and Chinese language instructors, Asian history and literature professors, and fellow students of the region. Our department head, Professor Peterson, was firmly ensconced in a spacious corner office on the first floor. He spent his days editing works on Chinese intellectual history, pausing every so often, I imagine, to ponder once again a key passage from the writings of Confucius or Mencius. Whenever I passed his office, I could always count on seeing his dog sprawled out on a rug just in front of the desk. Oblivious to the students and administrators who drifted in and out of his office throughout the day, Professor Peterson's dog didn't have to worry about her future.

That day, I must not have been in much of a hurry either, for as I made my way to class, a sign on the hallway bulletin board caught my eye. It advertised the Princeton-in-Asia program, which offered recent graduates the opportunity to work in Asia for a year or so. I had known about the program, of course, but most of the jobs I'd heard about were English-teaching positions in high schools and colleges in China and Japan, places I'd already studied and visited. The prospect of returning didn't interest me. What I did find intriguing though, was a small announcement, buried among a sea of others, for a possible job opening—in Laos.

The opening was for a language and marketing consultant at the National Tourism Authority of the Lao People's Democratic Republic, or Lao PDR. The National Tourism Authority, or NTA, was the Lao government's central office for tourism development, planning, and promotion, and was located in Vientiane, the capital. That's about all the detail the job notice contained, and a conversation with the staff inside the program office didn't reveal much more. They told me that Princeton-in-Asia had never before sent anyone to Laos, and, in fact, they weren't even sure the job really existed. They had little idea of what the experience would be like, and couldn't guarantee me anything. As for money, the Lao government wouldn't

7

be paying me anything, but Princeton-in-Asia would put up enough for housing and food. I was on my own for travel and other expenses.

At that point, I knew next to nothing about Laos. I had come across a reference or two to the country and its people in the context of the war in Vietnam. In its attempts to thwart the ascendant communist movement in Vietnam and Laos in the 1960s and 1970s, the US had dropped enormous quantities of bombs on Northern Laos. The CIA had trained and supported a guerrilla fighting force in Laos made up primarily of the Hmong, a minority ethnic group, many of whom are now living in the US. Just before handing over power to John Kennedy in 1960, President Eisenhower had told the young leader that Laos was "the key to the entire area of Southeast Asia." If Laos fell to the communists, in other words, the entire region would follow. At one point, the US Embassy in Vientiane was the largest in the world. Nevertheless, Laos is now depicted as a sideshow to the main event, a mere historical footnote. Laos' place in the world today is rarely considered—it certainly had never come up in conversation with any of my professors or classmates at Princeton.

But while I may not have known much about Laos, I already knew that I wanted the job.

————

Once I had been accepted for the position at the NTA, I sought out as much information as I could about Laos. My thirst for knowledge had an urgency that dwarfed my enthusiasm for the classes in which I was enrolled at the time. I enjoyed learning about the history of jazz and the American occupation of Japan, but my interest in these subjects lacked the immediacy of my need to learn about this small country in Southeast Asia.

Finding information about Laos wasn't easy. Not only has so little been written about the country, just a handful of films about Laos have ever been made—and they don't tend to be very good. As a first step, I went where any good student would go in search of knowledge: the library. I felt certain that the fifty-odd miles of shelves in Princeton's labyrinthine Firestone Library would hold at least a few answers to the questions I had about Laos. Sure enough, buried among the hundreds of books about Asia's major powers, I found a few about Laos. I used these in order to get a handle on the essentials of Laos' history and culture.

It didn't take long before I was hooked.

What you first notice about a map of Laos is perhaps the country's most mixed of blessings: it is entirely landlocked, sharing borders with China and Burma to the north, Thailand to the west, Vietnam to the east, and Cambodia to the south. It has had little easy access to international trade over the centuries, but at the same time has suffered from heavy-handed meddling by its neighbors and other outside powers. Constant invasions from Siam and China were a feature of the country's pre-colonial past, before the French took over and incorporated Laos into Indochina, along with Vietnam and Cambodia, in the late nineteenth century. The US' perception that Laos could not be "lost" to the communists led to intense American involvement in Laos after it achieved independence in the 1950s. And the Soviet Union showed a keen interest in Laos' well-being at the height of the Cold War. On the other hand, many today believe that Laos has an opportunity to capitalize on its location at the intersection of major trading routes in the region. In fact, this was the key, to the hopes for Laos' future, to which my soon-to-be colleagues at the NTA clung.

Laos covers an area of about the size of Great Britain, and is dominated by the Mekong River, the twelfth longest in the world. More of this great river (the "Mother of Waters") runs through Laos than any other country in Southeast Asia, most of it freely. This promises to soon change, and when I left for Laos in 1998, at least twenty or so damming schemes were in the planning stages; every week during my time there, it seemed, I would hear of another hydro-electric project "in the works." The Mekong River Valley provides Laos with its best agricultural zones, and with the fish that—along with rice—are a staple of the Lao diet. The Annamite Mountains run parallel to the Mekong through almost half the length of Laos. The terrain in the north is marked by steep and jagged mountain slopes, while the south benefits from fertile plains such as the Bolavens Plateau, where most of Laos' coffee is grown. The country's highest peak is Phu Bia, which lies just south of the

Plain of Jars, a series of lush, grassy, rolling hills in the northeast of the country.

Laos sounded like a beautiful country, but what I learned about its climate gave me pause. Like most of mainland Southeast Asia, there are three main seasons. The rainy season, marked by the arrival of the monsoon between May and July, can last until as late as November. During this season, the weather is hot, sticky, and wet; daytime temperatures average thirty degrees Celsius in the lowlands and 25 in the mountain valleys. The monsoon is followed by a dry, cool season from November until mid-February, during which the temperature in the Mekong River Valley can drop to as low as 15 degrees Celsius. The third season, dry and hot, begins in late February and lasts until May; temperatures in Vientiane can reach a blistering 38 degrees Celsius in March and April. I'd been born on a gray, misty day in London, and at Princeton that's the kind of weather I still found most comfortable. How would I survive in a climate that offered relief from the heat for a mere four months a year?

Poring over the pages of these works, I also began to learn about Laos' extraordinary ethnic diversity. The country's population stands at just under five million, and with only twenty people per square kilometer, it has one of lowest population densities in Asia (in neighboring Vietnam, it's 230 people per square kilometer). The Lao government likes to divide the population into three main ethnic categories, according to the elevation at which they live: Lao Soung (higher mountain), Lao Theung (lower mountain), and Lao Loum (lowland). About half the population are Lao Loum, 20–30 percent are Lao Theung, and 10–20 percent are Lao Soung. This is a somewhat arbitrary categorization, as there are at least 68 different ethnic groups in Laos, each with its own linguistic, religious, and culinary traditions. In general, however, the Lao Loum live in the Mekong River Valley, subsist on wet-rice cultivation, and practice Theravada Buddhism. The Lao Theung live on mid-altitude mountain slopes, are largely animist, and suffer from the lowest standard of living of the three groups. The Lao Soung live at altitudes of 1,000 meters above sea level and higher, and have traditionally relied on the cultivation of dry rice and opium. Laos' ethnic Chinese and Vietnamese communities are strong, dominating the business communities in the country's urban centers.

Buddhism is the main religion in Laos, and nearly two-thirds of the population are Theravada Buddhists. Introduced in the late thirteenth and early fourteenth centuries, Buddhism was heavily promoted by King Fa Ngum, the first monarch of the unified Lan Xang Kingdom, or the Kingdom of the Million Elephants. Theravada, or Hinayana (Lesser Vehicle) Buddhism, which originated in India and reached Laos via Southeast Asia, is the earlier and more "pure" of the two major schools.

The other school, Mahayana (Greater Vehicle), is a more expansive Buddhism practiced in North and East Asia. The objective of Theravada Buddhism is to attain nirvana, the ultimate end of physical existence—and thus, all suffering—on this earth. Most Lao Buddhists are of the Lao Loum majority, and regularly donate money and food to the monks at their local village temple in order to acquire merit and help them to achieve this end.

As I read about the country's culture and religion, I became increasingly excited about going to Laos. What intrigued me most of all, however, was a fact that didn't seem to fit the image of a deeply religious developing nation: Laos was a communist country. The Lao People's Democratic Republic, the *Satalatnalat Passatipathai Passason Lao*, was founded on December 2nd, 1975, when the communist Lao People's Revolutionary Party took over from the Royal Lao Government in the wake of America's defeat in the Vietnam War. The king was deposed, the monarchy abolished, and a new class of revolutionaries took their seats in the ministries in Vientiane. To this day, the Party remains the primary ruling institution in the country, exerting considerable influence on people's everyday lives. Power within the Party lies in the nine-member Politburo, the 49-member Central Committee, and the Permanent Secretariat. Currently, the secretary general of all three bodies is the same man, President Khamtay Siphandone—one of the original "cavemen," the revolutionaries who orchestrated the war against the Americans from their secret headquarters deep inside caves in Northern Laos. The National Assembly is the nation's sole legislative body. Representatives, almost all of whom are Party members, are elected by the public and meet once a year to rubber stamp Central Committee decisions and prime ministerial declarations. Only four independents were allowed to run in the 1997 elections,

11

when voting was compulsory and strictly monitored. There is little real opposition to the Party, and no free press.

Although most of my friends in the States couldn't understand why, this was the aspect of life in Laos that I found most alluring. They wondered why I would want to waste my time in a place where political freedom was limited, and people were being thrown in jail for speaking out. And besides, wasn't communism dead? Why bother with a failed political and economic experiment? But I wasn't another John Scott, the famed "American worker in Russia's city of steel" and author of *Behind the Urals*. Along with other Westerners enamored with the communist experiment, Scott had traveled to the Soviet Union in the 1930s to report on the great successes of collectivization and the joys of Soviet life. Of course, long before I became a college senior, Scott had been discredited and communism dismissed. I wasn't looking for a viable political alternative to free market capitalism—I was simply curious. Communism in Laos struck me as an anachronism. I could scarcely understand how it had survived in a country in which eighty percent of the population works in agriculture, fishing, and forestry. What relevance did the theories of Lenin and Marx have to a place with no workers? Where was the proletariat that would unite and overthrow the ruling elite?

After they took power in 1975, the communists did attempt to make some drastic changes in Lao society. The new government confiscated private property, collectivized farms, and sent around 40,000 citizens to re-education camps in the countryside. As a result, more than 300,000 Lao fled across the Mekong to refugee camps in Thailand, and then on to new homes in the US, France, and Australia. However, this early communist zeal resulted in colossal failure and popular resistance, and in 1979 the government abruptly reversed course and embarked on a process of reform in agriculture, monetary policy, and commodity pricing. The economies of urban centers like Vientiane had been transformed since the mid-1980s, when restrictions on private enterprise and ownership of private property began to be lifted. This turn to the West accelerated when the Soviet Union collapsed in the 1990s and Russian aid—nearly half of all foreign aid received by Vientiane in the 1980s—quickly dried up. Almost as soon as the Russian technicians and diplomats were gone, the Lao government began looking to donors like

Sweden, Japan, and Australia to replace their former benefactors. In exchange for new aid, the Lao government agreed to further liberalize economic policy, soon developing a foreign investment code that was among the more liberal in Southeast Asia. Thailand and the US now top the list of foreign investors.

But while much has changed since 1975, the Lao People's Revolutionary Party still has a firm grasp on power. After all, along with its Vietnamese counterpart, it had triumphed over the world's greatest superpower, and the Lao rightly remain proud of this victory. The cavemen had risked their lives in the great battle against the American "imperialists," and they were not about to go away now. What I knew about the legacy of America's war in Indochina—from the bomb craters that dot the landscape to the countless citizens who fall victim to mines each year—made me angry, and, as an American myself, I wondered how I'd be treated in Laos. Would I be welcomed by the people I met? Or would they challenge me to justify America's actions in their country? Would I be regarded warily and followed closely by government officials? Or would I be accepted as a friend?

While these questions might have led some to shy away, they were among the main reasons I wanted to go. I had to see what life was like in one of the world's last remaining communist nations.

I was sure I wanted to go to Laos, but I remained perplexed as to why the NTA would want to hire someone like me. After all, I didn't speak a word of Lao, a language that is very similar to Thai but has nothing at all in common with Japanese or Chinese—the languages I had spent so many hours in Jones Hall studying. I knew little about Laos and its people. And, although I had been a tourist often enough myself, I had no experience in the tourism industry. All I had going for me was an ability to speak English rather well, French much less well, and a solid liberal arts education. The fact that I had gone to good schools was of course irrelevant—as I would soon find out, no one in Laos had ever heard of any of them. So what was a communist government's department of tourism doing hiring an American just out of college?

13

The answer was to be found in the state of Laos' economy, one of the ten poorest in the world. Industry is almost non-existent, and the economy is overwhelmingly dependent on foreign aid, pumped into the country by bodies like the United Nations, the Asian Development Bank and the World Bank, and individual donor countries. The Asian economic crisis of the 1990s, particularly the currency woes in Thailand, had had a devastating effect on the Lao economy, sending the kip, Laos' currency, on a deflationary free-fall. Despite government attempts to keep it under control, Laos had a thriving black market for currency exchange and the trade of untaxed imports from Thailand and Vietnam. In 2000, Laos experienced an impressive real GDP growth of 4.5 percent, but GDP per person was stuck at a mere 272 dollars. Foreign aid accounted for half the country's budget.

By 1998, some in Laos' leadership thought they had come up with a solution to the country's economic woes: tourism. As part of its general policy of economic liberalization, the government had begun in the early 1990s to allow international visitors to enter the country. This marked a major policy shift for the regime, which had kept the country almost completely isolated from the outside world since 1975. After the decision to open up, tourism in Laos quickly took off. Between 1990 and 1997, tourism arrivals increased at an annual rate of 74 percent. In 1990, only 14,400 people visited Laos, but by 1997 this figure had risen to 463,200. The NTA's statistics indicated that revenue from tourism had grown to 73,276,904 dollars in 1997, from just 24,738,480 two years earlier. Already, Western backpackers were beginning to discover the wonders of a country that had been off-limits for more than two decades.

Nevertheless, Laos had a long way to go before it could hope to catch up with the well-developed tourism industries in Vietnam and Thailand. The number of tourists had grown, but it remained tiny in comparison to the number visiting Laos' Southeast Asian neighbors. As a result, the Lao government decided to designate the 1999–2000 season as "Visit Laos Year." And it gave the NTA primary responsibility for the campaign's success. But while government officials had indeed decided to commit to the development of tourism, they remained deeply divided about the effects tourism would inevitably have on Laos' culture and people. When

Party officials looked to Thailand, they saw a country overrun with tourists. The Lao government wanted nothing to do with the booming sex trade, rampant over-development, and environmental devastation Thailand had experienced in the post war years. They knew as well as anyone about the resort areas in Thailand that only a decade before had been pristine, but were now so crowded and polluted that even tourists were going elsewhere. Some Party officials were also deeply suspicious of the influences tourists would have on political and social stability. For many, tourism conjured up images of long-haired hippies traipsing through the countryside, searching for drugs and spreading crazy new ideas about freedom and democracy. (This image was not so far from the truth.) An influx of foreigners threatened to undo the hard work the Party had put into securing and unifying the country.

The challenge faced by my friends at the NTA was to figure out a way to develop the tourism industry in a way that would help the country get richer while at the same time preserving the delicate cultural and natural heritage that attracted visitors in the first place. So how did I fit into all this? As far as I could tell, they wanted me to help them develop the skills they would need to handle a large influx of tourists. I would teach them basic English, and help them to develop information materials about what to see and do in Laos. But I would also work with them on how to promote Laos as a destination that would attract the "right" kinds of tourists. I would be an unpaid consultant, thinking through the issues and trying in some small way to contribute to a carefully considered, healthy approach to the development of tourism over the next decade or so.

While I was excited by the prospect of working at the NTA, I knew that I'd be struggling with many of the same doubts about tourism that were troubling Laos' government officials. I had done a fair amount of traveling in my life, and I had been to places that had been completely transformed by the arrival of tourists. Often without even knowing it, tourists can easily disrupt a local economy, introduce unhealthy habits to the local community, and destroy ancient cultural traditions. I had contributed to this process myself. If successful, I knew that approaches like eco-tourism and cultural tourism had the potential to create incentives for the protection of natural resources and cultural traditions that were threatened, while at the same time helping people to earn money. But it was a difficult balance to strike. I was also doubtful of my ability to contribute anything worthwhile to the challenge that confronted the folks at the NTA. There were people out there who did tourism development consulting for a living—I would end up meeting quite a few—and I was not one of them.

I had my doubts, but when the time came for me to leave for Laos, I couldn't wait. Sure, I didn't have all the right skills, but I was prepared to use those I did have to contribute in any way I could. Above all, I was eager to learn. I saw in Laos the opportunity to gain a different perspective on the world. To experience life under one of the few remaining communist regimes around. To confront the problems of international development. And to come to terms with being an American in a land where, not so long ago, Americans were the official enemy. I was about to take a giant step across the globe, but I was ready. I was 22, and it was about time. After all, if what I really wanted was something different, I couldn't get much more different than Laos.

The General

A boss must love his subordinates;
a grandfather must cherish his grandchildren.
Lao Proverb.

When I told people in Vientiane where I worked, they usually showed little interest. The *Hongkan Tongtiow Hengsad* sounded like just another link in the endless bureaucratic chain that was Laos' government. The people I met during my first few months in Vientiane, Lao and expatriate alike, were invariably familiar with where I worked. A whitewashed concrete box that seemed to have fallen out of the sky and landed on Lan Xang Avenue, the wide central boulevard in Vientiane, my office was hard to miss.

Lan Xang Avenue had been known as the "Avenue de France" when the French had been in charge of Indochina, and even today the folks at the NTA like to refer to it as Vientiane's own Champs Elysée. Even though Vientiane had only a few paved roads—and not a single functioning cinema—when I stepped off the airplane in 1998, the parallels between Laos' capital city and Paris were not entirely misplaced. Just a few minutes away from my office, Lan Xang Avenue ends at a traffic circle resembling the Étoile, at the center of which stands the Patuxai, Vientiane's very own Arc de Triomphe. The Patuxai (Victory Gate) was completed in 1969 in memory of the Lao killed in wars before the communist victory. It's also known as the "Vertical Runway," as the project was finished with cement donated by the Americans and intended for the construction of a new airport in Vientiane. Despite the French inspiration, Buddhist imagery is present in the Lao-style moldings, and the frescoes under the arches represent scenes from the *Ramayana*.

Adjacent to the NTA was the Morning Market, or Talat Sao, a maze of individually-owned stalls selling everything from antique textiles and carvings to household appliances, from jewelry and silk to electronics. The Talat Sao was where I'd head on a weekly basis during those initial months—before I learned better—to exchange my US dollars for Lao kip. I would sheepishly duck into one of the stalls at the Talat Sao and behind a merchant's counter in order to engage in this illicit transaction. If I was lucky, my partner in crime and I would escape the notice of the stern (but sorely underpaid) policemen who patrolled the market. As the value of the kip continued its downward slide, I'd emerge from the Talat Sao with increasingly unwieldy and conspicuous piles of Lao cash.

At the other end of Lan Xang Avenue was Laos' Presidential Palace, originally built as the French governor's residence. The French took control of Laos in 1893 and administered the territory directly through the *résident supérieur* in Vientiane. After independence, King Sisavang Vong, and, later, his son Sisavang Vatthana, used the palace as a residence when visiting Vientiane from the royal seat in the city of Luang Prabang. It is now used for hosting foreign guests of the Lao government and for meetings of the presidential cabinet. The president himself does not live here; these days he lives in a far more grandiose affair near the outskirts of town. The area surrounding the Presidential Palace was once the administrative center of French rule. This neighborhood includes the French Embassy and residential complex, the Catholic church, built by the French in 1928 and still offering daily services, and a number of administrative and residential buildings.

The communists followed the lead of the post-independence royalist regime and set up shop in the buildings the French had bestowed on Vientiane. Unfortunately, the NTA wasn't nearly important enough to have made it into one of these grand edifices. A relatively recent entrant into the bureaucracy, the NTA was located in the sort of bland concrete structure that inspired neither awe nor confidence in the government of the Lao People's Democratic Republic. So, needless to say, people around town weren't all that excited by my place of employment. On the other hand, when I mentioned the name of the man for whom I worked, they could scarcely believe it. A look of astonishment would come over their faces, and they would struggle to accept the truth of what I'd said.

"You work for the General?"

"Yep. The General."

"General Cheng?"

"That's right. The General."

"Wow. The General."

The chairman of the NTA was Cheng Sayavong, a general in the Lao People's Army and, when I arrived in Laos, the richest man in the country. He was born in 1936 and grew up in Savannakhet, on the border with Thailand in Southern Laos. His distinguished military career had spanned more than four decades, reaching back to the early days of the revolutionary struggle. In 1957 and 1958, he had participated in paratrooper training at the military academy at Pau in France. His involvement in the revolutionary movement had begun soon after he returned home in 1960. He fought against the Americans alongside Khamtay Siphandone, the leader of the revolutionary forces and today the aging president of Laos.

After the communist victory in 1975, Cheng rose to the rank of colonel and was sent to the Soviet Union to attend military school in Odessa and the University of Army Engineers at the Kroutchev Academy in Moscow. In 1985, back in Laos, Cheng achieved the rank of general.

It was also in 1985 that the government put the army in charge of developing some of the country's most inaccessible areas. General Cheng was appointed president of the military-owned Phattanakhet Phoudoi Company—*phoudoi* means something like 'rural mountain'—that operated in Central Laos. Thus was the city of Lak Sao born. Lak Sao, or "Kilometer 20," sits near the border with Vietnam, southeast of Vientiane. In 1985, it didn't even exist. The region was "an abandoned forest area with tigers. There were only seven inhabitants," Cheng has said. "It was imperative to rescue these underdeveloped areas." Access roads on both the Vietnamese and Lao sides of the border were built. In 1987, Cheng constructed a village, complete with a sawmill, an orphanage for minority children, and a wildlife protection project. Soon there were more than 12,000 residents living in the prosperous commercial town.

But Cheng's rapid development scheme came at a cost. Intense logging for export to Vietnam, much of it controlled by the military, devastated the natural environment. The proposed construction of a hydro-electric dam in the area allowed loggers to clear vast areas of virgin forest before the project had even been approved. Vendors at the market at Lak Sao sold all sorts of birds, reptiles, and other critters that were no longer found in the wild.

One evening early in my stay in Laos, I met Bounthang, a university student who had grown up in a small village just a few kilometers from Lak Sao. We were at the home of Rachel, a French girl about my age—though years beyond me in sophistication and style—who taught French at the Centre de Langue Française, just across the street from the NTA. At this point, I hadn't known Rachel for very long, but there weren't very many expatriates in Vientiane (and the number of foreigners my age living there was few indeed), and I saw her all the time. It was difficult not to get to know other foreigners in Vientiane rather quickly, as everyone showed up at the same parties, ate at the same restaurants, and hung out at the same cafés. Rachel and I had had a number of awkward conversations, none of which had amounted to much. But I had been quietly pining over her since we'd first met, and in fact had come around to her house that evening hoping to find her alone.

Instead, I found Bounthang lounging about on her veranda. Bounthang had left Lak Sao as a young boy, long before General Cheng and the Phoudoi Corporation had arrived, and now studied French and civil engineering at the National University. During his vacations, he returned home to visit his parents, who were rice farmers in his childhood village. His parents had been on the receiving end of Phoudoi's grand strategy in Lak Sao: round up Lao of diverse ethnic backgrounds—most of whom had no previous experience with wet rice cultivation, a practice common only among the country's ethnic majority Lowland Lao—stick them together in farming villages, hand them heavy farming equipment, and expect them to farm. Bounthang's parents' lives hadn't improved much since he left, even as the landscape around them had been transformed. Each time he went home, Bounthang was amazed by the rapid development of his homeland—and the power of General Cheng.

"*J'ai peur de Monsieur Cheng.* He scares me," Bounthang said in perfect, unaccented French as he blew a puff of smoke into the air above us, where it disappeared into the relaxed swirls of the ceiling fan. Bounthang was not at all what one might have expected from a boy who had grown up in a village near Lak Sao. He was handsome and refined, and his fine features and easy manner disarmed even me. It soon dawned on me that Bounthang and Rachel were more than mere acquaintances. I put aside my jealousy for the moment, and tried to find out more about my boss.

"What do you think about what Cheng has done at Lak Sao?" I asked.

"The town was once successful, but there's nothing there anymore. *Il n'y a rien.* No trees, no animals. They are all at the market." Bounthang spoke of the Phoudoi experiment with disgust, but he had not allowed his cynicism about his homeland to impede his hopes for the future.

Cheng had made a bundle of money from the development of Lak Sao. In 1996, when Phoudoi's power was at its height, the company exported nearly forty million dollars worth of timber. Between 1984 and 1994, Phoudoi earned 105 million dollars, or forty percent of Laos' total export earnings. But soon the General became a bit too ostentatious for his fellow Party cadres. He built homes all over the country, flew to and from Lak Sao in his own army helicopter, and began to receive foreign guests as if he were Laos' president or prime minister. Among the international community, his dubious approach to the environment was well known: according to one American journalist, Cheng was "a singularly venal Party official known for murdering anyone who noted that the logging was an obscenity."

So, in 1997, he was transferred to a new job. That's how he ended up as chairman of the NTA. And that's how I came to know General Cheng Sayavong.

———————

The first day I showed up at the NTA, I was told that, in my capacity as a tourism development consultant and walking English resource center, I was expected to serve as the chairman's personal language tutor. In fact, I was asked politely if I might be interested in practicing conversational English with General Cheng, but I understood that I had no choice in the matter. "Practicing conversational English" with the chairman would turn out to be quite a challenge, as the man barely spoke a word. Like many Lao of his generation, his French was not bad at all, but he'd never really bothered to study English. Far more serious a problem than this, however, was the fact that Cheng was simply never around.

The chairman had no regular schedule; he was in when he was in, and out when he was out. No one in my office could tell me more. When the general's English lessons had first been discussed at the office, the staff had seemed enthusiastic. After much delay, the boss had been located and he had even agreed to a regular schedule: Tuesdays and Thursdays at one o'clock. Looking back now, I cannot remember a single lesson that took place during these appointed hours. At first, I spent many a lonely hour loitering outside his office, waiting for my star pupil to arrive. But I soon found out that in order to learn whether or not I had the slightest chance of teaching Cheng on any given day, I couldn't simply wait around. I would have to go straight to the source: the General's chauffeur, Oudom.

Oudom was a jolly fellow, short and plump. His every feature, from his face right down to his feet, was perfectly round; there wasn't a sharp edge to his body, or his personality. He remained at the General's beck and call throughout the day, using his free time to clean and polish one of Cheng's vehicles: his office car, a black sedan with tinted windows, or his personal four-wheel-drive Pajero, used for the weekend getaways at which Oudom's presence was always required. As far as I could tell, Oudom's close attention to the gleam on his boss' cars was a lost cause, as the clouds of dust that billowed through the streets of Vientiane were inescapable. No car could remain shiny for more than a few seconds in this glorious capital city. But Oudom was happy to do it. He made good money, and the job was secure.

When the General first arrived at the NTA, the government had automatically provided him with a personal secretary. One secretary wasn't enough for Cheng, however, so he brought in his own. He also surrounded himself with a number of familiar faces from his former career, military types who tended to pal around with one another at the office as if they were still back at the barracks. One was Cheng's personal assistant Khit, who was known as the office clown, a court jester of sorts who pranced about the NTA poking fun at his colleagues and provoking spontaneous laughter in anyone who happened to be nearby. There wasn't an ounce of fat on his body, and Khit's extraordinary elasticity lent itself to his unbridled antics.

But not everything about Khit was funny. Whenever he traveled outside of Vientiane, as I would later find out, he carried a handgun in his briefcase. Khit could be deadly serious. As Cheng's long-time aide, he was supposed to know his every move, and to anticipate his every need. If ever he happened to be on an urgent mission for the chairman—making a photocopy, perhaps, or typing up a document—no amount of joshing would lead Khit to crack a smile.

But even with two personal secretaries, there was only one man who ever knew where Cheng actually was. If you needed to see the chairman, you went to Oudom.

Scheduling anything with the General was a lost cause. It was an unwritten rule at the NTA that *he* scheduled meetings with *you*. This I learned well before our first lesson. One Monday afternoon, I was teaching my advanced English class—happily explaining the nuances of the word "hangover" to my students and colleagues— when Khit suddenly walked in and announced, "The chairman wants to see you. It's time to learn English."

"But I'm teaching *these* students now," I protested. I had been making progress with a sticky grammatical point just prior to our brief digression into the intricacies of being drunk in English, and I didn't want to give up now. "I thought we'd decided on a schedule."

"The General is free *now*," Khit insisted, and swiftly turning on the heels of his low-cut, black leather boots, walked out.

Exasperated, I looked to my students for support. How could the chairman decide on a whim that he wanted to study and just expect the rest of the staff to give up their only chance to practice English for the week? And what about me? I wasn't some sort of dial-a-teacher that you could simply order on demand. This was an outrage! Right? Unfortunately, my valiant call to arms fell on deaf ears. While my students were disappointed at the rude interruption, they told me not to fight. If the General wanted to learn now, he would learn now. That was the way it was going to be. Don't ask questions, Mr. Brett. My students began packing up their things, and, just like that, class was dismissed. They taught me among the more important lessons I would learn about life in Laos: whatever your own views might be about the situation, you'd better keep them to yourself. If I wanted to get anything done at the NTA, I soon realized that I'd have to put aside my personal feelings in order to avoid conflict and to please those in control. As far as General Cheng was concerned, my opinions were irrelevant.

Inside Cheng's office, I may have been the teacher, but the General was always in charge. His office suite was twice the size of the International Co-operation Unit, where I worked along with three other members of the staff. He used one room—which contained a full sofa set and two coffee tables—to greet the steady stream of guests that came to pay their respects to the General: from Taiwanese businessmen to Malaysian diplomats, everyone wanted an audience with Cheng. The second room contained his desk and a large wooden table surrounded by chairs, which was used for staff meetings—and our English lessons.

When I knocked on the General's door that first time, Khit opened it and showed me to a seat on one side of the meeting table. The General sat just opposite me. At the end of the table sat Khit, whose role it was to translate my sentences into Lao whenever the General could not understand. As the General spoke no English, this occurred after every other phrase. Of course, Khit couldn't speak

English much better than his boss, so he ended up doing a whole lot of listening. And whenever the General needed something, Khit's job was to fetch.

"How about a blackboard?" the General asked in Lao. "I can't learn without a blackboard. Who learns without a blackboard?"

"A blackboard, sir?" Khit asked.

"I don't really think we need one," I suggested helpfully.

"Get me a blackboard," the General insisted.

"Yes, sir," said Khit before scurrying out and obtaining one from the Marketing and Promotion Unit next door. After he returned, Khit erased whatever had been written on the board and propped it up against the wall just behind me.

How important could those marketing notes have been, anyway?

Khit's actions were indicative of the way most things were run at the NTA. Whatever work employees at lower levels might have been doing paled in comparison to the immediate needs of their superiors. Long before I had the chance to get to know him, I learned that the NTA was run as Cheng's personal fiefdom.

———— ———

Cheng was powerful, but in fact he struck me as a rather gentle man. I found it difficult to reconcile his reputation as the "singularly venal Party official" who inspired fear in the hearts of so many with what I knew about him. A foot shorter than I, and at 63 a bit heavy around the middle, he wore large glasses and a broad smile. He had inherited a no-nonsense, business-like approach to work from his days in the military, and had little time for pleasantries. But he invariably spoke in a low, soft tone, and only rarely raised his voice. His handshake was warm, and I felt the faint urge to give him a hug every time I saw him, as if he were my own grandfather. His wardrobe contained only one business suit, a dismal gray affair that he almost never wore. On official outings, he preferred instead to sport a casual Thai silk shirt and his favorite Nike baseball cap. It was the aura of power that surrounded the General, more than any brute force, which discouraged people from challenging him.

I was certainly taken by his power. I knew I'd been hired to help the NTA as a whole, not to serve as Cheng's personal assistant.

While Cheng's learning English certainly had the potential to be useful to the NTA, I imagined that it would end up doing far more for any personal business enterprises he might be pursuing than it would for the development of tourism. Nevertheless, the prospect of close access to a man who was so well-known—and feared—throughout the country was alluring. And so, though he made little progress in conversational English, and though it took time away from the work I was doing that was clearly of more benefit to the staff of the NTA, I continued to teach General Cheng.

One weekend, I tagged along with Cheng and his four-year old grandson—and Oudom, of course—for a trip to the General's country house on the outskirts of Vientiane. Cheng had one daughter, three sons, four grandchildren, and countless homes. In Vientiane alone, he owned at least three. This particular one was as large as a small hotel, and was situated in the middle of a vast plot that had once been a farm. But while the house was big, it was not the kind of place you would expect the wealthiest man in Laos to reside. The building itself was made of concrete, and contained little wood; the columns and railings, benches and picnic tables had been painted to look like natural teak. This was ironic indeed, considering General Cheng's deep involvement in the lumber trade at Lak Sao. You'd have thought he would have been able to get enough real wood for his own house.

The veranda out back was surrounded by a railing topped with a series of ersatz Roman figures, now completely covered in cobwebs. Weeds were already beginning to emerge from Bacchus' head. The gods presided over a man-made fish pond, a favorite accessory of the Lao upper class in Vientiane. These ponds were usually muddy and always seemed overwhelmed by expanding algae; at Cheng's house, the fish remained invisible until the General threw in some food and attracted a pack to the surface, to the delight of his grandson.

Throughout the day, in fact, Cheng's attention had been entirely consumed by his grandson. As I watched them play together outside, I realized that neither the activities of the NTA nor his private business enterprises were of the least importance to Cheng anymore. At this point in his life, all that really mattered to him was his family. He had participated in the Lao revolutionary struggle, witnessed the birth of a new nation, risen through the ranks of a young military, and helped to develop at least a part of the Lao economy. In the process, he had also amassed quite a bit of wealth, and a degree of notoriety in Laos that was unsurpassed.

As I spent more time alone with Cheng, the rage toward him that had built up inside me dissipated. My thoughts of people like Bounthang and his family, who had suffered while Cheng had prospered, and the way Cheng had made use of his position in order to further his personal wealth—all of this began to fade away. For at the end of the day, I realized, this man, as feared as he was admired by his fellow countrymen, was just another grandfather playing with his grandson. Just one more caveman discovering the joys of old age. And just another wartime hero, secure in the knowledge that he would live out the rest of his days in the comfort of continuous revolutionary struggle.

Lent's Over

It was 4:00 in the morning. Just a few minutes ago, I'd been fast asleep in my bed. Now, the insistent sound outside my window kept me awake. *Bong, bong, thwak*. Then silence. *Bong, bong, thwak*. Again, silence. Two beats of a gong, followed by a single beat of a drum. *Bong, bong, thwak*. The steady rhythm drew me out of my stupor and over to my bedroom window. I looked out at the sky above the temple just across the street. A full moon filled the early morning sky with light over Vientiane, this City of the Moon. The sun hadn't yet risen, but I knew what day it was: *Awk Phansaa*, the end of Buddhist Lent.

———

I considered myself lucky to be lying in this bed, in this house, in this neighborhood, located in the historical and spiritual center of Vientiane. I was surrounded by the most important Buddhist temples in the city—and some of the most beautiful French colonial architecture. When I'd first arrived at the airport, Khit and Oudom had driven over in the office van to meet me at the gate. I wasn't sure that someone would meet me when I arrived, and of course had no idea what that someone might look like. And while my photograph may have been sent to the NTA at some point in the months preceding my arrival in Vientiane, I'm sure it hadn't found its way to Khit's desk. But it wasn't hard at all to find each other, because at that point Vientiane International Airport didn't really have gates. Not much seemed to have changed at the airport since the early years of the Cold War, when the facility had first been built. There were only one or two flights a day. The loudspeaker announcements were intermittent, and only in Lao. The toilet door let you in, but not always back out again. On my way from the plane to the terminal, I had seen a lone farmer on a bicycle making his way slowly across the crumbling runway. I loved it.

That first day, Oudom had driven me directly from the airport to the Pangkham Guesthouse, where I spent my first week in Vientiane. The Pangkham was a nondescript Chinese-owned hotel. It certainly wasn't anything to write home about—and, ungrateful son that I was, it would be a few weeks before I wrote so much as a postcard—but its central location gave me a chance to explore the downtown. Not far from the NTA, the Pangkham was situated just off Samsenthai Road, which was the main drag running through Vientiane's prosperous commercial district. Only a decade ago, this area had been a ghost town; most stores had been shuttered and unoccupied, as the Party had yet to initiate its economic reform program or to open up Vientiane to foreign influences. But now, this was the busiest part of town, and the Thai-owned Lao Hotel Plaza around the corner from the Pangkham was a monument to the city's recent economic growth.

Along with Setthathirath and Fa Ngum roads, Samsenthai was one of Vientiane's three main thoroughfares, each of which ran perpendicular to the grand Lan Xang Avenue. A few small streets ran through the neighborhoods between Fa Ngum and Setthathirath, which was named after the king who moved the capital of the Lan Xang Kingdom from Luang Prabang to Vientiane in 1560. Chao Anou Road is the namesake of King Anouvong, the ruler of the

Kingdom of Vientiane from 1805 until 1828. Anouvong launched an ill-fated attack on neighboring Siam in 1826, prompting a fierce response that resulted in the obliteration of the city in 1828. The Siamese re-settled large numbers of Vientiane residents to North-eastern Thailand (even today, there are more ethnic Lao living in Thailand than in Laos), and captured Anouvong and brought him to Bangkok, where he died in custody.

The Siamese attack on Vientiane in 1828 left the city in ruins. When Francis Garnier, a French explorer, arrived in the city less than forty years later, he was appalled by the destruction he found on the site of the capital: "The absolute silence which reigned in the enclosure of a city that formerly was so populous and so wealthy astonished us," Garnier wrote in his *Mekong Exploration Commission Report*. "Fire and slavery after victory are, for most of the Asian races, the final outcome of a conquest. In the ruins and the solitude of Vienchan we find a striking example of this brutal destruction."

East of Chao Anou is François Nginn Road, named for a member of a late nineteenth-century Indochina exploratory mission led by Frenchman August Pavie. Born to Cambodian parents in Phnom Penh in 1856, Nginn studied at the École Coloniale in Paris and took the name François after becoming a naturalized French citizen in 1906. After working as a secretary, guide, and interpreter for Pavie—who eventually awarded him the cross of the French Legion of Honor—he entered the colonial government in Laos as an administrative and commercial officer. Nginn retired to Vientiane and died there in 1916. Of course, most people in Vientiane had no idea this street was named for Nginn. Residents of the capital city almost never used the names of streets. If you were to ask for directions, any reference to street names was futile—landmarks such as temples, restaurants, and water towers were far more helpful. Even if they did know the story of François Nginn, many in Vientiane probably preferred not to think of his contribution to their nation's history. After all, his story embodied the legacy of the colonial rule of the French and their penchant for employing other Southeast Asians to rule over the Lao, whom they considered lazy and inefficient.

The city center is dotted with temples that were destroyed when the Siamese invaded but have since been rebuilt. The *sim* of Wat Chan, located at the intersection of Chao Anou and Fa Ngum roads, houses a large, bronze seated Buddha that actually survived the destruction, in addition to a series of beautifully carved wooden panels. Wat Mixai, on Setthathirath Road, is built in the Bangkok style with a surrounding veranda. Two guardian giants stand at attention outside the heavy gates, and there is a lively elementary school on the grounds. Wat Ong Teu, just up the street, is named for the large "Heavy Buddha" found at the rear of the *sim*. Originally built by King Setthathirath in the mid-sixteenth century, it was reconstructed by the French and the Lao in the nineteenth and twentieth centuries. Home to the Buddhist Institute, a school for monks who come from around the country to study here, Wat Ong Teu is one of the most important religious centers in Laos. Given the constant flow of students through its gates, there was always a group of novices gathered outside in the gardens surrounding the temple, talking or playing cards. Wat Ong Teu was my favorite of all.

As I walked through the streets of the city center that first week, piecing together the capital's story with the aid of the occasional street name, I was overwhelmed by its rich history. In Vientiane, the past did not seem distant at all—it was immediate and palpable. In the neighborhood's varied architectural styles I could see the centuries of conflict and change, the waves of competing foreign influences that had shaped the city over the centuries. But whenever I paused for a moment on the temple grounds, I could feel the strength of Lao culture, the spirit of a way of life that has endured. It was here that I wanted to live.

So it was with the greatest delight that I came upon the small, handwritten sign in the window just along the street from Wat Ong Teu. It read, in English, "House for Rent." I stepped back from the window to take a look at the place, which was a two-story Chinese shophouse that had recently been painted a bright, vibrant yellow with a white trim. The house was graced by a second-floor balcony that overlooked the street below, where a family of chickens loudly objected to my presence. I knocked on the door and soon found myself inside, taking a tour with the landlady, who spoke a smattering of English and French.

On the first floor, the front room, at one time perhaps the eating area for a small noodle shop, had been converted into a sitting room with beautiful hardwood floors and simple rattan furniture. The wooden cabinets were filled with a collection of old lacquer boxes that had belonged to the landlady's mother, who had used them to store betel nut. The rear of the house contained a large kitchen, dining area, and bathroom. Upstairs, there were two bedrooms, each with hardwood floors, a double bed, and a desk—which was key. I had an idea I'd be doing quite a bit of writing. The house didn't have air-conditioning, of course, but the large and powerful ceiling fans put me at ease. There was no hot water, but I convinced the landlady to install in the shower one of the small electric water heaters I'd seen at the Morning Market.

The house was so extraordinary that I wondered aloud why anyone would ever want to leave. The landlady explained that her family was moving to a new place she and her husband had just built on the outskirts of town, and they needed someone to take care of the shophouse, which had been in the family for generations. After negotiating for a few minutes, she and I agreed on a monthly rent that even I, on my limited stipend, could afford. I told her I'd take it, and we shared a bottle of drinking water, a staple of life in Laos, in celebration.

The sound I heard early that morning as I lay in bed was emanating from the tall drum tower in the grounds of Wat Ong Teu. The monks were calling nearby worshippers to celebrate one of the country's most sacred and beloved festivals. *Boun Awk Phansaa*, in late October, the eleventh month of the lunar calendar, marks the end of the monks' three-month rains retreat. During the retreat, which takes place during the long rainy season, monks must spend each night in the *wat*, or temple, where they live, study, and work. After *Awk Phansaa*, they are finally allowed to travel freely throughout the country to visit family and friends. It is an important occasion, and to mark this day, a monk is often presented by the faithful with a new set of brilliant, saffron-colored robes.

By seven o'clock, I was wide awake and had already prepared my offering for the morning's *takbaat*, or alms-giving ceremony. I placed my gift of bananas, Vietnamese sweets, and sticky rice in a glistening silver bowl, designed especially for the purpose, that I'd found buried deep within my landlady's closet during a desperate search the night before. My next-door neighbor, Sumali, helped me to arrange my rather pitiable offering in a style appropriate for the special day. Sumali, who was my age, was dressed in her finest *sin*, the traditional sarong-like skirt of Laos, and *pa biang*, a sash draped loosely over the shoulders and across the chest on special occasions. I was used to seeing her hanging around her house in a T-shirt and jeans; this morning, she was strikingly beautiful.

After we had finished our preparations, we went across the street to Wat Ong Teu. We walked past the monastic quarters that sat directly opposite my bedroom window. This morning, the building was empty. Though a rich combination of colonial French and traditional Lao architecture, the dormitory was a modest affair indeed; I imagined that the monks, glad that Lent was finally over, had been quick to get out.

At the entrance to the *sim*—the chapel where monks are ordained, and the most important building in any Lao temple—we removed our shoes and stepped up onto the front terrace. The *sim* had been covered with a fresh coat of paint, the same rich saffron hue as the monks' new robes. Just above the terrace, a carved wooden façade filled with mythical figures like the *naga*, or water serpent, and the half-bird half-woman *kinnari* graced the front of the building. Through the main entrance, I saw the feature for which Wat Ong Teu was most renowned: the sixteenth-century bronze statue of the Buddha that weighed several tons. Purple, red, and silver gems gleamed from the base of the great statue, which dominated the rear of the chapel.

Sumali and I sat among the other worshippers who crowded the terrace, facing the golden Buddha, and carefully placed our bowls of offerings on the floor before us. I noticed that some worshippers' silver *takbaat* bowls were inscribed with the seal of the pre-revolutionary Royal Lao Government, a three-headed elephant. The seal, however hidden, was a potent symbol of the past; its subtle re-emergence in Vientiane was an indication of the gradual opening up of Laos' political system. As I tucked my legs beneath me as neatly as I could, I saw a large, contemporary statue of a monk just in front of me and to my right.

"Who's that?" I asked Sumali.

"He's the big guy, the head monk," she replied with a whisper. "Here, look inside."

In the center of the chapel, in front of the Buddha, sat an elderly monk who was conducting the morning's ceremony. This was the deputy patriarch of the Lao *Sangha*, or monastic order. He was the leader of the temple's Buddhist Institute, to which monks from all over the country came to study Buddhist doctrine, and thus he had his official residence here at Wat Ong Teu.

As the deputy patriarch read the ancient *Pali* scriptures into a microphone, his steady recitation was broadcast throughout the temple. His voice was a strict monotone, and faintly soporific. As it washed over the worshippers, it nearly put me to sleep. My cumbersome legs, unaccustomed despite months of living in Asia to sitting on the floor, were already reminding me that they weren't designed for this sort of thing. Just as I was about to slip into a state of numbed semi-consciousness, the deputy patriarch completed his recitation and the melancholy chords of traditional Lao music crept out of the speakers.

We walked over to a tent that the monks had set up on the main plaza of the temple grounds, and lined up behind the crowd, our bowls at the ready. As we waited for our turn to place our offerings into the larger bowls inside the tent, I noticed that almost all of the worshippers were women.

"Where are all the men?" I asked.

"Women like to give alms. Men don't," replied Sumali with a grin, her lips pursed. She was a woman of few words, but her simple response pointed to a central truth about religious life in Laos: it was the women who kept the temples in business. This extraordinary devotion was despite the clearly inferior position traditionally accorded to women in Lao Buddhism. Snooping around in the office, I once came upon an old essay by Phagna Ingpeng Suryadhay, who had been Laos' ambassador to the US in the 1950s. "Here is the philosophy of Buddhism and the one we follow," he wrote in 1970:

Since everything changes, why insist on an ideal solution for all problems when it would be preferable to follow the middle course? This explains why our morals and traditions are suffused with so much amiability and tolerance. . . . As well, don't look to complicate things in Laos. Take things as they come and as they are arranged. . . . A Lao woman herself must prostrate herself at the feet of her husband each night before going to sleep in order to ask for forgiveness for all the bad things she did during the day. She cannot sleep on the same pillow as her husband, for he has a pillow placed higher than hers. What is more, they cannot sleep just anywhere on the conjugal bed, but invariably to the left of her husband, to permit him, at the first signal of danger, to grab his sword quickly. During a meal, she cannot begin to eat until her husband has arrived at the third mouthful. During conversation, she can never cut off her husband.

Buddhism offered many benefits to Lao women, but a way up and out of the morass of sexism was certainly not among them.

The only man at Wat Ong Teu that morning, I put a bit of my modest wealth in each of the row of bowls inside the tent—a banana in this one, a ball of sticky rice in the next, a candy bar in another. We made these simple offerings in order to earn merit in this life, which would hopefully be returned to us in the next. On our way home, Sumali pointed out four *that kaduk*, or bone stupas, that sat just inside the temple walls. She explained that over the years our landlady's family, prominent merchants since the early twentieth century, had been a great benefactor to Wat Ong Teu; the parents' and grandparents' ashes were interred in these stupas. Their dates were engraved on the front of the pyramid-like structures. The grandfather had lived from 1930 to 1994, the grandmother from 1931 to 1996. Placing a small amount of sticky rice on the base of each stupa, I paid my respects to my surrogate ancestors, whose photographs were on prominent display in my bedroom.

That evening at 8:00, I met Sumali in front of her house for the *bientiene*, or candlelight procession, around Wat Ong Teu. We prepared our offerings—this time, small bundles of flowers, incense sticks, and orange candles—and crossed the street to the temple. As soon as we entered the grounds, the procession began. A smaller group of worshippers, mostly young people, had returned to pay their respects to the monks and to wish for good luck. The women had swapped their *sin* for more casual attire, and some were even dressed in jeans. At the front of the circling crowd walked the resident monks and novices, led by the deputy patriarch.

We filed in behind the monks and used another worshipper's candle to light our own. As we turned the corner of the *sim*, I caught a glimpse through one of the windows of the great Buddha sitting inside—as serene as ever despite the din of the evening's activities. Two young monks sat in front of the Buddha, reciting from their scriptures, their words broadcast through two large speakers placed outside. The chapel's ornately carved shutters, painted bright red and gold, depicted scenes from the Lao version of the central Hindu epic, the *Ramayana*. In the glow of the candles, the characters seemed to come to life: the hero Phra Lak triumphed over his evil brother Phra Lam and went on to become the true leader of the people of Vientiane. The burning incense created a magical haze on this cool October evening, and the flames from our small candles flickered faintly in the eyes of the two *naga*—central figures in Lao mythology—that guarded the temple entrance.

We circled the *sim* three times before following the crowd over to a longboat that had been placed in the grounds. After the monks lit the candles that graced the seats of the boat, we each placed our palms together and performed a *nop*, the formal Lao greeting, three times before laying our floral votives inside. The candles, flowers, and incense soon caught fire, but no one seemed at all worried by the growing flames. As the crowd began to disperse, monks strolled about setting off fireworks into the night to celebrate their newfound freedom. One novice marched about with a long, tube-like rocket in his hand, periodically setting off a fountain of sparks into the sky. He appeared in the dark to be a young sorcerer, casting a spell over the evening with his wand. Children, delighted and frightened at the same time, squealed and ran for cover behind their parents' knees.

Back at her house, Sumali and I sat outside munching on boiled peanuts, one of her favorite snacks, as we waited for a group of her friends to arrive. I knew that it wasn't easy for her to be sitting here alone with me, a foreign man about her age. Just think of what the neighbors might say! A young Lao woman had to be more cautious than women in West when it came to how she acted and the company she kept, lest she develop the sort of reputation no woman anywhere in the world would want. Then again, Sumali didn't seem all that worried. Even under the watchful eye of her mother, an elderly woman who did little but watch the world go by from inside the cramped quarters of their one-story home, Sumali could at times be quite flirtatious.

Sumali lived with her mother and elder brother. The family seemed to rely on the brother's ad hoc motorbike repair business to get by. He also trained the family's chickens to fight, and entered them into competitions every weekend. The cocks struck me as particularly vicious—for two years, I made sure to keep my distance—so I wouldn't be surprised if his winnings substantially supplemented the family income.

As we sat together, Sumali took the opportunity to tell me about one of the most popular legends of *Awk Phansaa: Bang Fai Phanyanak*, or the Fire-Shooting Serpent of the Mekong. According to this legend, at the bottom of the Mekong, about sixty kilometers south of Vientiane, there lives a great water serpent. On the eve of *Awk Phansaa*, the serpent shoots a stream of fire from his mouth and out of the water, spraying light into the dark sky above. Every year on this night, thousands of Lao and Thais gather to watch the mysterious pockets of light rise one hundred meters above the river and then disappear. It always takes place in the same location, and always on the eve of *Awk Phansaa*—though the exact date of the festival changes every year.

"Oh, come on. *Koi baw seuah chao*. I don't believe you—there's no such serpent," I said.

"*Mee tae*. There is so," Sumali insisted. "I used to say I didn't believe, but then I saw it with my own eyes. And now I know, the serpent exists."

No one could quite understand this phenomenon, and I heard a different explanation each time a Lao told me about the legend. Some wondered if there wasn't some sort of chemical reaction occurring under the water. But why only on *Awk Phansaa*? Perhaps a few mischievous Thais were playing a trick on the crowds. One of my colleagues at work had also been to view the light display, and he insisted that there was a city underneath the Mekong that was also celebrating *Awk Phansaa*. According to him, the lights that jumped out of the river were really fireworks being set off by the celebrants below.

As Sumali tried in vain to convince me of the truth, her girl-friends showed up.

"*Oh, mee falang!* It's a foreigner!" one exclaimed. "He's cute. Does he speak Lao?"

All of this fuss never amounted to much, and I knew it was mostly a game. But I couldn't help but wonder if these girls were actually interested in me. Or was I merely an object of curiosity?

After I had established my credentials, we all set off for the banks of the Mekong. Candlelight glowed from the windows and court-yards of our neighborhood's closely packed homes. The calm quiet belied the intense activity within. Grandmothers and granddaugh-ters worked side by side constructing *khatong*, or miniature boats made from banana leaves, flowers, and incense, which they would later set adrift on the river in an ancient Lao tradition known as *Lai Hua Fai*.

As soon as we passed out of our village, the calm became a maelstrom of live music, cheering celebrants, and laughing children. Nearly every house near the river had been converted into a make-shift restaurant. In the driveways of old colonial villas, residents had set up small stands selling grilled chicken, sticky rice, and that inimitable elixir of life in Laos: Beer Lao. In 1999, Beer Lao had sold 33 million liters of beer and made 150 billion kip, and by the end of 2000 it would own nearly 100 percent of the domestic market.

On Fa Ngum Road—the namesake of the founder of the Lan Xang Kingdom—which runs along the Mekong, the crowd was so thick that we were soon swept away in a sea of merriment. After struggling for a few minutes to walk in a particular direction, we gave in and became one with the mob. Wherever the crowd went, we followed. Along the riverbank, stands selling Thai and Viet-namese toys had been set up under tents. Occasionally, the jolting sound of a firecracker pierced the night air.

"*Ao nyang baw, monsieur?* What would you like?" an elderly woman called to us. "How about these *khatong?* Very beautiful." I wasn't a tough sell, and quickly bought two boats decorated with bright orange and purple flowers. Armed with our *khatong,* Sumali and I traipsed over the muddy flats and down to the river. Drunken men, relieving themselves in the dark, dotted the landscape around us. Near the water's edge, young couples and families alike gathered to release their boats into the Mekong, an act of offering to the powerful spirits of this, the world's twelfth-longest river.

In the autumn breeze, it was a challenge to keep our candles lit as we sent our own *khatong* on their way downriver. When they floated away, our natural banana-leaf models were soon overtaken by a very different kind of miniature boat, made from bright pink plastic and shaped like lotus blossoms: imports from Thailand. In the weeks leading up to the end of Buddhist Lent, the Lao government had issued a statement encouraging citizens to refrain from using these Thai models in an effort to protect the river environment. Not many got the message. These plastic models invariably stayed lit the longest, and their owners seemed happy with their purchases.

The Mekong, sprinkled with flickering lights drifting by, mirrored the clear night sky above. But despite their beauty, these small lights actually represented our evil spirits being sent downriver, far from Vientiane. I wondered if villagers further downstream would be nearly so pleased when they woke up the next morning to find these decidedly non-biodegradable boats on their shores.

Satisfied that our boats would stay afloat long enough to drift away, we trekked back up to Fa Ngum Road to a large concert stage erected right on the riverfront. The energetic singer wore an orange nylon shirt and tight white jeans, and constantly ran his hand through his greased hair as he sang a mix of Thai and Lao pop songs. In front of the stage, hundreds of teenagers attempted to dance to the music, jumping up and down in place and occasionally throwing their hands in the air with carefully restrained abandon. These kids had never known life in the Lao PDR at its most strict, in the late 1970s and early 1980s, when women were prohibited from wearing anything else but the traditional *sin*, and men couldn't even wear jeans.

In front of the stage, young men and women alike were dressed almost uniformly in blue jeans. Drunk on Tiger brand whiskey, groups of boys swayed back and forth, stumbling as they made their way to the dance floor. "Hallo!" they cried out when they saw me. On the edge of the crowd, pairs of young men stood as nonchalantly as possible, cigarettes in hand, arms draped heavily over one another's shoulders. This generation may have tossed out many of the traditions of old, but it continued to preserve perhaps the central prohibition of Lao society: men and women never touched in public.

The young people around us showed no signs of stopping, but Sumali, her friends, and I were tired. We were getting old, it seemed. The full moon above guided our way back to Wat Ong Teu. We said good-night and I went upstairs to bed.

The next morning, I woke up earlier than I'd have liked, as Sumali and I had planned to head down to the river once again. But she and her mother had set up a small shop outside their house in order to capitalize on the steady stream of people already making their way down our small alley. Sumali's mother had bred goldfish throughout the year, and was now selling them in old whiskey bottles to the children who passed by. Business was swift, and her mother needed help, so I walked down to the river on my own.

Today was Vientiane's Water Festival, or *Boun Nam*, held each year in association with the end of Buddhist Lent. This festival has its origins in an animist focus on the spirits of the soil and water; the community looked to the spirits to protect the kingdom and to ensure agricultural prosperity in the coming year through the annual cycle of flooding and drainage of the rice fields. These days, boat-racing competitions dominated the festivities. Throughout the morning and into the afternoon, races were held on the river in front of Fa Ngum Road.

The races had clear roots in Laos' royal heritage. During the Water Festival in Luang Prabang, when it was still the royal capital, the king's boatmen would remove the royal barges from a shed behind the palace and enter the Mekong nearby. They would row north to the spot at which the Mekong and the Nam Khan rivers converge, to a collection of rocks where a group of *naga* was said to rest. The boatmen would place floral arrangements and candles on the rocks, and then pray to the water spirits to protect the kingdom before retracing their journey to the palace.

On this day in Vientiane, onlookers lined the riverbank, jockeying for a glimpse of the racing boats. Many in the crowd were clearly not from Vientiane, and they stood out. These country folk seemed bewildered, overwhelmed by the whirl of activity that surrounded them. While most urban folk showed little to no interest in me—one of very few foreigners around—these men and women were as agog as their grandchildren when they saw my white face. They reminded me of an old Lao saying Sumali had once taught me: *Gai gan ban fa gap din.* The difference between their lifestyle and that of their fellow citizens here in the big city was as great as "the distance between the sky and the earth."

Each race began with a gunshot. Once they were off, the long, slender boats glided gracefully through the tepid waters, slicing through the stillness. The contestants, about fifty to a boat, had trained for months, and they were ready. Each oar moved in perfect time, as if the men were part of a single organism. Traditionally, different villages within the city formed the teams and competed against one another. In recent years, as Laos had opened up to the forces of market capitalism, large companies had begun sponsoring teams as well. Today, Pepsi had a team, as did Beer Lao.

Thirty-six boats competed in the races: 26 in the men's and another ten in the women's. The competition was run as a single-loss elimination system, and the prize for the winning men's team was 14 million kip—at the time, about 1,700 dollars—and for the women, seven million. The races were certainly competitive, and onlookers cheered loudly for their favorites. But most rowers were really there to have fun, and when each race was over, both the winners and the losers exploded into a display of unbridled revelry. Boats rocked as teammates drank, danced, and sang, satisfied that all those months of training had finally paid off.

Back on Fa Ngum Road, I once again lost myself in the crowd. The temples along the riverfront had been turned into small carnivals with merry-go-rounds, bingo games, and fortune-telling monks. Vendors sold James Bond toy guns and model tractors. A Vietnamese circus had been set up on a corner, and the ringmaster stood outside, shouting through his microphone to the crowd to come inside. Marlboro representatives handed out free cigarettes on the street, lighter at the ready, just a few paces away from a government-sponsored anti-smoking poster.

Teenage boys, hand in hand, strolled from stall to stall and into the *bia sot*, draught beer shops that lined the riverfront. Powerful stereos inside these shops played the incessant whining that passed for contemporary Thai pop; the teenagers who sat and drank knew every lyric by heart. To these revelers, the boat races were almost peripheral, and only occasionally did they glance over to the water to see which team was ahead. Every once in a while, if in a close race the underdog pulled ahead at the last minute, the crowd would roar with approval.

I walked along the river past the starting line and into the neighborhoods and back alleys north of the center of town. These villages offered a peaceful respite from the festival activity, and they were dotted with houses that had been built by the French—one dated back to 1924. The temples here were deserted, as even the monks had left to take part in the festivities downtown. It had rained the night before, and in spots the mud was quite deep. I stopped to help a lonely *tuk-tuk* driver, stuck in a puddle, push his vehicle back on to solid ground.

Inside one house, the TV was on. I stuck my head in the door and found three men gathered on the floor of the living room around a rattan table, watching the boat races on TV. As soon as he saw me, Keo, the head of the household, invited me in for a drink. Glad for a break, I removed my shoes and joined them. The men were sharing a bottle of *lau lao*, or rice whiskey—Laos' ubiquitous and deadly version of moonshine. It is almost impossible to decline an offer of alcohol in a Lao home, so I downed a single shot, cringed, and quickly chased it away with a gulp of water. On the TV, the commentators were attempting to drum up excitement. They were engaged in the same mindless banter you might hear during an American football game on cable in the US.

In between each race, announcers read advertisements for the sponsors. These announcements were interspersed with Thai commercials for toothpaste and baby powder. The ads had been dubbed into Lao, a meager attempt by the government to limit the influence of Thai consumer culture. A promotion for the Lao national lottery boasted that the prize this month was 100,000 kip— about 12 dollars. The popularity of the lottery in Vientiane, I thought, was the result of a turn to the forces of chance in times of tremendous economic change and increasing uncertainty about the future.

Keo, for one, took the lottery very seriously. Every month, without fail, he would dutifully spend a few thousand kip at the Morning Market to buy two tickets.

"But how do you know which numbers to choose?"

"Aha! I ask the spirits."

Before buying a ticket, Keo never failed to consult the spirits, or *phi*, for some serious advice. One weekend, he told me, he'd spent more than four hours sitting outside his house near the river, eyes shut, conversing with the ghosts. They told him that the month's lucky numbers were 273 and 274, so he went ahead and bought these two tickets. He promptly lost.

"So what do these ghosts look like?"

"Oh, they're everywhere! You can't see them? They have strange faces and long feet, and they speak a different language than we do. But I can understand them."

Just then, a man stumbled in off the street. He was different from Keo and his friends. His skin was shades darker, and he wore an old business suit that was covered with dirt. In his hand he clutched a half-empty whiskey bottle and a shot glass. He was extremely drunk, and began to mumble incomprehensibly as soon as he stepped in—without removing his shoes, an entirely unacceptable act in Lao society. No one seemed particularly surprised, however, when he plopped himself down on the floor next to me. At first I could barely make out a word he said, but I soon realized he was speaking French and English. The simple phrases seemed to be coming from a dark place in his head, one that he had long since forgotten.

"*Bonjour, monsieur. Shake hands, shake hands,*" he said as he groped for my hand. "*Je suis un Laotien, comment-allez vous? Très bien. Shake hands, monsieur. Merci beaucoup, monsieur.*"

Eventually he passed out in my lap, and I helped Keo to lay him down on the floor. Who was this guy?

"Oh, don't mind him. He's just drunk," said Keo.

Not satisfied with this explanation, I pressed on. "But is he always like this? Is this usual?"

"He's not right in the head, you know," Keo explained reluctantly. "*Lao phi ba.* He's crazy. He spent twenty years in communist re-education camps up in Sam Neua. Twenty years! He was an official in the Royal Lao Army, a friend of the French and the Americans, and the communists wouldn't let him leave until 1995."

"What happened to him?" I asked.

"Well, he went crazy up there, and by the time he returned to this village, his wife had already left. Now he lives with his mother and drinks most of the day away."

Keo offered me another shot of *lau lao*, but I had to decline. Even on this joyous day, not all our evil spirits or unwanted memories could simply be sent downriver. A few ghosts stuck around to haunt us.

After I bade my farewells to Keo and his friends, promising to return one day to share another drink, I walked slowly back to Wat Ong Teu. The races were over, and teams were already heading back to their small villages, miles from Vientiane. The winners in both the men's and women's competitions were sponsored by Beer Lao—yet another triumph for the country's most popular beverage. The men's team had completed the 1,200-meter course in an impressive three minutes and twenty seconds.

On my way home, I ran into one team of men, dressed in identical blue T–shirts, gathered in the street near my house. They sang and danced, jostling one another and anyone else who seemed an easy target. Two women carried the team's supplies in a large bamboo basket. The team members soon boarded a large truck that was parked nearby; hard wooden seats had been added onto the back of the ancient vehicle, and I suspected it would be a very bumpy ride home.

"Did you win?" I asked one rower as he lazily hoisted himself onto the truck.

"No way! They beat us by a good ten meters!"

The team continued to make merry as their driver disappeared under the hood to tinker with the engine. There was no rush to get back, and before I finally went home, I shared a communal glass of beer in celebration of the village's loss.

Over the past few centuries, these streets had seen a lot, I thought as I forced down another swig of beer. The French had come and gone, kings had risen and fallen, temples had been destroyed and rebuilt, and counter-revolutionaries had been sent away and had once again returned home. But one thing had stayed the same. Every October, when the monks' retreat came to an end, Vientiane still took a moment to celebrate two things that never seemed to change: the beauty of a full moon and the glory of the Mekong.

The Prince

One fish can spoil an entire basket;
the sound of a single gong can fill the whole city.
Lao Proverb.

In a spacious, air-conditioned office just upstairs from
General Cheng—a few paces away, yet worlds apart—sat another
source of power at the NTA. Desa was the vice-chairman and the
director of a tourism project funded by the UN Development Program, or UNDP. He was worldly, cultured, and charming—in short,
a marked contrast to his boss. The General might have been kind
and soft-spoken, but he was still a rough and tumble military man,
a ruthless businessman, and a Party loyalist since the early days of
the revolution. In the end, I determined, the main reason he didn't
show up for our English lessons was because he simply didn't care;
learning a foreign language, and thinking beyond the narrowly
defined world over which he had such total control, didn't strike
the man as efficient use of his time.

Desa, on the other hand, was the NTA's resident sophisticate.
He was fluent in French and fully conversant in English. Whenever

a foreigner showed up at the NTA, chances were he was looking for Desa. Even if he wasn't, he would end up in Desa's office eventually, guided there by any staff member he might encounter in the halls. Speeches at international conferences, receptions for visiting delegations, study tours abroad, interviews with journalists—such tasks were inevitably reserved for Desa. If the vice-chairman couldn't remember an English word while he and I were chatting, he would mutter, *"Comment dit-on?"* and we'd switch into French. His face was perpetually graced by a bemused, even weary expression, and his legs were always crossed elegantly at the knees. The few strands of fine white hair that remained on his head were perfectly in place. His manner made it clear that nothing anyone said to him, in any language, would be a surprise. After so many years working in the government, he had seen it all.

During my first weeks at the NTA, I had quickly identified Desa as the one man I needed to know. He seemed out of place at the office, respected by his colleagues, to be sure, but set apart from them by a tangible mutual suspicion. Desa fascinated me, and I was determined to learn more about him and where he came from. This proved a difficult task, as he had seemed wary during our first few meetings. He dodged even my simplest and most naïve questions about Laos, and was always careful not to reveal too much about himself. Not only did he speak French with extraordinary fluency, but he had also adopted the intense reserve for which the French are known (and for which Americans are certainly not). But gradually, as the months passed, Desa opened up, and he began to tell me about his background. There was a lot to learn.

Desa hailed from Laos' pre-revolutionary elite. His father, it turned out, had as a young man married into the royal family of Champassak, Laos' southernmost kingdom. In the early 1940s, when Laos was still under French control, he had led the Movement for National Renovation, the goal of which was to foster the development of Lao literature, dance, music, and theater. Members of the movement took an intense interest in Lao history and identity, promoting the use of a national anthem and flag for the first time. But the movement didn't openly question French rule, so it was hardly a crusade for independence. In fact, since a central goal of the movement was to counter Thai influence in Lao affairs, the French saw a strategic interest in supporting his effort. Nevertheless, his cause marked the genesis of a genuine nationalist movement in Laos. When the Japanese arrived in Indochina in 1941 and called for an end to French rule, this nascent nationalism moved from the cultural into the political sphere, and ultimately led, in part, to full independence in 1954.

After World War II, Desa's father served as a minister in the Royal Lao Government. As minister, his personal crusade was to encourage the revival of genuine Buddhist practice in Laos. In May 1949, he wrote: "We have turned Buddhism into a doctrine of lethargy and resignation that is leading our race to its destruction." He oversaw a flourishing of the country's Buddhist associations and educational institutions, including the Pali College, founded in 1953. Fluent in French, he wrote perhaps the premier pre-revolutionary volume on Lao culture during these years. Its chapters on Lao religious practice, weddings, and literature remain among the best ever published. One day, Desa lent me his father's book, a well-worn volume with a faded red leather binding and gold-embossed title. Its pages had yellowed over the years, and by now a few were even missing.

"Please read it," Desa told me. "You could learn a lot. But please return it to me when you're finished. It's my only copy."

In 1960, Desa's father was asked by King Savangvattana to serve as Laos' prime minister. It was a time of intense political maneuvering in Vientiane: the communist forces were gaining strength in the provinces, and the country had returned to civil war in the wake of an attempted military *coup d'état*. Neutralist leaders were trying desperately to keep the country together through a series of ineffectual coalition governments. Both the king and the diplomatic community in Vientiane viewed him as a possible force for national unity, and they lobbied heavily to convince him to take over as the head of yet another caretaker government.

At the time, Desa was a student at the Lycée Vientiane, the capital's prestigious French-language high school. Preoccupied with his studies, and sheltered from the fighting, the war seemed far away indeed to the young man. One night, however, a messenger from the American Embassy showed up in the family's living room with two large suitcases. When his father opened them, he found stack upon stack of newly printed kip notes—a generous incentive to accept the king's offer. But he stubbornly refused. So the king appointed Desa's uncle instead, and Desa's father was named as deputy prime minister.

"My father was like me," Desa explained. "He tried to stay out of politics." In fact, many of the leaders of the Pathet Lao, Laos' indigenous communist movement, were friends of Desa's father. In the early days of the independence movement, he had worked alongside such central Pathet Lao officials as Prince Souphannouvong and Phoumi Vongvichit. When he became deputy prime minister, these men were serving time in a Vientiane prison, having been jailed after the formation of a right-wing government the year before. Soon after he took office, however, his former colleagues managed to break out. According to Desa, the jailbreak itself wasn't all that difficult. "They even convinced the prison guards to join them!" he recalled with a chuckle. Together, the men embarked upon a secretive four-month journey to the Lao communist headquarters in northern Huapanh province. "When my father later learned that they all had arrived safely, he was relieved."

Desa's father died in 1964, nearly a decade before the monarchy finally collapsed and Laos became a socialist republic. I could sense the nostalgia in Desa's voice as he spoke of his childhood and his father's efforts to promote traditional Lao culture. Every so often, a stream of government limousines would speed up Lan Xang Avenue past his office window—their sirens reminding us of the absolute nature of the Party's power—and Desa's face would betray his distaste for the current regime. It was as if he simply knew that things would have been better had the communists never come to power.

After graduating from high school, Desa completed his studies at university in Switzerland. He returned to Vientiane just a year before the communist victory, and applied for a position with the civil service. He was assigned to the Interior Ministry, but when the communists took over in December 1975, he was still in training. Desa was lucky: if he had been appointed to a full-time position, he would have risked being sent to one of the re-education camps, or *samana*. The new government, paranoid that those affiliated with the former regime would sabotage the Lao PDR, decided to isolate them at camps in the former communist stronghold of Huapanh. Many officials who were sent up north thought they'd be back home in Vientiane in a matter of months; some were even willing students of the new leadership's plans for political and economic development. In the end, these men ended up staying at *samana* for as long as ten years.

Desa was allowed to remain at the ministry, but his new supervisors refused to appoint him to an actual position with the civil service. "They could give me everything—a salary, a house—but not a job. They were afraid." His family name meant that, in the newly formed Lao PDR, he would always be on the wrong side. His father, after all, had been a high-ranking official in the former government, a good friend of the West, and a member of the royal family. He had been an enemy of the revolution. However, the new government could not resist Desa for long. Most of Laos' educated elite had already fled the country, joining relatives in France and the US who feared life under the communists. As a result, government officials with foreign language skills—or any kind of skills at all—were in short supply, and when the NTA was first founded in 1989, Desa was appointed vice-chairman. He had been in the same position ever since, serving under five different chairmen in ten years. "I am marked for life," he said. "I know my ceiling."

Desa knew that he would never move downstairs into the chairman's office. Because of his background, he would never be invited to join the Party. No matter how hard he worked, how many international seminars he attended, he would forever be regarded with suspicion in the hallways of the NTA. He would never be included in the most important meetings. In essence, he would never have any real power. Desa had not been an active anti-communist during the war. He hadn't chosen his family, but his name alone barred him from Laos' new ruling establishment. And his language skills and extensive foreign experience were only liabilities in the Lao PDR. Despite economic reforms and an effort to open up to the international community in the 1990s, the Party remained suspicious of anyone who had too much contact with the outside world—especially someone whose family had been on the other side. These days, Desa was simply trying to hang on.

————

As the director of a UN project at the NTA, Desa had a lot of contact with foreigners. He had to suffer the presence of innumerable international consultants and their wildly unrealistic ideas for developing tourism. (One Singaporean proposed that a computerized, touch-screen information booth be installed at the NTA. This, when we barely had enough money for toilet paper.) Desa dealt with the foreign businessmen who were perpetually unhappy with the NTA's efforts to promote tourism. And it was Desa who was ultimately responsible for deciding how to spend the UNDP project budget, which meant an endless stream of proposals to be reviewed, memoranda to be signed, and budgets to be approved. While most of his colleagues shuffled papers from one side of their desks to the other, trying their best not to offend the chairman, Desa actually had work to do.

On the other hand, his position did come with a few perks. For one, it guaranteed him the use of the UNDP project car, the white Mitsubishi sedan parked outside the NTA. And it ensured a steady supply of invitations to seminars and study tours in far-flung destinations like Thailand, Singapore, Japan, and Chile. A seminar on tourism for Lao officials in Santiago? You got it. It seemed at times absurd, but trips like this were supposed to help Desa and whoever else was chosen to go along, to better understand tourism planning and promotion. All they really did was to give them a chance to make a little extra money on the side, through the generous per diem that the UN allowed for international travel.

Was this corruption? Desa's actual salary was such a pittance, you couldn't blame him for jumping at the chance. Those few US dollars he could save by staying in cheaper accommodation and eating cheaply while overseas (if they spent less than their daily per diem, they were rarely required to return the difference) made a big difference to his wife and children. Or perhaps you could blame him. My contemporaries at the NTA would often complain, behind closed doors, that Desa liked to hoard all overseas opportunities. If an application for a seminar in Tokyo or a conference in Bangkok arrived in the mail, they lamented, the vice-chairman would simply sign himself up and go, with nary a thought to how a less senior staff member might benefit. This pattern, repeated in offices throughout Laos, left the government's younger staff with little international experience—just what they would need to lead the country to a better future. Perhaps they too just wanted the chance to make some extra cash, but my friends had a point.

In any case, Desa had a lot more on his mind than developing sound tourism policies. His teenage son had dropped out of school at 15, and was struggling to find a place for himself in the wilting Lao economy. What was the point in attending school when there would be no jobs waiting for him when he completed his studies? Desa's son spent his days hanging out with friends in a beer shop near the river. All of his friends owned motorbikes; whether they were stolen or purchased legally by their fathers—most of whom were civil servants—with the help of development aid, no one really knew.

"He wants me to buy him a motorbike, but I'm not sure," Desa told me. "If he wants to go somewhere, I'll just take him."

Desa had reason to be concerned about his son. Teenage gangs were rampant in Vientiane, as they had been for years. Many Lao men in their thirties still sported the tattoos they'd picked up from their days decades ago running with one of the capital's many neighborhood gangs. Drug abuse among teenage boys in Vientiane was on the rise, particularly the use of amphetamines—*yaa baa*, or "crazy medicine"—which were spilling over the border from Thailand. The city's public health system was completely unable to deal with the problem of drug addiction; victims were being treated in the psychiatric ward of Mahosot Hospital, the country's largest public health facility. The government was reluctant to openly acknowledge the serious problems with which Lao youth were struggling. So was the community. After Desa hinted at his son's troubles, I asked, "Do you ever talk with other families about these things?"

"Never," he replied quickly. "I can find a way to solve them on my own."

To Americans, the idea that young adults have a hard time during adolescence is nothing new. We understand that there are problems common to all teenagers, and this helps us to handle them. In fact, Americans are awash in the psychology of teenagers, as their escapades feature prominently on the nightly news and now dominate popular culture. At a time when teen queens like Britney Spears and Christina Aguilera reign supreme, we can scarcely escape adolescents and their endless woes. But in Laos, the very concept of adolescence was foreign. "It seems that children here, especially boys, always have problems at this age," said Desa. "I wonder why." He seemed unconvinced when I told him that boys around the world went through similar struggles in their teenage years.

"Really?" Desa replied. Just then, his mobile phone, purchased by the NTA, rang. It was his son. He hadn't been home the night before, and was calling to let his father know where he was. And, incidentally, to ask if he could borrow the car.

"As you can see," said Desa, with a wave of his hand in the direction of the troubled downtown, "there's nothing for him here. Maybe I'll send him abroad."

———

The day Desa was fired, it rained. The skies parted and emptied torrents of water on Vientiane. It poured down, beating on the roof of the NTA with such force that I could barely hear myself think. Deep puddles formed inside my office. My desk was wet. All work ceased, and the staff congregated on the balcony overlooking Lan Xang Avenue to observe the rain. In the hallways, the pounding of the raindrops was accompanied by hushed whispers. Did you hear about the vice-chairman?

As soon as I got wind of the news, I went upstairs to look for Desa.

I found him in his office, alone. The lights were switched off, and Desa was sitting at his desk, considering the piles of papers that surrounded him. The decision had arrived in the form of a prime ministerial decree, announcing that Desa no longer had a position at the NTA. Effective immediately, he was expected to report to work at the Ministry of Justice. There had been no warning, no explanation. And no job description. Desa had called a friend at Justice to see if he had any information. It was news to him, as well.

I, of course, was enraged. After so many years of service in this government, how could Desa be treated so poorly? It wasn't just, I argued. It wasn't fair. My young American sensibilities were offended by this transgression of what I considered to be *right*. But this wasn't only a question of justice; I was more than professionally involved. During my time at the NTA, I had come to view Desa not only as a teacher and colleague, but also a friend. I wanted to do something for him, but I was helpless. Desa, on the other hand, didn't seem nearly as agitated.

"You see, this is the situation here in Laos," he calmly explained.

While I was dejected, Desa was undeterred. Perhaps it had only been a matter of time. He already had another project up his sleeve, a private enterprise that would capitalize on his NTA connections. Desa's latest scheme was a Visit Laos Year 1999–2000 commemorative doll, Xang the Elephant. This plaster model of an elephant playing the *khene*, a simple bamboo pipe and the national instrument, would be produced cheaply in Thailand and sold to tourists in Vientiane. This project was a sure-fire failure—I knew of not a single tourist who would buy a plaster model of a pink elephant—but I didn't have the heart to tell Desa.

We bade farewell, and promised to keep in touch. Given the size of Vientiane, I knew it wouldn't be hard. I wished him luck in his new job, and he just smiled. Desa hadn't said as much, but I knew that he had no intention of following the prime minister's order to work at the Ministry of Justice. He had suffered long enough as an employee of the government. He was ready to move on. The regime would lose one of its greatest assets, but Desa would regain some of his dignity.

Outside the (now former) vice-chairman's office, I ran into a colleague in the darkened hallway. "You know what my father told me about the Ministry of Justice?" he asked me under his breath. "It's where they put people they want out." As the rain continued to fall outside, I gathered my things and wondered how I'd possibly get home on my motorbike. Desa was on his way out, but I imagined that he was happy enough to be leaving. And, hey, at least he had that UN project car to take him wherever was heading.

My Honda Dream

People in Vientiane don't walk. Nor do they ride bicycles. Even when no motorized vehicle is anywhere to be found, most Vientiane residents will refuse to resort to their pedestrian power. If they can't get a ride, they'll just sit in the shade and wait. It's too hot, after all, and no one's in much of a rush. The only people in Vientiane silly enough to walk around are the tourists—and the occasional expat. When I arrived, cars were still few, but the city had long been colonized by the motorbike. Not just any old motorbike, mind you. Only one model was worth your time: the Honda Dream II. Everyone in Vientiane owned, or desperately wanted to own, a Honda Dream. This was a powerful dream, and one from which the capital wouldn't awake any time soon. Not long after my arrival, I too was taken under its spell.

During my first few weeks in Vientiane, I relied on my feet and the occasional *tuk-tuk* to get around. Initially, riding in a *tuk-tuk*— a three-wheeled motorcycle taxi with two short benches strapped on the back, covered by a tarp and often painted in festive colors—was exciting. After flagging down a *tuk-tuk* and giving a general idea of where I wanted to go, I hopped in without the faintest idea of where I might end up. Some days it took ten minutes to get home from work; other days, it took an hour. Needless to say, I came to know Greater Vientiane very well.

A few roads in the city had actually been paved, and those that had been were graced with a series of mammoth potholes—and since the benches were rarely cushioned, a *tuk-tuk* ride wasn't always comfortable. There were no fixed prices for *tuk-tuks*, particularly for foreign customers, so bargaining was mandatory. Before even so much as touching the contraption, I'd have to engage in an elaborate negotiation as to the appropriate fare. Before long, the *tuk-tuk* became more tiresome than titillating.

Vientiane's public bus system, such as it was, wasn't much help, either. I never did discover the logic behind the routes, which mostly connected the downtown with the outlying neighborhoods. In any case, I doubt the established route mattered much, as the drivers seemed to stop wherever a passenger happened to live. They would stop at individual houses to deliver messages or packages. To drop people off, the buses would stop in places that appeared at first to be uninhabited. Not infrequently at such stops, a woman and her baby would step down from the bus and march off into a field toward a small hut in the distance. They would eventually be welcomed home by a sister cooking dinner. In one respect, buses in Laos were much more convenient than any in the developed world—they provided door-to-door service. But as a result, they took forever, and sometimes I wasn't up for a unique cultural experience. Sometimes I just wanted to get home.

When I'd decided that the Honda lifestyle was for me, I mentioned it to Oudom—General Cheng's driver, who was well-connected in the world of used motorbikes—and after work one day he drove me to one of the suspiciously numerous dealerships around town. From afar, these places didn't appear to be centers of commerce—there were no signs—but just residential driveways filled with old motorbikes. I had no idea what I was looking for, of course, but I quickly settled on a used Dream II, red and white trim, with about 100 cc of power. The horn was silent, the speedometer was broken, and the odometer had stopped keeping record long ago. To me these seemed like mere quibbles, and after a bit of bargaining, we arrived at a price of 750 dollars—a large percentage of my stipend for the year, but worth it, I convinced myself, by thinking of the *tuk-tuk* ride that awaited me if I didn't make the purchase. The bike came complete with a packet of documents, and, though I couldn't read a word, they looked legitimate enough.

It didn't take long to master the Dream. Unencumbered by unreliable bus schedules and unrelenting *tuk-tuk* drivers, I could control my own destiny. I had the freedom not only to travel back and forth between the NTA and my house with ease, but also to take long rides through the narrow, winding dirt roads of Vientiane, or to explore the countryside. These trips were often when I felt most at peace, when it was clearest to me why I'd come to Laos. Not when I was in the office struggling with the computer and battling split infinitives. Not when I was learning to dance the *lam vong* or make sticky rice. But rather when I was out on the road, the warm wind whipping at my face, seeing at least a part of the country, and meeting people along the way. It was also when I felt most free. Living in a place where one's behavior was tightly controlled and one's every movement watched, a motorbike was one of the best means of escape. On my Honda Dream, I felt as free as I ever had before in my life.

There were only a handful of traffic signals in Vientiane. (There were none anywhere else in Laos.) Despite their scarcity, these lights didn't receive much respect. Even when they were working, which wasn't regularly, no one really paid attention to them. Most drivers seemed to regard them as an inconvenience—a necessity, perhaps, but one imposed upon the city by outside forces of development, and not one to take very seriously. When I was driving around town and a traffic light happened to turn red, I would usually stop. As I waited for the light to change, a group of vehicles would gather behind me. Slowly, quietly, the pressure would begin to build. I would hear the impatient sound of depressed accelerators, and out of the corner of my eye would see the wheels beside me creeping forward. Soon, I'd feel my own wheels moving. At a certain point, a collective decision would suddenly materialize out of the fumes. As a group, we would take off without so much as a glance at the signal or the cross traffic. We'd decided that the time was right, and had gone for it. Overwhelmed by the power of the group, I found myself swept right on through the red light. The forgotten traffic signal was left behind in a cloud of dust.

———

Desa liked to call them *les mouches*. Flies. Dressed in drab green uniforms, they always seemed to be buzzing about like insects. They hovered over you, always ready to pounce. You wanted to swat them away, but were never quite sure that you could. Crime was on the rise in Vientiane, but the city's police force seemed to spend most of its time engaged in one activity: inspecting papers. At a certain point in the evening, usually around nine o'clock, but a bit later on the weekends, the police would suddenly emerge from the shadows. They would set up shop along the city's roads in a few strategic locations, often just around a corner or beyond a traffic light. When the spirit moved them, they'd select a motorbike or car and pull it over, furiously blowing their whistles.

The first time this happened to me, I dutifully stopped and presented my foreign ID card. Was this what he wanted? I also handed him the pile of incomprehensible papers I'd been given with the motorbike. But this wasn't enough; the officer seemed to want something more than my ID. He handed the papers back and spoke for a few minutes in a calm, didactic tone. Given my rudimentary Lao, I couldn't decipher his subtle hints, however, and I politely said good-night and went on my way.

It was never clear to me why the police stopped people. Drivers in Vientiane were more fastidious than most in Southeast Asia about wearing their helmets. Drunk driving was widespread, but the police didn't target drivers who were under the influence. Were they checking for stolen motorbikes? Motorbike theft in Vientiane was rampant, and there was a huge trade in pilfered Honda Dreams. Red and white, as it happened, was the preferred color. But how could a policeman have identified a stolen vehicle? They were usually repainted, and they all looked exactly the same. Even the regime's original reason for conducting spot checks—to keep tabs on people's movements in, out, and around the city—was untenable.

The police were outnumbered and under-equipped; they had no cars of their own and had to share motorbikes. All I could conclude about this police activity was that it was merely an end in itself, a way for the government to announce its presence and insert itself into people's lives and to keep them guessing. For the officers themselves, it was probably also a way to make a little extra money on the side.

After a while, I just stopped stopping. I ignored *les mouches*. As I drove past them in defiance of their orders, I could hear their whistles in the wind behind me. But I wasn't worried. They would have to abandon their position to come after me, and there was a surplus of unsuspecting drivers. I probably shouldn't have been so cavalier. While the law in Laos requires arrest warrants issued by a prosecutor, and the Lao constitution provides for procedural safeguards, the police weren't known to respect these provisions. They often used arrest as a means of intimidation and to exact bribes, and found it easy to rely on exceptions to the warrant requirement for "urgent" cases. And while the law provided for a one-year limit for detention without trial, in practice this was often ignored.

But on my Honda Dream, I felt invincible. And even if a policeman did decide to hop on his motorbike and follow me, I could always drop the name of my boss and star English student. One mention of General Cheng would likely have swatted away even the most zealous of flies.

The Game

The leg of the elephant closes the beak of the bird.
Lao Proverb.

"It feels good to talk to you, you know," Mon told me as she glanced nervously at the door.

Mon's desk in the International Co-operation Unit at the NTA sat just across from mine. Our office was a modest affair, presided over by two lazily creaking ceiling fans that just barely cut through the thick humidity. Forgotten faxes and memoranda fluttered in the gentle breeze below. A heavy layer of dust coated the furniture. The scene was dimly lit by a set of flickering fluorescent lights. A computer sat in one corner but it was almost always turned off; at any one time, there was only enough electricity for the fans, the lights, or the computer. If I switched on the light, the fans would stop turning. If I turned on the fan while Mon was using the computer, it would begin screeching and then crash. I liked to refer to the International Co-operation Unit as the ICU—this place did not offer any intensive care, but it certainly could have used some.

For my part, it felt good to talk as well. I had already been at the NTA for months, but I felt I hadn't accomplished anything. I was accustomed to drawing up objectives, completing projects quickly, and pointing with satisfaction to concrete results. At the NTA, this approach clearly wasn't going to work. When I had proudly presented a work plan to Desa—whom I'd adopted as a surrogate boss, though he had known nothing of my plan to work at the NTA prior to my arrival—he had regarded it with his usual bemused nonchalance. "Good luck, Mr. Brett. *Bon chance*," he said. Work plans, I quickly learned, meant little when the only resource you had to offer the Lao government was yourself.

My English program was going nowhere. On top of the usual problems with attendance that you might expect to accompany an instruction program that took place during office hours, my heart just wasn't into it. I seemed to spend most of my time editing the flurry of faxes that surrounded General Cheng's frequent trips to meet with his counterparts in neighboring countries. I would encourage whoever had written the fax to sit down with me and follow along as I re-wrote it, but who wanted to bother? I hadn't even come close to confronting the issue of how tourism could be developed successfully without destroying the country's unique beauty.

The main problem was that no one at the NTA really knew what to do with me. One day, I'd arrived at work only to find that my desk in the ICU was gone. My chair was still there, perfectly positioned behind the neat pile of dust that had accumulated over the years in the spot where the desk had been. But the desk itself had disappeared. After some investigative work, I learned that it had been moved to another room. Overnight, the minister of commerce, General Cheng's boss, had decided to transfer a few of his employees to a room in our building. They needed more desks, so mine was the first to go.

After a few days, the desk had miraculously reappeared. It seems the Commerce bureaucrats had grown weary of their re-assignment, and the NTA had reclaimed the space. It wasn't the best working environment, and it certainly helped to have someone around who was willing to talk. My conversations with Mon always made me realize that, in the end, any concerns I had were inconsequential.

Mon and I were alone in the office that morning, but as we talked, one of us always kept an eye on the door. We had an unspoken agreement: if anyone entered, our conversation would come to an abrupt end. What Mon had to say might not please her boss.

In the early 1980s, at the height of Soviet influence in Laos, Mon had won a government scholarship to study Russian language and literature in the Soviet Union. Of all the programs available to Lao students back then, scholarships to study in the USSR were without doubt the most prestigious. It was a time when Laos' revolutionary leader and president, Kaysone Phomvihane, was consulting regularly with Soviet leaders. Stocky Russian technical advisers—or 'Soviets!' as they were known to children in the streets of Vientiane—were among the few patrons of the city's nightclubs. When Mon had applied for the scholarship, she had expressed interest in the fields of political economy, international law, and medicine. She hadn't the slightest desire to study Russian literature. But when decision time came, the government informed her it was Russian literature or nothing, so she spent six years struggling through Tolstoy, Dostoevsky, and Chekhov at the University of Kiev. Ultimately, she wrote a thesis comparing Lao and Russian literature.

"In Russia, I had no Lao books," Mon explained, "so I just tried to remember the stories my mother had told me as a child, and wrote about them." Mon was one of a handful of staff at the NTA who spoke excellent English. Although she was in her late thirties, and by now a mother of two, her cherubic face lent her a refreshing air of youth. She possessed a playful spirit that managed to shine through even in the stifling environment of Laos' bureaucracy. Each day, she came to work dressed impeccably in a *sin* and silk blouse, in accordance with a dress code enforced to encourage traditional customs. Whenever we met outside the office, however, the *sin* was replaced by blue jeans and a T-shirt.

Many Lao of Mon's generation had left home during the Cold War to study alongside their socialist brothers and sisters in Eastern Europe. Most of them would have much rather gone to the US to study English, but considering the geopolitics of time, that was out of the question. As a result, many Lao returned home saddled with all sorts of languages they would never use again—Hungarian,

Polish, Czech, Bulgarian—and ended up having to learn English anyway when the Cold War finally sputtered to an end. Very few came back convinced that the socialist path suited Laos. After all, by the time many of them arrived in Eastern Europe, students there had already begun to challenge the very system that the leaders of the Lao PDR were attempting to emulate.

After Mon returned to Vientiane in 1987, she was luckier than most, quickly finding a job as the project manager for a privately funded reproductive health project at the Lao Women's Union, the organ of the Party responsible for women's issues. Within a year, she was married, though to hear her tell the story, it was hardly love at first sight: "I didn't think he was so bad looking. And my mother felt it was time for me to get married. So I agreed."

I had met Mon's husband, a doctor, a number of times at NTA gatherings. During these encounters, he had barely uttered a word or cracked a smile; his personality made for a sharp contrast with Mon's indefatigable effervescence.

When her husband won a scholarship from the Australian government to study medicine in Sydney in 1993, Mon dropped everything and went along for the ride. She spent her time in Australia learning English and looking after their only son. The scholarship allowed the family to save a great deal of cash in Sydney; money that they would ultimately use for a new car when they got back to Vientiane. Did the Australian government envision its scholarship awards being used for family automobile purchases? Not likely, but the money meant a great deal to Mon. Every morning during my time at the NTA, Mon would drop her son off at school before driving to the office in her bright red shell of a car, which wasn't much larger than my Honda Dream.

Before she left Australia, Mon had tried several times to contact the reproductive health project back in Vientiane to ensure that she'd still have a job when she returned. But she never received a response. When she arrived home, she found that someone else had moved into her office. Her boss had simply given her job away, claiming that the correspondence had never come through.

A gust of wind rushed through the windows of the ICU, and the door swung open. Mon turned around and looked behind her. "Oh, it's only the wind," she said, relieved, as I stood up to close the door. When she knew it was safe, she continued. After her job at the reproductive health project fell through, she again lucked out and, through the help of a college friend, secured a position at the NTA. At first, things went well; the work was interesting, and she even had the use of an office motorbike. She soon became the head of the ICU and received nothing but good reports from the then chairman, Souk. He summoned her to his office numerous times a day to ask for her advice and to assign her major projects.

Then, one day, the calls just stopped.

Mon was removed from her position as director, and Khom, a bureaucrat from the Ministry of Information and Culture, took over the ICU. In the Lao PDR, Khom had two things going for him that Mon didn't: he was a member of the Party, and he was Vietnamese.

Since its earliest days, the Lao revolutionary movement had been fostered, you might say controlled, by North Vietnamese communists, and political ties between Vietnam and the Lao PDR remained tight through the 1990s. Although Khom's English skills were hardly up to the job of directing international co-operation activities, the fact that he was Vietnamese was highly valued. Soon it was Khom who was getting all the calls, while Mon waited for her phone to ring. However, all the ICU files from Mon's tenure as director remained locked in her file cabinet—and she held on to the key. Whenever Khom wanted to access an old memo or project report, he had to ask Mon first. In the game of Lao politics, this was one of her chips. She had few others.

With the arrival of a new chairman at the NTA in 1997, Mon had hoped for a change. But when General Cheng came in, the old chairman, Souk, simply refused to leave. He was demoted, but hung on to his position as the head of the People's Revolutionary Party organization at the NTA. This meant that he was responsible for all major personnel decisions. At each office of the Lao government, there was a structure for the recruitment and training of new Party members; at the NTA, of a staff of forty, 13 were members. This select group met once a month to set the NTA's agenda. The Party functioned in much the same way as a private recreation club might in the US. You could only become a candidate for membership if a current member proposed your name to his colleagues in the Party. If the entire group agreed, two Party members would be assigned to closely follow your progress over the course of one year, keeping track of your working habits and personal lifestyle.

If, at the end of that year, you hadn't made any serious mistakes, you just might be admitted to the Party. Your acceptance would be followed by a year of training, during which you would attend the monthly meetings and go through intensive instruction on Party doctrine and government policy. The Party did not often expand; existing members were likely afraid of newcomers who might upstage them and threaten their hold on power. In all, Party members made up less than two percent of Laos' total population. Mon remained stuck in the other 98.

At first, she had some luck with General Cheng, meeting frequently with him on issues related to international co-operation, and even traveling to conferences abroad with him and his wife. She had the ear of the new chairman—but, always the professional, she failed to exploit it to her own advantage. While she worked as hard as possible to get the job done, her colleagues spent their time and energy cultivating the right personal ties. As the general was so often absent, he had little idea of what actually went on inside the NTA. Far more than previous chairmen, Cheng relied on his closest staff to guide his decisions about assignments and promotions, and Mon was out of the loop. By the time she returned from a month-long tourism-management training course in Tokyo, the requests had stopped coming, and she was once again isolated and without work.

"I don't understand what happened," said Mon. "There was no problem with my work." It just didn't make sense.

———

Suddenly, the door to the ICU flew open and a short, pudgy man strode in, stomach first. It was Souk, the ex-chairman. Immediately, and according to plan, Mon and I turned our attention to the intricacies of the computer operation manual, and I pretended to be giving her a short seminar on the joys of file management in Windows 95. Souk poked around for a few seconds, perhaps checking to see if Khom was around, and then left without a word to either of us.

"Do you think he heard us?" Mon wondered aloud. "His office is just next door, you know. The walls here are quite thin."

Talking with Mon taught me that you had to play the game, and play hard, if you wanted to succeed at the NTA. Mon had yet to fully understand that pure ability counted for little in the Lao government. She hadn't played hard enough, and as a result she wasn't sure where she stood. That week, she had been informed that she would be sent to an all-expenses-paid, ten-week English-language course sponsored by ASEAN, the Association of Southeast Asian Nations. She would study English in the context of Laos' integration into Southeast Asia's regional forum. Most NTA staff would have been overjoyed at such an opportunity. Imagine, two months of English training, absolutely free! But Mon wasn't happy at all. She knew why she had been chosen over staff members who were in far greater need of language training: she had nothing better to do at the office.

It was definitely risky, but Mon seemed to find a certain relief in discussing her situation with me. The product of a culture that frowned upon openly expressing personal frustration, perhaps she saw in me an outlet for her true feelings. I was an outsider, disconnected from Vientiane society, and thus there was little risk that I'd ever discuss her story with a family friend or relative. Using a language that wasn't her own, speaking about her life in Lao society with someone who was safely removed from it, was for Mon a liberation of sorts. For me, on the other hand, talking with her was problematic. Our conversations led me to question my own motivations for living in Laos. What was my role here? What were my responsibilities to her? Shouldn't I take some action on her behalf?

Listening to her story, I found myself wanting to storm into Cheng's room to tell him the truth about the office, about who was competent and who wasn't, who deserved to be commended and who should be fired. But I knew that Mon would never allow me to do such a thing. It would only reflect negatively on her if I, a

Westerner, were to criticize the NTA on her behalf. As was so often the case, I had to contain my own outrage in order not to worsen the situation into which I had stepped. If I couldn't teach people English or help shape the development of Laos, at least I could listen. Sometimes that is contribution enough.

"It's good to talk to you, you know," Mon said again, before suggesting that we have lunch at the small noodle shop next to the office.

At the very moment we left the ICU, Souk stepped out of his adjoining office. He followed us down the stairs and out into the parking lot, never uttering a word. When he finally got into his car, Mon laughed uneasily. "Why did he leave right now?" she asked. Together, we wondered: was he keeping an eye, and an ear, on the two of us? Was he uncomfortable with the idea of one of his employees spending too much time with the only foreigner at the office?

Mon was worried, but not enough to cut off our conversation. If Souk had heard her complaints, so what? In a way, she *wanted* him to hear. She needed him to acknowledge the frustration he had caused—praising her abilities and contributions one week, then simply ignoring her the next. He needed to realize that it wasn't right to run an office based on personal whim, making personnel decisions without regard for ability. How could the NTA ever hope to accomplish anything, let alone in a professional manner, if each member of the staff was constantly worrying about where he stood—and where he might be standing next week?

Over a bowl of steaming *feu*, Chinese noodle soup, Mon kept talking. As always, the soup was served with a plate piled high with fresh greens—cilantro and mint, bean sprouts and lemon—that one added for taste. On the table sat an assortment of Lao and Thai condiments like fish paste, chili peppers, and hot sauce. I usually stayed away from these deadly bottles. Mon, on the other hand, dumped a healthy dose of each into her bowl. Just one whiff of the spices caused my nose to run.

Mon was thinking seriously of leaving the NTA. She was looking for a job in the private sector, and had already applied for a position at the UNDP. It looked as if the Lao government was about to see another of its most capable employees walk out the door. In fact, brain drain was a dilemma that had faced the Lao PDR ever since 1975. It began with the escape of most of the educated elite across the border to refugee camps in Thailand. And it continues to this day, as the government loses its best and brightest to the private sector and the international development community, or to university programs and jobs abroad. Why work for peanuts in an organization that clearly doesn't value your skills?

If Mon had quit the NTA for the private sector, the professional rewards and the security—not to mention the money—would have been far superior. Still, she was reluctant to leave. She liked working for the government, helping her country to develop, if only in a small way. Her reluctance to leave was not motivated only by altruism: she also liked the perks associated with civil service work, like international travel. Working for the UNDP, Mon would have made nearly fifty times her NTA salary, but would have had little opportunity to leave the country. The same went for the private sector: she would make more money, but she'd be stuck.

In the end, I knew, the main factor that kept Mon at the NTA had little to do with free trips abroad. It was a matter of pride. If she had resigned, it would have been an admission of defeat. Already, I knew, people at the office were beginning to talk about Mon behind her back. Why was she being passed over for major assignments? her colleagues wondered. She must have done something wrong to deserve this treatment, right? Mon could only imagine what they'd say if she had left: "See, I told you so—she couldn't stick it out. She's leaving after all." She would have had to admit that she had been forced out due to the machinations of a few washed-up Party cadres. And since she couldn't bring herself to do that, Mon stayed, waiting patiently for the phone to ring.

But not, I thought, forever.

Revelations

One mercifully cool evening in mid-January, I set out for Ming's office to pick her up for our weekly dinner. My Chinese friend's company was located in a series of rooms on the second floor of the Ministry of Information and Culture guesthouse. The MIC was the least expensive hotel in Vientiane—and, without a doubt, the most dismal. It was the kind of place that appealed only to backpackers for whom finding the cheapest and most miserable accommodation possible was an almost all-consuming challenge. Even if the price was right, why anyone would put up with the dark hallways, dirty walls, and surly employees that were the hallmarks of the MIC experience was beyond me.

Whenever I dropped by to pick up Ming, I always encountered a small crowd of hotel employees lounging in the lobby, watching TV. They were all intensely curious about my affairs with the young Asian woman who worked upstairs, and—no matter how engrossing the particular Thai game show or soap opera—all eyes were on me the moment I entered the building. By the time January had come around, I'd taken to marching into the lobby, bellowing, "*Sabaidee, tuk kon!* Hello, everybody!" and, without missing a beat, heading upstairs to Ming's office. While my bravado certainly left them speechless, it did nothing to satiate their curiosity. Relations between white men and Asian women were always cause for wild speculation in Vientiane. Even the most innocent of interactions was interpreted as a sure sign of romantic involvement. Considering the depth of our friendship, I'm sure my friends at the MIC figured that Ming and I were already married—or at least that we should have been.

Once safely outside the clutches of the MIC guesthouse, Ming hopped on the back of my motorbike and we drove across town to the Liao Ning dumpling shop, the newest Chinese restaurant in Vientiane. The owners, who had immigrated from Liao Ning, a small city north of Beijing, had opened the place only a few months before, but already it was known for its heaped servings of pork-filled dumplings, served steamed or crisply fried. Located on the bottom floor of a simple shophouse around the corner from my office, Liao Ning just barely earned the appellation "restaurant." A few mismatched tables and chairs had been cobbled together to form the dining area, and the lone woman who worked in the kitchen was unable to handle more than two customers at once. But the food was excellent, the prices reasonable, and the staff invariably pleased to see us. Liao Ning was usually filled with an odd mix of recent Chinese immigrants and young Western expats. Lao people weren't interested.

As soon as we took our seats, Ming set about her usual routine of cleaning her own place settings. First, she thoroughly wiped the plate, spoon, and teacup with a napkin, then disappeared into the kitchen to deal with the chopsticks. The Liao Ning wasn't the cleanest place in Vientiane, to be sure, but I just couldn't bring my-self to wash my own dishes. The very idea struck me as absurd. Ming's actions were typically Chinese, of course, but they were also emblematic of her entire approach to life: whatever she felt had to be done, she did it. What others thought was essentially immaterial.

Ming was a rare find in Vientiane. One of the strongest and most forceful personalities I had encountered in Laos, she spoke fluent

English, producing flawless sentences at rapid speed. She looked straight at me during conversation, establishing a direct eye contact that was unusual, even unsettling, in a Southeast Asian context. Most Lao avoid direct eye contact at all cost. In the West, speaking while looking someone "straight in the eye" is seen as a sign of honesty and trustworthiness; in Laos it is viewed as circumspect. Perhaps the worst way to get a point across to a Lao colleague was to look right at them. Rather than putting him at ease, it put him on edge.

Ever energetic, Ming's speech was marked by constant expressions of playful incredulity. "Oh, *really!*" she would cry in response to any mildly controversial statement I happened to make. I often saw my friend around town, slowly pedaling her two-speed bicycle as the traffic around her flew by. From afar, I could always spot Ming because of her flowing summer dresses and wide-brim straw hat, the very style worn by rice farmers to shield them from the sun. The bright floral patterns she favored never failed to break through the clouds of dust on Vientiane's streets.

Ming worked as an interpreter for a company that was under contract with the Chinese government to build a Lao "cultural hall" in Vientiane. A gift from the Chinese, the gargantuan building was under construction, but already it dominated the Vientiane skyline. Its façade was typical of the architecture of China after Mao: white-washed walls dotted with eerie metallic-blue windows. In a cursory nod to the culture it was built to showcase, traces of traditional Lao design graced the edges of the building. But no flourishes of pseudo-Buddhist imagery could hide the fact that the entire project was out of place in Vientiane. In fact, its style was diametrically opposed to all that I considered Lao. Whereas Lao architecture was understated and subtle, designed to maximize interaction with the natural elements, this hall was imposing and inescapable—much like China itself, you might say. And not even Ming, deeply involved as she was with the intricacies of the company's management, could tell me what the building would ultimately be used for. "We just have to finish it on time," she told me. "That's the important thing."

This emphasis on a speedy completion had led to a few gross errors. When the Lao government had first accepted the project, Ming's company had sensibly suggested an underground parking lot be incorporated into the plans. But the Lao government had dismissed the offer as too expensive and time-consuming, insisting that visitors could just as easily park on the streets nearby. As the sprawling building neared completion, the prime minister's office belatedly realized that there *weren't* any streets nearby. So in order to make room for a parking lot, the company was ordered to demolish a group of buildings, left over from the days of French rule, adjacent to the project site. Overnight, the families who had lived here for decades were unceremoniously kicked out of their homes. And by the next evening, in the name of progress, a piece of Vientiane's architectural heritage had been rendered a pile of bricks.

The National Culture Hall was a perfect example of how foreign aid could go horribly wrong. The Chinese were aware that it was a fairly useless project. The officials in the Lao PM's office knew it. Ming and her colleagues knew it. And my neighbors, whose lives it was somehow supposed to improve, certainly knew it. No one really wanted the thing, but who was going to refuse a free building?

"I know that this project doesn't help the Lao people," said Ming. "It only helps the Chinese government. They want Laos' vote in the UN." The rumor around town was that the Chinese president was even thinking about coming to Vientiane upon completion of the project—the first visit by a Chinese head of state to Laos anyone could remember. Even after a half a century of independence and a quarter century of communist rule, Laos remained a pawn in the grand game of international politics.

At the Liao Ning, Ming and I ordered a plate of steamed dumplings and two glasses of weak Chinese tea, and settled in for the long wait while our food was prepared from scratch. In the meantime, Ming told me about her experiences as an employee of a Chinese company overseas. Hers was not simply a job, I discovered; it was a way of life. She was required to work seven full days a week, despite the fact that, by law, Chinese workers were granted weekends off. "The Chinese government and the Chinese Embassy know, but they keep silent."

What about the law?

"It doesn't mean anything. The Chinese people can write the most perfect laws in the world, but they are the worst at carrying them out. If I run a red light in China, and the officer is my classmate, he'll let me go. But if I have no connections, I have to pay."

Ming ate three meals a day at the office, slept in the company house, and was even expected to vacation with her colleagues. Over the Chinese New Year holiday, Ming had wanted to take a few days off to travel by herself, perhaps just over the border to Nong Khai in Thailand. But her boss wouldn't hear of it. The office was going up to Luang Prabang for the weekend, and Ming would be coming. And she would have fun. It would have been considered ungrateful, even treacherous, for her not to have joined the group, so she acquiesced and went along.

Ming, who was 26, came from Kunming, the capital of Yunnan province. She and I were close in age, but our backgrounds could scarcely have been more different. Ming had been born into a period of unimaginable chaos: China's Cultural Revolution, a time when Mao's Red Guard was terrorizing the country and anyone with an intellectual background was labeled an enemy. Ming's mother, a highly regarded doctor, had been the best student in her class at medical school, a distinction that now spelled disaster. When the Red Guard took over, she was one of the first to be sent to work in a remote village miles from Kunming. She took Ming with her. Ming's father, a chemical engineer, was sent off to work in another distant rural town, and he took Ming's younger sister along with him.

During the Cultural Revolution, all able men and women in China were forced to work full time. Since Ming's mother ran the only clinic in the village almost single-handedly, she had to leave Ming unattended in their apartment during the day. Ming saw her mother only briefly at dinner time, when she would return from the clinic to prepare some food before heading out once again to study the writings of Mao with her *danwei*, or work group—often until midnight. No childcare was available for Ming, as her identity papers listed her as a resident of Kunming, and only local children were accepted at the village children's center.

Of course, Ming wasn't the only one who found herself in this situation. "Oh, everyone has the same story to tell," she assured me. Each day, once her mother and all the other parents were safely out of sight, Ming would climb on top of her kitchen table, out through the window, to the street below. She would make her way to a large field nearby where the other abandoned children all gathered to keep themselves entertained, requiring a fair amount of improvisation. One of their favorite activities was to capture, kill, and cook small animals over an open fire. "I ate all kinds of strange food at that time—mice, rats, lizards."

The children were happy enough with their independence, but they soon learned that the consequences of the Cultural Revolution could be deadly. One evening, while her parents were out at a political education session, one of Ming's friends set out for the field on her own. When her parents came home late that night and found her missing, a village search committee was sent out. The next morning, on the outskirts of the village, only her clothes were found.

The girl had been attacked and killed by a wolf, but even this incident didn't put an end to the madness in the village. And the Cultural Revolution hadn't put a dent in Ming's parents' unwavering support of Mao, a figure they continued to worship. "He is like a god to them, even now," said Ming.

So who did they blame for the excesses of the Cultural Revolution?

"Just 'crazy people,' I guess."

Ming had begun to lose faith in the Chinese version of communism long before she first came to Laos, in 1995. Even prior to the Tiananmen Square massacre of 1989, she had come to doubt that the West was the source of all that was evil and corrupt in the world. "There were two truths in China when I was growing up: the truth in the textbook, and the reality outside," Ming said as we sipped our tea still waiting for our dumplings to arrive. "The textbook said that socialism was the best, that socialist countries were the richest, but we all knew this wasn't true. But no one said anything. We just lied. Even my parents, they lied. If they wanted to stay home from work to be with their children, they couldn't tell their superiors. They had to make some excuse that would demonstrate their devotion to the party, so they said they were sick. We all lived a lie, every day." But Ming had continued to believe that the Chinese government was fundamentally good, and that it had the interests of the Chinese people at heart.

That all changed when she got to Vientiane. Through her job, she observed first-hand the deep-seated corruption of the Lao government, and came to realize that her own government was operating under the same flawed system. Ming was responsible for taking care of the delegations from China's Ministry of Foreign Affairs that came to Vientiane to monitor her project's progress. "They just wanted to stay in the best hotels, eat the most expensive food, and have a nice time." She was surprised by their disregard for the good of the people, Lao or Chinese. But she knew the deal: her company used the Chinese government's money to entertain its officials, thus ensuring that its contract would be renewed in the future.

During her first year in Vientiane, Ming fell into a period of confusion, even despair, which was entirely out of character for this determined young woman. She began to question the entire world in which she'd been raised. "I decided that I couldn't return to China, that I'd go to live in America." She rejected communist ideas and even challenged traditional Chinese morals. At night, she went out to nightclubs—though, she assured me, she never touched any alcohol. She befriended a group of Western men, a wild bunch who talked openly and almost incessantly about their sexual exploits. "I had all sorts of bad thoughts then, about boys, about what I wanted to do with them. I knew that if I had the chance, I'd do it. I thought, why should I waste my youth?"

She had a plan, and was just waiting for the chance to execute it. Then, it all fell apart.

One weekend, she took a trip with a group of Chinese friends to Tad Leuk, a waterfall that lies just a few hours south of Vientiane. As a dare, she and two others decided to walk across the river at the top of the waterfall: "We stepped along the rocks, holding hands, and all of a sudden—I'm sure it wasn't my fault—my friends slipped and fell into the water, and pulled me down with them." The three were whisked away by the speed of the water as it rushed towards the falls. Ming grasped in vain for a branch or stone. Soon, she felt herself falling. "I felt water pouring down all around me. Then I hit a rock, and felt a huge bump on the back of my head. I thought to myself, 'This is it. This is my life. And what have I done with it? What was the meaning of it?'"

She survived with only minor injuries, but she checked into Mahosot Hospital just in case. Since the medical care at Mahosot was nearly non-existent, her friends suggested that she see a

Taiwanese doctor who was living in Vientiane at the time. But, they warned Ming, there was something she should know: the doctor was a Christian.

"At that time, I knew nothing about Christianity. Like most Chinese people, I just thought it was something foreign, something strange—nothing to do with me! But I was curious, and I thought maybe I could get a free Bible from her, so I agreed!" Reading material in Vientiane was scarce and, sure enough, when she arrived at her bedside, the doctor brought a Chinese-language Bible for Ming to read.

With little else to do, Ming began leafing through the Old Testament. She was surprised by how negative the whole thing was. "From Adam and Eve all the way through to Abraham and his sons, everything was bad. Nothing nice. I thought, 'Where are all the good things?' Then I read the New Testament. And there was one phrase I remember: 'Ask and you shall receive.' 'That's it,' I thought. I just have to ask, and my questions will be answered."

Soon after checking out of the hospital, she joined a Taiwanese church group and began her journey through the world of Christianity. She stopped hanging out with the same crowd of Westerners. All of a sudden, she'd encountered a concept of love that she had never before known. "In communism, we are taught to hate. If your father is a class enemy, you must hate him. The only love we are taught is class love. But Christianity teaches real love, for all people. Love your neighbor as yourself."

Not at all religious myself—I hadn't been to a church in years— I felt the conversation veering into vaguely uncomfortable territory. Just when it was getting a bit too heavy for my tastes, the food thankfully arrived. Ming discreetly bowed her head in silent prayer before digging in. She seemed secure in her new-found belief in Christianity, but I could sense that she was struggling to reconcile her Chinese heritage with the Western concepts of individualism and free choice that she'd encountered in Vientiane. "I just can't talk to them," Ming said of her Chinese colleagues. They couldn't understand why she had adopted a "foreign" religion, or why she chose to spend time with foreigners. If she needed religion, why not Buddhism? Many were wary of any non-Chinese, particularly Americans. As an American man, of course, I was a central target of their suspicions. When we went out for dinner, Ming often requested that we meet at the restaurant; she preferred not to suffer the scrutiny of her colleagues when I picked her up at the office.

In fact, everything about Ming's life in Laos was risky. Freedom of religion was guaranteed by the constitution, and Christians were permitted to practice their faith. But the constitution also prohibited "all acts of creating division of religion or creating divisions among the people," and Christianity had come under increasing scrutiny. In 1999, district authorities—with the support of the police and military forces—orchestrated a renunciation and church-closing campaign in Savannakhet. By the end of 2000, fewer than half of the province's churches remained open. In Vientiane, where a similar campaign was launched, officials demanded Christians renounce their faith or face arrest or imprisonment, and more than ten churches were closed. Around the country, about 95 Christians were arrested, and 25 remained in detention without trial at the end of 2000.

As a foreigner, Ming was safer than Lao Christians, but she wasn't immune: the government wasn't afraid to target non-Lao accused of proselytizing in defiance of prohibitions. It didn't happen often, but foreigners working for evangelical groups operating under the guise of providing social services like education were subject to arrest and detention.

Ming's religious affiliation wasn't the only thing that set her apart. Her association with foreigners, her desire to eat out with friends or even alone every once in a while—all were liabilities. But by removing herself from the world she knew back home in Kunming, Ming had learned so much and experienced so many new things that the risk was worth it. That's not to say that all of her questions had been answered. In fact, she seemed to welcome my own skepticism about the Christianity she had accepted.

I was suspicious of the Christian organizations I'd encountered in Laos, whose members often proselytized under the guise of English-language teaching or some other form of aid. They seemed to offer attractively simple answers to deeply complicated questions. How can you know that there is a God? Is the Bible the Truth or simply a convenient fiction? Hadn't Ming just replaced one dogma with another?

"Communism is a religion, yes," she said. "Like a religion, it can never be realized. You can never prove that it's right."

Unlike so many of Vientiane's expats, who whiled away their time pining for home over beer on the banks of the Mekong, for Ming, living in Laos had been a tremendous transformative experience. She now openly challenged what her government told her, expressing controversial views over dinner on everything from China's role in Tibet to its campaign to enter the WTO. Just as I had come to view America in a different light during my time in Laos, Ming had gained a new perspective on her own country. Laos was a prism through which we could more clearly view the places we called home. For Ming, Vientiane had turned out to be a city of revelations, where she had learned more about the world—and about herself—than she ever would have if she had stayed in China.

"Sometimes it's good to look at your country from another place," she told me as we waited for the check. "Sometimes you don't like what you see."

I agreed with her. But I had trouble reconciling what I knew about Ming—her curiosity, flexibility, and dynamism—with her strong religious convictions. How had she managed to achieve such clarity so quickly, to suddenly accept that there was a single answer to her problems? I had never experienced the sort of revelation she had described to me. Much as I had tried over the years, I had never managed to find the Truth. And for all of its extraordinary contributions to the world, religion had always struck me as a potentially dangerous force. I had always tried to see things from all sides, to try to understand every possible perspective. It's true, this usually left me confused—and dissatisfied. In a sense, clarity was just what I had come to Laos to attain, but my time there had only made me more confused about the world.

Laos had long been a laboratory in which the great powers freely conducted experiments on how to structure society. Imperialism, independence, capitalism, communism, socialism, development, evangelism, nation-building—Laos had seen it all. But what was to be learned from all this experimentation?

If Ming could find the answer, why couldn't I?

Funny Money

"So, what did you do this weekend?"

Thus began many a Monday morning English lesson at the NTA. Ill-prepared for class, as I was so often wont to be, it was this question that I'd use to kick off a lesson with my advanced students. The idea was to buy myself some time as I mulled over how on earth we were going to spend the next hour and a half together. Usually, however, my students had no interest in assisting me in this endeavor. Rather than expound upon their favorite weekend leisure activities, they preferred instead to sit in silence and stare. One Monday, however, I did get a response. Seng was the only student who had shown up that day, and in answer to my simple query, he taught me an economics lesson that I'd not soon forget.

"What did I do this weekend. . . ? I worked."

At the NTA, Seng definitely stood out. He was one of only a handful of employees from Laos' ethnic minorities. Most of my colleagues were Lao Loum, the lowland Lao who have always ruled

Laos. Seng was Lao Theung, the poorest of the country's ethnic groups. According to government calculations, about half the population was Lao Loum, while thirty percent was Lao Theung. The government trumpeted the nation's ethnic diversity at every opportunity. Female representatives of each of the three main groups invariably showed up on printed currency, government billboards, and in official festivals and parades. The number of minorities in the National Assembly was representative of their proportion of the population at large. At the NTA, I translated many a speech for vice-ministers and deputy prime ministers that made a point of congratulating Laos' ethnic minorities for their contributions—never quite identified—to the success of Visit Laos Year 1999–2000.

Seng had been born roughly thirty years before in a rural village just north of Luang Prabang. His parents had converted to lowland rice cultivation under a government relocation plan targeted at ethnic minorities when Seng was only a child; his parents were still farmers in the same small village. After completing his studies, Seng moved south to the capital to make his fortune. Things hadn't turned out quite as he had hoped. As we sat alone in the classroom at the NTA, he told me about his life in Vientiane outside of English class. For weeks now, his one-year old son had been very sick and needed medical attention badly. But good quality, affordable healthcare was hard to come by in a country in which the economy was spinning wildly out of control. The kip was sinking fast, and Seng was struggling just to keep his head above water.

When the Asian economic crisis descended on the nations of Southeast Asia in 1997, Laos was hit hardest of all. The country's fledgling economy was so dependent on Thai investment, and on the Thai market for its exports, that it simply could not stand on its own. When the Thai baht began to slide, the kip abruptly collapsed. Laos saw a greater depreciation of its currency and a higher inflation rate than any other country in Asia. The kip was still sliding when I arrived in Vientiane, when one US dollar was worth about 3,800 kip on the black market. A month later, it was 4,200. By the time summer came around, the exchange rate had reached 9,000 to the dollar. No one even bothered with the official bank rate. The kip had depreciated more than seventy percent, and inflation had surpassed 100 percent. By March 1999, the World Bank had decided against granting a 20-million-dollar credit to the Lao government due to its failure to meet conditions of reform and restructuring to which it had previously agreed. Even worse, as the currency took a nosedive and prices soared, salaries remained the same. In 1997, the average civil servant had been paid a monthly salary worth twenty dollars, but by mid-1999 it was the equivalent of only ten.

That is, if they were being paid at all.

On the morning Seng and I spoke, the staff at the NTA had not actually been paid in more than three months—the office had run out of money, and the central government wasn't about to supply any more. Even when my colleagues did receive their salaries, the money just wasn't enough to survive. With prices rising daily, they couldn't buy what they had been able to in the days before the crisis began. At the market, the average price of meat rose from $1.75 to $2.60 per kilogram, almost overnight. Seng told me that he was now paying more than two dollars per kilogram for beef and pork, a dollar for fish, and a dollar and a half for chicken. As he and his family attempted to stay afloat in a sea of fluctuating currency exchange rates, skyrocketing prices, and absurdly low salaries, Seng found that his hands were tied more tightly than ever before.

No one had any idea how large the country's foreign reserves were; it was a closely guarded state secret. International economists guessed that 100 million dollars, or just two months of imports, was optimistic. They explained that the depreciation of Laos' currency was the result of a severe balance of payments deficit—for every dollar of export, Laos was importing two dollars—that had been exacerbated by shrinking export growth during the economic crisis. A steep contraction in the Asian market for timber—regrettably one of Laos' major exports—had led to a ballooning of the trade deficit. Foreign direct investment had also dried up; investors had their own crises to deal with at home. And the possibility of a bail-out by the IMF or the World Bank seemed unlikely, as the Lao government was unable—or unwilling—to meet the strict conditions set by the international lending agencies.

Seng and his wife, a nurse at Mahosot Hospital, did what it took to get by. To save on housing costs, they lived with their child on the empty, unfurnished second floor of the NTA. They were able to make a bit of extra money this way, as Seng also served as a night guard for the building. Their living space was a gloomy affair, with few windows and none of the comforts of home. The unpainted walls were coated with a thick layer of cobwebs, and boxes of unwanted government papers sat in a corner of their modest kitchen.

Because his wife was a nurse, Seng's son was guaranteed a place at the hospital's day-care center. But the center was filled with so many sick children that Seng feared a stay there would do his son's health more harm than good. And Seng couldn't afford to pay for care at one of Vientiane's private children's clinics. Doctors at these clinics were known to refuse to tell their patients what type of medicine they had prescribed, in order to force them to return to the clinic each time they needed care. The doctors would crush the particular medicine into an unidentifiable powder and hand it to the patient in a small paper funnel. To make sure you got the right stuff, then, you always had to visit the clinic—the much cheaper pharmacies weren't an option.

On the weekends, Seng explained, his work did not stop. To help make ends meet, he and his wife produced a popular Lao candy made of peanuts and sugar, and sold it to a vendor at a market just out of town. On Friday night after work, under the sole working light bulb in their makeshift apartment, they would boil pure sugar in a large vat. When the sugar had melted, they would add the crushed peanuts. They poured the mixture onto long, flat baking sheets, rolled it into a thin layer, and let it harden overnight. On Saturday morning, they would cut the candy into small squares and wrap the individual pieces in plastic. Seng would then get on his motorbike and head out of town to the market, where competition from other candy suppliers was fierce. Seng's vendor would pay him only after every piece had been sold.

Seng didn't always think his life would end up this way. After he graduated from high school in the early 1980s, he had been granted a scholarship by the government to study in the Soviet Union. Seng saw the scholarship as a tremendous opportunity to gather knowledge that he could later use to help his own country to develop. And it was an extraordinary achievement. People like Seng faced deep-rooted discrimination in Laos; even today, state and Party officials are known to deny qualified people from ethnic minorities the opportunity to study abroad. Generally, given their remote habitats, minority tribes have difficulty influencing government decisions regarding spending and the allocation of natural resources. But Seng was lucky enough to spend six years studying engineering in the Ukraine, and he loved every minute of it. Well, perhaps not every minute.

When he first arrived in the USSR, he admitted, he was a little homesick. The winter was cruel, and he wasn't used to the faceless concrete apartment buildings in which everyone lived. "But after some time," Seng told me, "it was okay." Before long, he found a Russian girlfriend and moved into her apartment near the university. One night, he invited a fellow Lao exchange student, Bounnyang, over to the apartment for drinks to meet his girlfriend and one of her classmates. Bounnyang showed up with a case of beer and some dried, salted fish, a typical Russian snack. The four of them imbibed quite a bit that night, and Bounnyang ended up sleeping with the classmate of Seng's girlfriend.

When Bounnyang completed his studies in chemical engineering in 1994, he proposed to the girl, and they were soon married at a small church in Odessa. She moved with him back to Vientiane and quickly found work at the Soviet Embassy. The transition wasn't so easy for Bounnyang. He applied for a position with the government; with his strong scientific background, he was sure he'd be offered something at the Ministry of Science and Technology. But no positions were available to Lao citizens who had studied abroad. Everyone knew that Bounnyang was far better qualified, but those who had stayed behind had filled all the jobs—every desk at the ministry was taken.

Nearing graduation back in the Ukraine, Seng also asked his girlfriend to marry him. But she refused; her family, who lived in an apartment only a block away, would not allow her to leave the country. Upon returning to Vientiane, Seng was offered a job with the NTA. The position had nothing whatsoever to do with what he had studied in the Soviet Union, but at least it was a job, and Seng was glad to have it. Eventually, his girlfriend married a Russian man, and Seng later married a Lao girl. He wasn't sure if his ex-girlfriend even knew—it had been years since they'd last exchanged letters.

Bounnyang was never able to find a job with the government. When Seng and I spoke, he was working as a delivery man for the Beer Lao Company in Vientiane. He drove from one beer shop to the next, ensuring that all the inventories were in order. His wasn't a job that required a degree in chemical engineering. At Beer Lao, Bounnyang was making more money than he ever could have as a civil servant, but he still dreamt of one day actually putting the skills he had learned in the former Soviet Union to work. Every once in a while, Seng visited Bounnyang and his wife at their house on the outskirts of Vientiane. It was a far cry from Seng's spartan apartment at the NTA. They lived in a neighborhood of large villas, most of which were rented by foreign expats. Just like Seng and his wife, they had a one-year old son.

"When I go to visit, we speak Russian and talk about the past," Seng said.

"Do you sometimes feel uncomfortable when you go to his house?" I asked.

"Oh, no," Seng assured me. "Because I know that he is a close friend." Bounnyang may have been a close friend, but Seng must have recognized the irony in their relationship. Seng had realized his dream of serving his nation in a government position, and now he lived on an empty floor of his office building. Bounnyang, a trained chemical engineer, had been shut out of the civil service—and he lived in a fancy house in the suburbs with a foreign wife, a car, and cash to spare.

After English class was over, I spent some time in the Statistics Unit helping Seng write and edit the 1998 Statistics Report on Tourism in Laos. But first, I had to take a trip to the only functioning office latrine, my personal roll of toilet paper in hand—soft and welcoming in comparison to the scraps of waste paper someone had kindly placed in a basket inside the stall. After I returned to the office, we popped the Spice Girls into the CD player and worked together to produce an English-language document that actually made sense, a rarity indeed at the NTA. Towards the end of the day, as he was piecing together a map of Laos to include in the report, Seng suddenly looked up from his desk.

"Mr. Brett, do you think the Lao economy will survive?"

Not grasping the gravity of his question at first, I laughed it off. "Oh, sure it will, come on. It's okay." I turned my attention back to the truly riveting paragraph on the screen; a convoluted, statistic-ridden text about tourist arrivals and departures.

"No, Brett, do think it will *survive?*" Seng insisted.

Taken aback by his sudden and intense concern, I walked over to his desk and asked him what was up. The night before, it turned out, he had heard a Voice of America broadcast on his short-wave radio that had reported that the Lao economy was about to collapse. I had always thought of VOA as a dusty vestige of the Cold War, but even today, Lao who spoke English well enough tuned into the US government broadcasts regularly in order to get a different perspective on news about their own country.

"What happens to my savings if the government runs out of money? Won't the banks be empty?" he asked.

"Well, what does the government tell you?" I wondered aloud.

"Nothing!" Seng replied. "They just keep saying that everything is okay."

Throughout my time in Vientiane, the government had been essentially silent on the issue of the nation's precipitous economic decline. In the local newspapers, officials acknowledged Laos' financial difficulties only with empty calls for unity, patriotism, and increased devotion to the People's Revolutionary Party. But the people were worried, and they were beginning to demand explanations. As I listened to Seng talk about the dire economic situation, I sensed an apprehension in his voice that I'd rarely encountered in Laos. I wanted to comfort him, to tell him that things would be all right. I wanted to provide some answers.

But what was I supposed to say? What did he really want from me? Answers? What did I know about economics, anyway? Only what I'd read in books or gleaned from theoretical discussions at school about growth and contraction, inflation and unemployment. I had spent some time studying Asian political economy, reading and writing about the post-war economic miracle and social change in East Asia. But Seng knew so much more about the world, and about living, than I did. He had a wife and child, and faced responsibilities and concerns that dwarfed my own. All I really had to worry about was which restaurant I'd go to for dinner that evening. Chinese noodle soup or Vietnamese spring rolls? Throughout my life, I'd been given so much: a supportive family, extraordinary educational opportunities, the chance to live and work abroad. All I really knew about suffering was what I'd read in books or seen on stage. But there was nothing theoretical about the economic crisis in Laos. It was about people's lives.

And Seng was asking *me* for answers?

In Laos, I often found myself in this position. It was one that I found unsettling. Here I was, 23 years old, fresh out of the ivory tower. For most of my life, I had been told what to do—what papers to write, what courses to take. And now, as a "consultant" of sorts at the NTA, I was expected to tell others what to do. Not only how to speak English, but also how to do their jobs. But what did I know about their jobs, or about how to develop tourism in Laos? Just about the youngest person at the office—in a society in which age was traditionally respected above all else—I was among the least qualified to provide advice on sound and sustainable development policies for Laos' future. It is true, I had been offered opportunities most of my colleagues could only dream of. Sure, I knew more about technology and current affairs than any of them. I could use the Internet and name Israel's prime minister. But they had far more to teach me than I did them about the way the world worked.

In fact, I did have a few words of comfort to offer Seng. I knew from my informal discussions with visiting officials from the Asian Development Bank and other agencies that fears of a collapse of the Lao economy were largely unfounded. Despite all the negative talk, some economic indicators didn't look all that bad: while the average growth rate for Southeast Asia in 1998 had been well below zero, in Laos, it had been about four percent. Within the region, severe contraction in Thailand and Indonesia had actually been offset by this positive growth in Laos, which had been largely fueled by a major hydro-electric dam project.

Furthermore, for the average Lao citizen out in the provinces, the Asian economic crisis meant very little. The vast majority of Laos' five or so million citizens were agricultural workers who lived in a subsistence, non-market economy. As I told Seng, the farmers down south were not about to stop farming just because of a little kip fluctuation up in Vientiane.

But my explanation would offer little consolation to my friends at the NTA. The farmers might not have been suffering as a result of the economic crisis, but Seng and his colleagues certainly were. They belonged to the one sector of the Lao population that could not ignore the regional economy: the middle class—its entrepreneurs and civil servants.

After we had finished talking, Seng took one look at the work that remained on his desk and—although closing time was still an hour away—packed up his things and left. The annual statistics report could wait until tomorrow.

In an economy that required constant ingenuity just to survive, he had more important things to do.

The Consultants

Even with his four legs, the animal slips;
even with all his knowledge, the scholar makes mistakes.
Lao Proverb.

Thomas had a problem.

A consultant with the German government's official development agency, Thomas had been working in Laos for more than two
years. With a professional background in biology and a strong interest in environmental protection, he had been responsible for
co-ordinating Laos' National Wildlife Day in 1997. It had been a
great success, but one that had yet to be repeated; for reasons not
at all clear to Thomas, there had been no mention of National Wildlife Day since. Even more discouraging, the environmental edcation
project that Thomas used to run out of the Department of Forestry
had simply disappeared.

"So what's happening at Forestry these days?" I asked Thomas,
a balding, soft-spoken man nearing his fifties, during our first conversation over a beer by the pool at the Lane Xang Hotel.

"Nothing," he replied with a weary sigh. "Nothing's happening.
One day I came back from holidays and my staff was gone. They

had all been transferred to other offices. Now I basically just do paperwork."

In fact, most foreign experts in Vientiane had a horror story or two to tell about bureaucratic inertia and corruption at Forestry. When the Lao government established 17 National Biodiversity Conservation Areas (NBCAs)—totaling about ten percent of the country's land mass—and placed them under the jurisdiction of the Department of Forestry back in 1993, many environmental organizations and foreign governments had been taken in by this superficial commitment to the environment. A flourish of development aid activity in the field of conservation soon followed, and consultants from around the world descended on Vientiane.

By the time I arrived, most NBCA projects were already as stagnant as the Mekong. Overwhelming obstacles like illegal logging, wildlife poaching, and the government's nearly complete failure to enforce conservation regulations had left international aid workers feeling frustrated and helpless. Environmental experts seemed to be packing up their things and fleeing the country with a haste that rivaled the exodus of Lao citizens after 1975.

So why didn't Thomas just join the crowd and head back to Germany?

"I don't like Germany," he said.

He was disgruntled with his situation at the ministry, but he wasn't about to leave Laos. He liked living in Vientiane. His wife, a Filipina who was the lead singer for the house band at the Novotel, also enjoyed life in Laos. So Thomas needed to find a new job. And not just any job—he had a few strict requirements. First was that, "I must stay in Vientiane, not in the provinces. Maybe a short trip occasionally, but I cannot live out there."

So now, the Germans' top priority was to find Thomas some work. That's how he and Martin, a fellow consultant in the field of geology, ended up at my office one Monday morning for a meeting with Bounh, Desa's replacement as the director of the UNDP project. The Germans were armed with a spanking new development aid proposal: an all-expenses-paid eco-tourism consultant stationed at the NTA. The consultant would assist the government by working with local communities and the private sector to develop eco-tourism projects in the National Biodiversity Conservation Areas.

"Usually, we would need you to write a detailed terms of reference for the office back in Germany," Martin explained to Bounh over a UNDP-funded Nescafe. "Then they would choose someone who fit the position exactly. But, luckily, in this case we already have somebody in mind."

And who would that be? You guessed it: our friend Thomas.

This all sounded great to my NTA colleagues, of course. As long as the government didn't have to spend any of its own money, it would happily accept just about any aid project a foreign consultant could come up with. Garbage cans for urban centers? Great! Red-tape reduction for the PM's office? Why not! A foreign aid project to co-ordinate existing foreign aid projects? Come on in!

With so many international aid agencies and NGOs lining up to pump money into the country, government officials barely had to lift a finger. And, busy sifting through the endless torrent of new aid proposals, bureaucrats certainly didn't have a chance to propose their own ideas.

At first, the NTA hadn't quite understood Thomas' proposal. As Martin had explained to me the day before meeting with Bounh, whenever the Germans looked into starting up a new aid project, they first distributed a questionnaire to the government in order to assess its needs in the area concerned. At the NTA, this questionnaire had somehow ended up in the mildly capable hands of Nee, of the Hotel Training and Management Division. Using her extremely limited written English skills, Nee had dutifully filled out the questionnaire and sent it back. When Thomas reviewed the responses, he noticed something was amiss: they had nothing at all to do with eco-tourism. Instead, Nee had requested that Thomas provide customer-service training for hotel and restaurant staff in Vientiane.

"But I'm a biologist!" Thomas had protested.

In any case, each of us—Thomas, Martin, Bounh, and I—knew that the questionnaire completion exercise was little more than a farce. Its contents were irrelevant. For, in essence, Thomas was going to be working at the NTA whether the NTA liked it or not.

When Martin had first mentioned the project to me, he had presented it as a done deal. "It seems we need to find somewhere for Thomas to work, and somehow NTA is it."

I never mentioned it to Thomas, but his modest eco-tourism consultancy project embodied everything that was wrong with development in Laos. His very approach had doomed the project to failure from the outset; like so many aid workers before him, he had put the cart before the horse. Rather than making a genuine effort to discern the needs of the Lao government in a particular area, researching what had already been done and proposing a project accordingly, the Germans had simply come up with something that fulfilled *their* immediate need: putting one of their frustrated consultants back to work. In fact, an eco-tourism development project was already well underway at the NTA, but the Germans didn't even seem to know about it.

Whether or not the project was necessary was immaterial. They just needed to find Thomas a job.

"In fact, tourism is not my specialty," said Mr. Kawabata with a slight chuckle over his chilled asparagus soup at Le Vêndome restaurant. A Frenchman ran this modest eatery in the center of Vientiane, just around the corner from my house and a few paces from the riverfront. Le Vêndome was a favorite haunt of Kawabata's; in fact, it was the sole restaurant in Vientiane, save his hotel dining room, to which he had ever ventured.

Kawabata was a consultant with Japan's official development agency, assigned to advise the NTA for three months on how it might expand access to the Japanese tourist market. It was a field in which he had limited experience, and this evening, with the aid of a bottle of Chardonnay, he wasn't afraid to admit it.

As I swatted the occasional mosquito away from my plate, Kawabata told me his story. It was difficult to pay close attention to his every word, as his appearance offered numerous distractions. His hair was perpetually out of place, despite the healthy dose of grease he used to try and keep it under control. He donned a pair of large eyeglasses, which insisted on sliding down to the tip of his nose during conversation; the thick lenses and heavy black plastic frames were straight out of the 1950s. And he spoke in short, awkward spurts that sometimes gave the impression of an officer barking commands rather than a colleague making conversation.

Kawabata had been a casualty of the bursting of Japan's economic bubble in the mid-1990s. When he was laid off in 1997, he had been working at Tokyo Steel for nearly 35 years. So much for lifetime employment. Luckily, with the help of his former employer, he had been able to quickly secure a position as a "senior research consultant" at an international tourism development institute in Tokyo. Overnight, he transformed himself into an expert on tourism development in the Third World—and ended up in an office adjacent to the ICU at the NTA.

Kawabata's transition to tourism development in Laos was rather hurried, as I discovered when I first ran into him in the hall outside his office. After introducing ourselves and making pleasant conversation in Japanese for a few minutes, we exchanged cards. On his I was surprised to find the logo of the Tokyo Steel Corporation. This was the same card, I supposed, that he'd used while living and working for Tokyo Steel in Michigan in the late 1980s, a time when the Japanese economy was still on the rise and Japan's corporations had outposts all over the American economic landscape.

Now Kawabata lived with his wife and two sons in Japan's Saitama prefecture, smack in the middle of the Tokyo suburbs. Though they were both nearing thirty, his sons, like most unmarried Japanese, still lived at home—it was cheaper, and, in any case, more in keeping with the central Confucian value of filial piety. Kawabata commuted into Central Tokyo each morning by train, a long ride that gave him a chance to read his favorite conservative daily newspaper. Back in Japan, he lived in an ocean of conformity.

During his first two and a half months at the NTA, Kawabata accomplished precious little. He sat in his air-conditioned office, an unwieldy Japanese-English dictionary at his side, and dutifully scrutinized the English-language *Vientiane Times* in an attempt to understand the scintillating articles. Every once in a while, he would come up with a few recommendations for the NTA staff. Once, he fired off a three-page memo to the head of the Marketing and Promotion Unit, pointing out all the typographical mistakes in the English-language "Visit Laos Year 1999–2000" brochure. Kawabata spoke English very well, but his written skills still had a ways to go. He ended up replacing the NTA's errors with ones of his own.

During the final two weeks of his contract, however, Kawabata struck gold. Over dinner, he let me in on his minor triumph: the discovery that there was a ceiling on the number of tourists Laos could ever hope to attract. Considering the limited flight capacity into Vientiane, and up north, at the time, Kawabata argued, the NTA would be unable to expand tourism much beyond 1999 levels. The country would need to improve international air access and domestic air travel, and soon. I congratulated him on his observation, but not before noting that there was little, if anything, the NTA could do about it. Kawabata's pride was undiminished, however, and he waited until just the right moment before he revealed his discovery to the rest of the staff.

The moment came a few days later, when he was scheduled to give a presentation to summarize the findings of his mission. As he slowly made his way through his notes and prepared to unveil the great revelation, I could sense the excitement gradually welling up inside him. Unfortunately, Kawabata's excitement was not contagious—his presentation style left something to be desired. He rattled off statistics from his triumphant report without once looking up: 5.9% Japanese travelers, 4.3% male backpackers, a 5% market share. The numbers just kept on coming. Most of the staff in attendance hadn't the faintest idea what Kawabata was talking about, and when he finally dropped the news about the flight capacity problem, it fell on deaf ears. The only reason half the room had shown up in the first place was for a break from work and a free soft drink.

As Kawabata plowed on, Khit and others madly flipped through the presentation materials in a vain attempt to follow along. The confusion on my colleagues' and students' faces was painful to witness. The office cameraman had been brought in to document the session, and I prayed that he wouldn't focus on Mani of the

Statistics Unit. Her expression betrayed the reality that she could barely introduce herself in English, let alone digest reports on the intricacies of tourism development. Kawabata occasionally tried to ease the tension with a joke or two, but they inevitably fell flat. When they did, his lonely chuckles came across not simply as awkward—in this context, they struck me as almost maniacal.

Kawabata was a kind man, and well-intentioned, but to my colleagues he appeared as the archetypal "Ugly Japanese." He had marched into the office and, without any knowledge of the language, culture, or political system, demanded changes that the NTA simply couldn't carry out. The staff loved to make fun of Kawabata behind his back: his anachronistic fashion, the corner of his shirt that peeked out of his perpetually undone zipper, his disheveled hair. But Kawabata's main obstacle wasn't his flawed appearance. It was the content of his consultancy. An employee of the Japanese government concerned almost exclusively with the Japanese market, Kawabata's advice would always be circumspect at the NTA.

For in the end, Kawabata's failure came down to one grand miscalculation above all others: he and his supervisors assumed that the Lao actually *wanted* more Japanese to visit their country.

"I've had better luck with Africans," Nigel whispered to me under his breath before sighing in exasperation. Nigel was an international tourism marketing consultant who had been assigned by the UNDP to work with the NTA. We were standing in the frigid, air-conditioned conference room of the Royal Hotel, where Nigel was trying in vain to conduct a marketing workshop for bureaucrats and those in the tourism industry. I had just dropped in to see how things were going: not very well, it seemed.

"There's a real problem with lateral thinking here," said Nigel. "These people just don't know how to work together."

So far, the workshop participants had spent the morning playing around with colored slips of paper. The yellow pieces, I learned, signified tourism attractions; the green ones, problems with those attractions; and the blue ones, possible solutions. Participants had been grouped according to region—North, South, and Central Laos—and had begun by writing down every tourist attraction they could think of on a yellow slip, then sticking them up on the wall. After an hour or so, it had dawned on one participant that some organization was necessary, so the slips of paper had been grouped according to province. This task alone had taken more than an hour, for, despite working in the industry, most hadn't a clue where the tourist sites were actually located.

By the time I'd arrived, the workshop had succeeded in creating little more than complete confusion. There were slips of paper everywhere, decorating the walls and strewn about on the floor as if in the aftermath of a ticker-tape parade. Most participants had already given up, their attention spans spent and their stomachs grumbling.

According to Nigel, the task of the day was actually to establish travel itineraries in each region that could be easily marketed abroad. But many participants seemed to think that simply putting the names of tourist sites up on the wall was enough. After having done that, they relaxed. Most were content to sit quietly in the air-conditioned meeting room, sipping the complimentary drinking water, and waiting until the first coffee break mercifully arrived. Officials from the more remote of Laos' provinces seemed excited just to be in the capital, delighted by the free pens and lined note-books provided by the UNDP.

"Just another five minutes, and then I want everyone sitting down so we can attempt an analysis . . . of what we're doing," announced Nigel, hopefully.

A towering, jovial Brit of about sixty, Nigel had been hired for two three-month stints at the NTA. He was paid 10,000 US dollars a month, the usual rate for UN consultants. Not all of my colleagues knew just how relatively astronomical Nigel's salary was—about 500 times the average civil servant's—but they had a good enough idea. And, in private, they all agreed: there had to be better ways to spend 60,000 US dollars in development aid.

In addition to touring the country with Bounh and giving marketing workshops in Vientiane, Nigel's main task at the NTA was to develop a comprehensive tourism-marketing plan for the country.

In the process, he had used a portion of the UNDP project budget to hire a friend's design firm back in England to come up with a logo for the new campaign—the "Magic of Laos." The result of six months work was an impressively heavy English-language report that drew largely on his past experiences in the developing world, particularly Africa. In parts, the plan seemed to have little to do with the situation in Laos itself.

In any case, the likelihood of any recommendation in the report actually being implemented was extremely slight. It would be months before the document was translated into Lao, so most NTA staff remained in the dark as to its contents. After a translation was completed, high-ranking government officials would have to approve the report before anything in it could even be considered. By the time we reached that point in the process—if indeed we ever did—Nigel would have long since moved on to his next assignment. A few months after Nigel left Laos for the last time, he sent me a brief e-mail. He had another project up his sleeve: "I have been speaking to the EU in Brussels," he wrote, "and there is a small fund for short-term support for SE Asian countries, which they seem not to know what to do with."

Free development aid! What an opportunity!

"However, it means the use of outside European-based consultants. I have been thinking of how we can get some more help to Laos. . . . I am going to suggest to Brussels that I undertake some detailed market research for the NTA in their potential core markets of France, Switzerland, Germany, the UK, and the Netherlands so that . . . they will have detailed background knowledge of what the needs of European markets are, who the main tour operators are, and also set up meetings for them. Can you ask Mr. Bounh if this would be helpful to him, and if it is I will draft a proposal that he can get the chairman to get the Ministry of Finance to deliver to the EU delegation in Bangkok."

In my response, I was as frank as I thought appropriate: "I'll mention your suggestion about market research to Bounh. Of course, I'm sure he'll say it's a great idea; as you know, the NTA will agree to almost anything that doesn't cost the NTA any money or political capital."

That was the last I ever heard from Nigel.

I may have given the consultants a hard time, but in truth I couldn't afford to be too critical. For wasn't I one of them? After all, according to my business card, I was a "consultant." And much of what I observed in Thomas, Kawabata, and Nigel, I saw reflected in my own work. With very little relevant knowledge, I was trying to change the way things were done. I made recommendations that I actually expected people to acknowledge. Fortunately, there was one central difference that separated me from the real consultants: money. My relative poverty, which had once so frustrated me, was in fact my best asset. My colleagues didn't think of me as a walking bank, the smiling face of a rich foreign government or international organization. Rather, I was a free agent, just a guy trying to help out. I had nothing to offer but myself and my thoughts. I was at liberty to actually get to know the people I was working with, to find out what they thought about the world and Laos' place in it.

Nevertheless, when I lay in bed at night, trying without much luck to fall asleep, and I thought about the future, I saw Thomas, Nigel, and Kawabata. I saw a man on his own, traveling from one poor country to the next as part of the international development caravan. Writing reports that no one would read. Sipping the local beer in hotel bars. And wondering what good he was doing.

Was this the man I wanted to be?

Another Quiet American

You can't teach a crocodile to swim.
Lao Proverb.

The day I first met Joe, it was raining. Hard.

The heavy drops had begun to fall as soon as I had revved up my Honda Dream and set out through the muddy streets of Vientiane for his house. Unlike my neighbors, I hadn't been deterred by the weather.

Whenever it rained, the capital came to a standstill. Anyone with plans to go out stayed home, and anyone who had planned to go home just stayed wherever they were. Those who were out on the road when the skies opened quickly sought the nearest cover—under a tree, perhaps, or a nearby living room—and the roads were suddenly cleared of traffic. It was as if everyone was living in Oz, convinced they would melt if they were so much as touched by a drop of rain. The only people crazy enough to be outside were the *falang*, the foreigners. If we had somewhere to go, no rainfall was going to stop us; you could take us out of the West, but you couldn't take the West out of us.

Joe lived in a spacious villa built in the early 1970s and hidden discretely behind a wall in Sapangmore village, a few minutes from the center of town. I always seemed to miss the turn that would take me down the narrow dirt road where Joe's house was. I would ride back and forth, wondering when to venture off the one paved road in the village. The streets in Joe's neighborhood would wash out with the slightest rain, so the ride could be treacherous. I wanted to be sure I had the right street before I took the plunge.

Deep purple bougainvillea cascaded over the upstairs balcony and down the façade of Joe's house. That day, small beads of rainwater had collected on the flowers' petals, and as I pulled into his driveway, I admired the understated beauty of Joe's garden. So rapt was I with the foliage that I promptly skidded on the thin film of mold that had covered the pavement, and toppled over, landing right at Joe's doorstep. I picked myself up and brushed myself off as best I could.

Joe's guard, an elderly man, came scurrying out from behind the house—not to help me up, but rather to open the gate to the driveway. He saw that I'd beaten him to it, and quickly retreated.

"Well, hello there!" said a voice from behind the bougainvillea. "Come on in!"

Joe emerged from the front door and, with a firm handshake, welcomed me inside. "How do you like the flowers?" He didn't seem to notice the dark brown streak that ran down the side of my right pant leg. If he did, he said nothing, so I spent the next few hours covered in mud, trying not to soil his furniture.

Joe was dressed in the uniform of the relaxed expat in Laos: a colorful silk, short-sleeved shirt—always untucked—and pressed khaki slacks. His 56 years hadn't been kind to his coiffure, and he'd lost most of the hair on top of his head. All that remained up there were two healthy tufts of gray perched above each ear. Joe's face was broad, pale, and smooth, almost shiny. The sheen was punctuated by a pair of bushy eyebrows that pointed upwards diagonally from his eyes. He was perfectly groomed, down to his fingernails; every strand of hair trimmed to equal length. When I excused myself to the bathroom to wash my hands, I found an array of grooming instruments neatly lined up on a dresser: nail clippers, a nose-hair remover, ear-wax cleaners, and an assortment of shaving para-phernalia.

When I'd finished washing up, Joe and I sat down in his living room to chat before lunch. At first, I wasn't much into the con-versation, as Joe was sitting just in front of a large bookcase filled with old novels and non-fiction volumes about Southeast Asia. My mouth fairly watered at the sight of so many English-language books, all in one place. I managed to pull my attention away from the smörgåsbord of literature and heard him explain that I'd caught him just in time, as he was leaving for a business trip to Singapore that afternoon. Just then, the guard slunk past us, carrying Joe's suitcase and jacket. As he was about to place the luggage on the floor near the front door, my host suddenly cut off our conversation and called out in English, "No, not there, Keo, not there. Put the suitcase out in the garage, and hang the jacket on the window handle. That's right. . . . Yes. . . . Oh no, not there." Exasperated, he got up from his chair, and, muttering angrily, performed the task himself.

"These Lao. I just can't understand it," he said. "They can't do two things at once. Can't fucking walk and chew gum at the same time."

Three decades before, Joe had been a pilot with the US Air Force in Vietnam. His years in the military had rubbed off on his approach to life, and he expected the tasks he assigned to be executed strictly according to instructions. Every aspect of his life was tightly regi-mented, each activity a part of a routine that could not be upset. That morning, he told me, the water in his neighborhood had been shut off for a few hours—a common enough occurrence in Vien-tiane—and he'd been unable to shave on time. Joe was just getting over this rude interruption of his daily schedule.

While a pervasive military air surrounded Joe, there was also a strong boyish quality to the man. It often seemed as if he'd never grown up. In conversation, whenever he came upon a subject that interested him, a magical glimmer would appear in his eyes and he would nearly jump out of his seat with excitement. The Internet, for example, fascinated him. He spent hours every day surfing the web and dashing off e-mails to an array of unwitting recipients—

from old college professors to President Bill Clinton. The Internet allowed Joe to close the gaping distance between his "home" in Vientiane and the rest of the world.

"Now they can't ignore me!" he said with a grin.

After six years in Vietnam, Joe returned to the States for college. "I studied political science . . . basically what you choose when nothing else is left." He was married to an American for a short while after graduation. When the marriage collapsed in the early 1980s, Joe left for Asia. He hadn't been back to the US since.

Joe led a quiet life in Vientiane. He rarely ventured beyond the gates at the end of the driveway that protected him from the outside world, and almost never went out at night. Each evening he would go to bed at 9:00, read for an hour, and then fall asleep. To relax, he listened to instrumental versions of Thai love songs; he no longer found much comfort in listening to Western music. "Sometimes I wonder if I'd even understand people if I went back to the US," he told me. "I've been over here for so long."

Joe visited Laos for the first time in 1987. He had been enchanted, and was drawn back to the region where he had once fought a war. A few years later, he moved to Vientiane and started a small business.

Then, in 1997, the Asian economic crisis landed in Laos with a deafening crash. Joe's Thai partner pulled out. By the time I met Joe, he had no regular income and was cutting costs wherever he could. To reduce electricity bills, all the lights in the house were off. He had cut the security guard to part time, and had come close to dismissing his cook, Sai—until he had tried to do without her.

Joe and I sat down for lunch in his dining room and Sai brought out a plate of BLTs and two bowls of home-made vegetable soup. Sai was an elderly Lao woman with a warm and gentle demeanor that was disarming. But I sensed that she was unsettled in Joe's presence, and the wan smile that broke through her discomfort was visibly forced. She was smartly dressed in a *sin*, and her hair was neatly tied up in a bun.

As we ate, I thought of Pyle, the CIA man and title character in *The Quiet American*, Graham Greene's seminal novel about the early days of the Vietnam War. In the book, Pyle's grand idea was that of a "Third Force" in Asia: the notion that, free of any colonial baggage, the Americans would be the force best suited to fight alongside "the people" for democracy in Indochina. "At least they won't hate us like they hate the French," Pyle said. And he was so sure that he was right.

Having lunch with Joe, I was reminded of just why Pyle's quaint theory had never really worked. Its premise was refuted on a daily basis amid the post-colonial bliss of this quiet American's life in Vientiane.

"Not bad," Joe said as we munched on the sandwiches. "Not bad at all, for Laos." He tossed off the remark as if it was the first time he'd ever tried Sai's BLTs—although I knew that this was his lunch almost every day.

Once we were finished, Joe rang the small silver bell on the dining room table to the right of his setting. "Dessert?" he asked, the glimmer of youthful excitement returning to his blue eyes. "I think we have lemon meringue pie today! Let me just check with the cook. Lemon meringue pie today, Sai? Yes?"

Sai wasn't quite sure what Joe was asking, so I translated. Joe had lived in Vientiane for nearly a decade, but he barely spoke a word of Lao. "Oh, so you're studying Lao," he said, once Sai had disappeared into the kitchen. "Good for you. I bet you like Lao food, too."

His compliment didn't seem entirely heartfelt: I might be studying Lao, Joe was saying, but I would never really learn the language. Expats never did.

After we'd finished dessert, Joe realized that his ride to the airport was late.

"These Lao, they just can't do anything right," he sighed. "You know, when the North Vietnamese fought with the Lao communists over here, they always put a Vietnamese at the front and one at the back of the troops—and one in the middle for good measure—just to make sure the Lao would fight!"

Even after so many years of living and working in Laos, Joe still expected people to be on time. "You know, this is what I can't stand about the Lao," he complained to Bat, his office assistant, who had been in charge of organizing Joe's ride to the airport. "You tell them to do one thing, and they do another. I just can't play these fucking games anymore."

Bat had been in the house throughout my visit, always lurking in the background. While Joe and I had been eating, he had pretended to be working in the small office that adjoined the dining room. But he had really been listening in on our conversation. Often I'd catch his eye as he nonchalantly shifted in his seat to get a better vantage point on the dining-room table. Once he saw me, he would quickly look down and pretend again to be engrossed in his work. In fact, there wasn't very much to do in Joe's office these days, and I sensed that Bat was looking for a way out.

When the driver finally showed up and whisked Joe away to the airport, I went back to the office to see if I might strike up a conversation with Bat. It didn't take much.

"Sometimes," he told me, "I feel like I was born in the wrong country. I feel ashamed to say it, but it's true."

Bat was full of energy and ambition. Dressed casually in faded blue jeans and a leather belt, to which he had clipped his cellphone, he exuded an intensity that said: this guy is going places, and will wait for no one. During the 1980s, Bat had graduated at the very top of his high school class, and had been sent by the government to study engineering in Czechoslovakia. His early success was the result not only of studying hard, but also of a continuous battle against the inertia of his parents, both farmers in a small village just outside Vientiane.

He had returned from Czechoslovakia excited by the prospect of assisting the government in the development of his country. But, like so many of his contemporaries, he found that he wasn't welcome. The very government that had sent him to study abroad, now refused to employ him. He would show up for appointments in bureaucrats' offices and, before he even had a chance to express his interest—let alone to present his credentials—he'd be politely told there were no positions available.

So Bat gave up on the civil service and embarked on a winding journey through Vientiane's private sector. Setting aside the Czech language he had spent so many years learning as almost completely without worth, he set about teaching himself English. By the time

I met him, he spoke almost fluently. Among other positions, Bat had worked in a hotel as a waiter, receptionist, and 'chambermaid'; with his brother in an import-export business; as a manager in a prawn-flavored-chip factory; and in the American Embassy as an assistant to the business consul. Certainly the worst job of the lot had been a stint as a pool hand at the Australian Embassy Recreation Club.

The Australian Club, or "the Club," as it was known to regulars, sat on the Mekong just a few kilometers from the center of town. It was a family-oriented place that offered Sunday-night movies and the occasional fancy dress party. Each afternoon, pasty white expats would gather by the pool with their children to sip beer and watch the sunset. Just beyond the fence, farmers tended to their paddies on the banks of the river. I went there only once in two years—the membership fee was far too expensive for my stipend.

"Before I took that job, I thought foreigners were different—I respected them," said Bat. His time at the club had changed his mind forever. According to Bat, the members were unrelenting in their pettiness, quibbling with him over the price of a hamburger or a fruit shake: "Sometimes they would even refuse to pay for food they had already eaten. I would bring the bill to a man, and he'd say, 'Talk to my wife.' But when I asked her, she'd tell me to ask her husband. They really didn't act well."

The most difficult part of all was that whenever the members had something to complain about, they would shout at him—even when it was clear that only his manager had the power to change the situation.

After he had bid his farewell to the Australians, Bat took the job as assistant to Joe. By the time we spoke, however, he was already thinking of leaving. "You know, I like to work, not just sit here playing games on the computer. Well, I don't play games all the time, but, you know. . . ."

It wasn't simply the fact that there was nothing to do that was leading Bat to consider other options. There was also Joe: "Sometimes he gets so angry at me—for no reason at all. He'll run into the office and ask for a file—*right away!*—and when I can't find it, he'll blow up." After offering his inevitable homily about why he couldn't stand the Lao, Joe would storm out. Then, a few minutes later, he'd slink back in. The file had been right next to his bed, where he'd left it the night before. He'd apologize to Bat, and things would be back to normal.

But not quite. For Bat didn't take such behavior lightly. He told Joe directly that such outbursts were not acceptable in Laos. And in the end, he usually ended up acting as a surrogate therapist for the suddenly reflective American, counseling him on "the way things worked" in Vientiane and offering advice on how best to get things done. Joe may have lived here for nearly ten years, but Bat, after all, was the one who knew Laos best.

"I grew up here," he said. "I am Lao, and I know what to do."

Bat agreed with me: Joe had been in Laos too long. He couldn't understand why Joe stuck around. "You know, foreigners have a choice. I don't. Sometimes when they start complaining about Laos, I ask, 'Why don't you leave? No one asks you to stay.' You know what Joe's plan for the future is? He wants to live in Laos, forever," he said with a look of disbelief. For upwardly mobile, highly motivated Lao like Bat, the option to leave the country without any hassle was a freedom they could only dream about. He couldn't imagine why anyone would choose to stay.

What, then, kept Joe in Vientiane? Like many expats I knew, Joe often professed his undying love for Laos: so many smiles, such a relaxed pace. On the other hand, he seemed to expend an enormous amount of time and energy complaining about it. He found fault with nearly everything: the people, the culture, the government— not to mention the help. Perhaps it was just the power of the familiar. When you finally settle down somewhere, entering your sixth decade, it is extremely difficult to move on. Once you're stuck, it's hard to get unstuck.

But I imagined that there was more to Joe's tortured love affair with Laos than that. Despite all the difficulties of living in Vientiane, the power outages and water shortages, it remained a far more attractive prospect for many expats than returning home. Leaving aside the house, cars, servants, and high standard of living, there was also the question of expectations. The very inefficiency and laziness that these foreigners lamented was a central part of Laos' attraction. Expectations were low. You could do very little work and still get by; no one questioned your productivity, as they would at home. Most long-term expats knew that the moment they stepped back on home turf, they would again be judged by Western standards. They would have to perform, or they would sink. And no one would jump in to save them.

In Vientiane, Joe was something special. "You're a kind of hero to the Lao, you know," Bat told me. "Even me; I like your white skin." A fetish for whiteness shaped the Lao world-view: from the color of your skin to the exterior of your house, the whiter the better.

In Laos, skin color was a class issue as well. Dark skin implied poverty, the need to spend the whole day working in a rice field under the hot sun. Thus dark skin was to be avoided at all cost. On sunny days in Vientiane, women and men alike would steer their motorbikes through the streets using only one hand. The other they used to shield their faces from the sun. If the roads also happened to be wet, many would lift their legs up above the motorbike's brake pedal in order to protect their clothes from the puddles. The result was quite an acrobatic feat: "Look, Ma, no hands—or feet!" My colleagues at the NTA almost always wore long sleeves, even in the most brutally hot weather. They frowned upon any leisure activity that involved sustained exposure to the sun. On a beautiful Sunday afternoon, rather than go out for a picnic, most of my friends preferred to stay inside and watch TV. It was less risky.

Despite a legacy of colonialism and unwanted foreign influence in their domestic affairs, the Lao still granted Westerners a measure of respect simply for being white. But back in America, Joe would no longer be a shining white face in a sea of brown. No longer a "foreign expert" with an ID card to prove it. In fact, he wouldn't be an expert on much of anything—except living in Laos.

As soon as Joe had left for the airport, his staff had taken over. The atmosphere brightened markedly upon his departure, even as the lamps remained unlit.

After I finished talking with with Bat, Sai showed me to the door. Her appearance had changed completely since lunch. Her hair fell freely around her shoulders, her shirt was untucked, and she wore a simple sarong and sandals. While only a few hours before she had been quiet, almost painfully demure, now she was talkative and playful. Who knows, perhaps she was surprised to find that an expat like me, white skin and all, could actually converse with her—albeit not very well—in her own language.

And without even ringing a bell first.

Vive la France

One of my favorite haunts in Vientiane was the Centre de Langue Française, a language and culture center funded by the French government and located on Lan Xang Avenue opposite my office. Set back from the street behind a wall, the modern white buildings of the Centre were surrounded by lush grass and palm trees. The interior was a far cry from what I was used to over at the NTA; the air-conditioned facility featured a high-tech screening room and performance space. The tile floors were cleaned and polished each night. The bathrooms even had spot lighting—and plenty of soft, white toilet paper. The reading area in the Centre library was filled with newspapers like *Le Monde* and *Figaro*, and magazines like *Paris Match*, and the shelves were stacked with copies of classics by Dumas, Verne, and Sartre. In the afternoons, the place would be filled with French expats reading the latest news and pining for *la vie en rose* back home.

Every Thursday evening at 7:15, I would head to the Centre for my advanced French class. My fellow students, who always showed up right on time, were mostly Lao men and women in their forties. They spoke French well, and rarely slipped into their native language, even during our breaks. Their passion for grammatical minutiae surpassed even that of my middle school French teacher, Madame Jouas, whom even today I can remember reciting irregular verb conjugations while my classmates snickered at the outdated fashions in the photographs of our obsolete 1970s textbook. Unlike my classmates back then, the students at the Centre adored French, and it seemed to me they came to class in part to keep the language alive—and perhaps to re-live, if only for an hour or two a week, the glory of French colonial power.

Our teacher in the *niveau avancé* was my good friend, Michel. A Parisian in his late twenties, Michel had come to Vientiane to complete the *service militaire* that France still requires of all its young men. Fortunately, he had been lucky enough to fulfill his obligation to his homeland without engaging in anything remotely militaristic, as the government permits its citizens to work for French companies or government agencies abroad in lieu of serving in the armed forces. In addition to teaching us every week, Michel was in charge of planning all cultural events at the Centre, including a regular film series and an annual singing contest. The job was perfect for Michel, who had studied contemporary jazz at the New Sorbonne in Paris and was passionate about the role of music and culture in people's lives—whatever their ethnic or national background.

It was impossible not to like Michel. Everyone who came within his orbit, Lao and *falang* alike, seemed unable to resist his charm. While he was thin and athletic, his uneven features and thick, dark curly hair didn't add up to any great physical attraction. But he had a powerful ability to make people feel comfortable, and a tolerance for different approaches to life that counted for much more than looks. Whenever I'd run into him by chance, perhaps careening around town on his third- or fourth-hand motorbike, a woebegone piece of machinery that made my Honda Dream look like a Harley Davidson, I knew I'd be in for a treat. I would inevitably catch his contagious enthusiasm for whichever topic was on his mind, even if I had no idea what he was talking about. Whether it was the completion of his latest cultural project at the Centre or the discovery of the perfect rice field in Vientiane from which to gaze at the stars at night, Michel always had something to be excited about.

One night, hosting dinner at his house in Sapangmore village, I remember Michel being very excited about food. He had just received an entire *confis de canard* from home, and couldn't wait to serve this traditional French delicacy to his friends. The fatty duck dish was so unhealthy that I was surprised the wily inspectors at the post office in Vientiane had even allowed it to enter the country. But it tasted good with the red wine flowing that night, and it provided the perfect accompaniment to a rather intense discussion we had begun. Michel had begun the conversation with the sort of statement he preferred: dramatic, controversial, and not entirely clear. *"Si on ne s'interesse pas a l'art,"* he said, *"on ne s'interesse pas aux autres."* If you're not interested in art, you're not interested in others.

For Michel, art was everything. I could have done without the musicians he preferred—the American jazz artist Carla Bley, for example, who assiduously avoided harmony in her compositions—but I appreciated his emphasis on the power and importance of culture. But what was "culture" in a place like Laos? In a country where there was no film industry and very few writers of note, the traditional markers to which the French and others in the West looked for signs of a vibrant popular culture did not exist.

At first glance, Lao people didn't really seem to be interested in 'art' as conceived in the West. Did that mean they weren't interested in their fellow man? The answer, of course, was certainly not. Michel and I agreed that if one expanded the definition of "art" to include the continuing dynamism of Laos' religious ceremonies and traditional customs, the people of Laos were certainly engaged in an attempt to understand the world around them through artistic expression. I tried my best to express these sentiments around the dinner table, fighting the impulse to speak in English. My conversations with Michel were always marked by a struggle between two languages: while I preferred to use French, he could be very insistent about practicing his English. Often, I'd speak in French, and he'd respond in English, each of us determined not to revert to our respective native languages. But discussions like these were a challenge, as I'd forgotten many of the basics of French that Madame Jouas had taught me.

If a refresher course in French grammar was what I needed, I certainly wasn't going to get it in Michel's advanced class. We didn't really *study* French under the tutelage of our *professeur*, who rarely prepared for more than a few minutes before each class. This was fine with my classmates, many of whom had busy lives. While they loved the language, they had no interest in homework. The only foreigner in the class other than me was the Polish ambassador, Henrich. In fact, he was Poland's ambassador, chargé d'affaires, and consular officer all at once. Times had changed since the glory days of the Cold War, when the Polish Embassy in Vientiane had been quite large. Now, after the inevitable downsizing that had accompanied the transition from communism to democracy, Henrich was the only Polish diplomat left. "Hey, it's a good way to save some money," he liked to say.

Another student was a Lao diplomat in charge of the Western Europe and Americas Division at the Ministry of Foreign Affairs. I'll not soon forget the class discussion on Francophone countries during which this student demonstrated his geographical prowess by insisting that Haiti was in Africa, and Egypt in Latin America. When we considered the question of why the French colonies in Africa had had so much trouble developing in the wake of independence, he exclaimed, *"Mais c'est parce qu'ils sont trop loin de la civilisation, bien sûr!"* Here was the considered analysis of a Lao diplomat: Africans just weren't civilized enough.

Most of my classmates had either studied in France or had been educated in French schools in Laos before the revolution. Some continued to incorporate elements of the *savoir vivre*—or at least the *savoir manger*—they had learned from French into their lives. One woman, as rotund as she was cheerful, owned a popular gourmet food shop and *fromagerie* near the center of town, Les Boutiques Scoubidou. Each week she would promise to bring to class a selection of her finest Camembert and Brie for us to sample along with a fresh *baguette* or two she'd purchased at the Morning Market. I sometimes felt as if, inside our classroom, the traditional narrative of colonial oppression and victimization had been turned on its head. Here, the "natives" were so eager to consume a foreign culture they considered more elegant than their own that they were willing to pay for the chance to do it.

I spent many an hour at the Centre, shooting the breeze with middle-aged Lao men and women who liked to reminisce about the days of French influence in Laos, long before the Americans showed up. They pined not for colonial rule, of course, but for a time when the idea of a powerful international community of Francophone nations still seemed feasible. I learned from these folks that there really had been something ennobling about the aesthetic values and cultural vocabulary that France had exported to its colonies as part of its *mission civilisatrice*. The French had never treated the Lao as equals, but their approach to colonization had lifted many in Laos— albeit those already at the very top of Lao society—up and out of the confines of their small country. Through the French, the Lao elite had been connected not only to a great power, but also to a network of countries with a common cultural heritage.

These days, the children of the elite were all learning English and desperately hoping to study in Australia or the US. French was the last thing on these young people's minds. America had so thoroughly triumphed in the global struggle for cultural pre-eminence— without much effort on the part of the US government—that France's attempts to promote *La Francophonie* in Africa and Southeast Asia seemed almost pathetic, a last gasp effort to stem the tidal wave of American pop culture that was flooding the developing world.

The language classes promoted French language and culture in an entirely artificial context, divorced from the demands of the world outside. During the day, the Centre provided French lessons to bureaucrats free of charge, a component of the French government's aid program. It was a nice gesture, and the Lao government wasn't about to refuse the complimentary instruction, but these employees had no use for the language at the office. If they were going to use any foreign language at all, it would be English. At the École Nationale d'Administration et Gestion, a French government-funded school of administration and management, students who aspired to study abroad were required to understand lectures about international economics and accounting in French. The top students were awarded scholarships to study in Thailand. What use for French would they ever have? This was an effective way to ensure that students learned the difference between *ceci* and *cela*, but as a means of advancing the power of French culture, it was hopeless. As Michel would say, *"C'est inutile!"*

On Thursday evenings after class, I would often linger at the Centre until the evening's film presentation. The French film series included screenings of everything from classics like Marcel Carné's *Les Tricheurs* to tremendously bad contemporary vehicles for Catherine Deneuve. You couldn't blame Michel for the unevenness of his selections: he was constrained by whatever happened to have been sent by the Foreign Ministry back in Paris. The projectionist at the Centre was an elderly Lao man who didn't speak much French—just enough to take people's tickets (a mere 500 kip per person)—and had yet to master the technology of the modern screening room he'd been hired to run. The Centre could easily have hired a technologically savvy young teenager to do the job, and paid him far less money, but this man was well worth keeping employed. He had a connection to film that extended far beyond his role as projectionist.

Our projectionist had once been a well-known actor, appearing in a number of important communist propaganda pieces in the 1960s and 70s. One Thursday, after a series of intense negotiations with government officials, Michel managed to retrieve such a film from the vaults of the Ministry of Information and Culture. In the comfortable cool of the Centre screening room, we watched Somouk Southipoune's *Boa Deng*, a pro-communist film that took place during the war. In the role of a dashing young Pathet Lao soldier, the handsome star on screen seemed a different person altogether from the old man with weathered skin and stooped posture that sat near the back of the room. Now that the Lao film industry had collapsed, he was out of luck. Forgotten by the Party, the only employment he could find was with the French.

Here was the French government in Laos at its best: using its resources to showcase the country's cultural heritage. For me, this further complicated the legacy of French colonial rule. While the French had mistreated the Lao, stunting the nation's political and economic growth, they had also bestowed important contributions that remain vital today. At the NTA, we knew that much of the country's tourism potential and its appeal to foreigners lay in the traces of French architecture, cuisine, and language that could still be found. And these days, it was the French government more than any other foreign donor that paid attention to culture. Even if the Lao were going to let a former film star languish in unemployment, the French, at least, were not.

Protest

Early one weekday morning in March, I was lying in bed, grateful for those few moments of silence before the neighborhood came to life. I relished this ephemeral quiet before the quotidian chorus of roosters, children, dogs, and motorbikes erupted. The calm before the storm, before the sun and the dust began to rise. It was the height of the dry season, and a thick haze of smoke—the result of slash-and burn farming on the outskirts of town—contributed to a heavy sense of foreboding in the air.

As I considered the day ahead, I knew that well before noon, the heat would have become almost unbearable, even in the shade, and most activity in town would have slowed to a halt. At the end of the day, I would scrape the dust from under my eyes and out of my nostrils before going to bed. As I tried to get to sleep with the help of my creaky ceiling fan, I would find myself pining for the wet relief of the rainy season.

The prospect of getting out of bed this morning, then, was hardly attractive. I lingered, enjoying the relative cool and listening for the hum of the day to begin. Suddenly, my reverie was cut short when the phone rang. I struggled out of bed to answer the call, which turned out to be from my energetic and easily excitable friend, Ming. She was already fully awake—and, well, very excited.

"Do you know what's happening?" she asked.

Other than the fact that I was being forced out of bed far earlier than could possibly have been just, even in an authoritarian one-party state, I had no idea.

"No," I replied.

"We are protesting this morning!"

"What?" A protest here in Laos? Impossible. "Who's protesting?"

"All the Chinese people in Vientiane."

"Where?"

"The American Embassy."

"Why?"

"Your government just dropped a bomb on the Chinese Embassy in Yugoslavia. Some Chinese people were killed."

This was news to me. Living in Vientiane, it was easy enough to slip out of touch with the world, and I hadn't so much as glanced at an international headline in weeks. Why would the US have dropped a bomb on the Chinese? I thanked Ming for the tip, slammed down the phone, threw on some clothes, and revved up the Honda Dream. Paying no mind to the maelstrom of dust, potholes, and open sewers, I arrived in record time at the embassy.

The US Embassy in Vientiane was housed in a sprawling compound near the center of town, a memorial to the excesses of an age when America had fancied itself in charge of the country. Like most of the buildings that had resulted from US influence in Laos, the architecture was uninspired, functional, and bereft of the charm of the remnants of the French presence that here and there graced the Vientiane landscape. Built in the 1960s, the embassy sat behind a thick concrete wall that was always covered with a fresh coat of blinding white paint.

These days, the American diplomatic presence was very modest. Each time I visited the embassy, the facility itself struck me as almost cavernous, far too large for the needs of a staff that had dwindled markedly since the end of the Indochina War. I pitied the foreign service officers and military attachés, maintenance workers and secretaries who toiled away in the lonely offices. Not much ever seemed to be going on at the embassy. But today was an exception.

Gathered outside the complex were nearly 100 Chinese men and women, loudly protesting the US-led bombing campaign in the former Yugoslavia. The campaign had been designed to force the hand of Serbian president Slobodan Milosevic, but somehow a bomb had landed on the Chinese Embassy in Belgrade, and the Chinese government was crying foul. The US claimed that the bombing had been a mistake, the result of an outdated map upon which the CIA had relied. But the Chinese didn't buy it, and today they were venting their anger. Large banners painted with black and red anti-American slogans rose above the crowd outside the embassy. The bold strokes of the Chinese characters screamed with outrage. The protesters, on the other hand, were rather subdued. Directed by disciplined organizers—mobile phones in hand—they chanted in unison from time to time. Every major Chinese business and citizen group in Vientiane was represented. The protesters were blocked from approaching the embassy entrance by a single Lao police officer, who didn't seem particularly threatened.

Another twenty policemen stood off to the side, awaiting further orders. They seemed as surprised by the entire affair as the small group of Lao that had gathered to watch from the safe distance of the ancient That Dam, wary of getting too close to the action. That Dam was Vientiane's Black Stupa, a crumbling stone structure that was slowly being overtaken by weeds despite a recent restoration. It sat just west of the American Embassy and was said to be the home of a seven-headed *naga*, which had come to life and protected local citizens during Siam's invasion of Vientiane in 1828. This morning, the *naga* showed no signs of stirring.

Finally, the police decided that something had to be done. So, as they usually did when all else failed, they began to direct traffic. Soon the air was pierced by the high-pitched police whistles: the mouthpiece of Lao authoritarianism. The police in Vientiane almost never spoke, but rather substituted toots on the pipe and incomprehensible hand signals for verbal communication. Still, it occurred to me as I watched the protesters that not once in Laos had I ever seen a whistle for sale. When I had played the part of a stuffy detective in the annual Christmas production of the Vientiane Players, a local expatriate theatrical group, our producer had had to procure a whistle from a party shop back home in London. The absence of whistles from Vientiane's markets wasn't surprising: the whistle was one of the strongest holds the authorities had over the people. In the wake of the failure of communism, words were empty—no one believed anything the government said. The whistle, on the other hand, was as effective as it had been in 1975. You couldn't question a whistle. You couldn't reason with sound.

After an hour or so, the American consular officer emerged from the embassy and sauntered over to the protesters to check out the situation. He didn't seem worried. I stood in the crowd, joking with the participants, delighting some with my limited Chinese-language skills. Things weren't so laid-back elsewhere in Asia on this day. In Phnom Penh, in fact, 300 Chinese marched on the US Embassy, armed with an angry protest letter. They broke through two police barricades before the Cambodian authorities opened fire with AK-47s and the crowd finally dispersed. No such disturbances occurred in Laos.

If the Chinese protest in Vientiane was non-violent, it wasn't exactly popular: it had been organized by the Chinese Embassy under direct orders from Beijing. And the Lao government, increasingly close to its large neighbor to the north, had actually given permission for the event in advance, well before the protesters had begun to gather outside the embassy walls. This was democracy, Lao-style.

The next evening, I had dinner with one of the protesters: my good friend and erstwhile Chinese teacher, Gong. Gong, in her late twenties, taught traditional Chinese dance, song, language, and history at the Overseas Chinese high school in Vientiane. The Chinese government had helped to found the school early in the twentieth century, but it was now entirely funded by the Chinese-Lao community in Vientiane. Much more important, Gong worked part-time as a Chinese-language teacher at the Interior Ministry. Most of her students were policemen.

"I think this job for me is very good," she told me in her halting English. Very good indeed, as Gong was working in Laos without a visa. She didn't even have a valid Chinese passport. Back in her native Sichuan province, when Gong had been accepted for a job with a Chinese construction company in Nepal, she had been issued a passport that was good only for travel between China and Nepal. When the job fell through, she crossed the border into Laos instead, and now she couldn't go home. She couldn't travel anywhere outside of Laos, for that matter, and if it weren't for her connections at the language school, she wouldn't have been welcome in Vientiane either.

"What about the Chinese Embassy? Can they help you?"

"No way," she continued in Chinese. "When I lived in China, I loved my country, and I thought my country loved me as well. But now that I live in a foreign country, I still love my country, but I realize that my country doesn't love me. *Mei you ai.* There is no love."

"Are you worried?"

"Well, there are Chinese police in Vientiane, I know. They come to find Chinese who have left the country illegally and are trying to emigrate to America. They could be anywhere."

"Have you seen any around town?" I asked.

"No, of course not. If I knew who they were, everyone would know."

Gong and I met for dinner every Sunday evening. The idea was to speak in Chinese for half the time, and English the other half. But since my Chinese, while limited, was a whole lot better than her English—and since Gong always had a tremendous amount to say—we ended up speaking almost entirely in Chinese. Meeting Gong for dinner was the one occasion in Laos when I had to be on time; if I was so much as a minute late, Gong would simply up and leave. Sometimes I'd arrive exactly on time, and she'd be standing outside the restaurant, pointing to her watch and shaking her head. A woman on the run, Gong did not like to wait.

A few weeks after moving to Vientiane, Gong had converted to Buddhism. For a while, she had made frequent visits to the temple near her apartment, and had even begun studying English with a monk. (For many Lao, the language classes offered in temples provide the only opportunity to study English.) But she soon became bored with Buddhism. Then, one day, she ran into a group of Taiwanese Christians, and, all of a sudden, converted to Christianity. Now she attended church every Sunday, one of only two Chinese in the mostly Lao congregation. Her plan for the future was to attend Bible school in Taiwan or Singapore, but she would have to wait until her passport problems were cleared up before that became a possibility.

"No problem," she would tell me. "I know that God will help me. I'm not worried."

As we discussed the situation in Yugoslavia over sweet peanut curry at Just for Fun restaurant—a laid-back hole in the wall run by a Thai woman and her family—Gong's pointed facial features and thin line of dark red lipstick accentuated her biting arguments. Gong was entirely different from Ming, whose fluent English and worldly manner betrayed her sophisticated urban background. Gong didn't have much time for manners, and usually got straight to the point:

"Look, I have no problem with the American people," she insisted. "The problem is with Clinton and the American government. He wants to take over Kosovo, Serbia, Russia—and then, what next? China!"

That morning, I had sought out a copy of the *Bangkok Post* only to find a photograph of protesters in Beijing carrying placards that depicted Bill Clinton with a swastika plastered on his forehead. This was a guy who, not two months before, had been fighting for political survival, battling an impeachment offensive that had stemmed from his wayward sex life. Now he was a Nazi? What Gong refused to believe was that Clinton was one of the least powerful "most powerful" men in the world; his hands were tied by an array of political interests and moral imperatives from which the Chinese president was free. Anyway, why would he want to bomb the Chinese Embassy? We had trade interests to promote, global security to protect. It just didn't add up.

My friend would have none of it. "Look, is Clinton a Christian?" Gong asked.

"Sure, he goes to church every Sunday," I told her.

"Then how could he drop bombs on Kosovo?"

A Chinese citizen using Christian morality to defend the position of her own government was a tad too much, I thought. All Gong had succeeded in demonstrating to me was the degree to which the Chinese people remained under the influence of an imperial dictatorial tradition. In China, one man alone *did* have the power to decide, and to destroy. But not in America.

When I first mentioned the Chinese protest in English class at the NTA a few days later, my students just laughed it off. Though the state media had been strictly instructed not to cover the event, they all knew what had happened. Vientiane was a small place, and there were very few secrets.

"Oh, that's just the Chinese," said Mon.

The protest had been the first to occur in Vientiane since 1975, and yet they feigned nonchalance. Hadn't they even been over to the American Embassy to check out all the action?

"Oh, no," said Mani. "I just watched it from my car window."

But the embassy was only a few minutes away.

"If we get too near, the police might think we are involved," admitted Mani. The rest of the class responded with a chorus of nods.

Could this kind of activity have been allowed if the protesters had been Lao?

"No."

But, when the demonstrators are from a foreign country, it's okay?

"Yes."

So why were they protesting, anyway?

Throughout the discussion, I'd noticed that Suphap—in English, his name meant 'Polite'—seemed to want to say something. "So what do *you* think, Suphap?" I asked.

It was an unfortunate fact that the English-language skills of Suphap—who happily enough was in charge of the NTA's Tourist Information Center—were nothing short of abominable. He could barely put together a complete sentence, and I often found myself intervening in order to prevent him from politely sending unsuspecting tourists off in entirely the wrong direction. In his garbled response, a mix of Lao and English, the only word I could make out was "bombie." But with a bit of help from his classmates, he eventually got his meaning across. He thought that the Chinese had protested for one simple reason: because a country larger and more powerful than theirs had harmed a group of its citizens. Suphap took it for granted that the US had bombed the embassy on purpose. And none of his classmates disagreed.

The legacy of the American military effort in Indochina—above all, its "secret," yet relentless bombing campaign in Northeastern Laos—lived on in Lao society. It wasn't immediately apparent in the streets of Vientiane. It didn't always filter through the friendly smiles and friendly shouts of "Sabaidee." The legacy of the war lay under the surface, but it was there. Sympathy for those who had come under American fire was the most important factor in shaping Lao public opinion about the Chinese Embassy bombing—far more important, even, than a Party-controlled national media that received its international news from the Chinese government.

After Suphap's contribution, the class fell silent. Not wanting the students to leave the room with an awkward feeling, I abruptly changed the subject. "If you could go anywhere in the world, and money wasn't a question, where would it be?"

Mon answered quickly: "Switzerland. It's beautiful."

Mani laughed and said she'd always had a thing for France.

And how about Suphap?

"America," he replied with a grin.

War

Wearing motley clothes makes the dogs bark;
trotting out old stories brings about disputes.
Lao Proverb.

Laos does not rank highly on many world records. With a population of just about five million, it isn't the smallest country in the world, and it certainly isn't the largest. An annual per capita income of less than 400 dollars means that it isn't the poorest or the richest either. There is one list, however, that the nation does top. Laos is the single most heavily bombed country in the history of warfare. During the conflict in Indochina, as a part of its "secret war" in Laos, the American military dropped more bombs on the country alone than it did during all of World War II, and three times as many as it did during the Korean War. The bombing cost US taxpayers 7.2 billion dollars, or 2 million every day from 1964 through 1973. Most Americans have forgotten these astonishing facts—if indeed they ever knew them to be true.

I, for one, had no idea until I moved to Laos. And even while I was there, it was easy enough to forget. Although the war in Indochina had ended less than three decades before, the entire conflict appeared at times to have been relegated to the deep recesses of the Lao collective memory. Not once did a Lao friend ever raise the subject of the war in conversation. Lao my age and younger, while certainly aware that a major conflict had taken place, could be vague on who exactly had been involved. And when I revealed my nationality to Lao who had been alive during the hostilities—even to men who had fought against the Americans and their allies—I never encountered a scowl or so much as a strange look. On the surface, at least, I was presented with nothing but smiles and overwhelming approval.

"America?" people would exclaim after I had told them where I was from. "Oh, very good! America number one!" When other expats, European or Asian, introduced themselves to my Lao friends and colleagues, I listened for the reaction. No other country received such a positive response as the US.

If you looked closely, though, evidence of the war and America's involvement in Laos was not hard to find. A sign for the "Lao American Association"—an organization supported by the US in the 1970s to promote American culture and the English language in Vientiane—still stood outside the complex now used as the headquarters of Laos' state news agency. US Army parachutes shaded vendors selling fresh fruit juice and beer on the banks of the Mekong. In the countryside, families used empty bomb casings as planters or pylons. By recycling the remnants of this dark period in their history, most people seemed to have moved on. Or had they?

Every so often, the smallest of things would remind me that the war wasn't such a distant memory after all. Once, toiling away at my desk in the ICU, I looked up to find my colleague, Souksan from the Marketing and Promotion Unit, standing before me, smiling. Souksan's smile was ever present, and it was contagious. It disappeared in only the rarest of situations, such as when he attempted to formulate complete sentences in English—and even then only for a moment. Though his English was terrible and his computing skills minimal, Souksan had been put in charge of producing the brochures the NTA distributed to tourists. He didn't mind the job, really, especially since it meant he was able to use the new scanner the office had just acquired through the UNDP. Boy, did Souksan love to scan. Graphics were never a problem in NTA brochures, for Souksan seemed to spend most of his time taking photographs and scanning them into the computer.

As I saw it, my job was to make sure that the text of Souksan's brochures was readable, and that the design fit into the broader marketing scheme for Visit Laos Year 1999–2000. I had a difficult time convincing Souksan that the NTA should develop a set of uniform marketing materials; each time he put together a brochure, which seemed to be weekly, it had an entirely different look and a new take on the English language. But my frustration hardly had a chance to surface when I was working with Souksan, who was relentlessly upbeat despite the odds stacked against him. Even his name, in English, meant "Happy."

Happy asked me to look over a draft of a new brochure he had been working on. He pulled a chair up next to mine and, since I required it of any staff member who wanted my help, began to edit the brochure along with me. We made some truly daring alterations, like changing "now clothes" to "new clothes" and eliminating English words that even I could barely understand—terms like "simonize" and "circumambulate." Heaven knows where he came up with this vocabulary; he certainly hadn't studied it in my inter-mediate English class. By working through the awkward language, we tried to make Laos sound as if it were, in addition to being a "unique tourist destination" (as Souksan had put it), a relatively nice place to visit.

Souksan soon lost interest in the task at hand, and left me to it. As he played around with the computer, I plowed through a series of incomprehensible descriptions of Laos' tourist attractions. The brochure took me on a bumpy journey through the country's highlights: Vientiane, the political capital and home to the majestic That Luang stupa, the symbol of Laos; up north, Luang Prabang, the former royal capital and World Heritage site; and Wat Phu Champassak, the ancient Khmer temple complex in Southern Laos.

Then came Xieng Khouang. This northeastern province is home to the Plain of Jars, a landscape of rolling hills throughout which large jar-like structures, said to be more than 2,000 years old, are scattered. No one has ever been quite sure what to make of these "mysterious" jars. Perhaps humans had used them as sarcophagi, or for wine production or rice storage. Regardless, the Plaine des Jarres, in French—or PDJ, as the US military liked to call it—had also been an important battleground during the Indochina War. The North Vietnamese and the Pathet Lao had numerous camps in the area, from which they launched a major anti-aircraft operation. Residents of Xieng Khouang lived through daily bombing raids by American planes, and constant ground combat between US-trained forces and the communists. Nearly every town and village in the province was bombed between 1964 and 1973. In 1969 alone, 1,500 buildings in the provincial capital and another 2,000 on the Plain itself were destroyed. Even today, Xieng Khouang suffers from the legacy of war; more than sixty citizens a year fall victim to unexploded ordnance like land-mines and cluster bombs.

In this section of Souksan's brochure, to my surprise, the English was absolutely perfect. "Xieng Khouang province," it read, "offers the beauty of high, green mountains combined with rugged karst limestone formations. The original capital of Xieng Khouang, Muang Khoun, was almost totally obliterated by US bombing in the 1970s, and its inhabitants consequently moved to nearby Phonsavanh." Whoever had written this paragraph certainly hadn't minced words. The phrase "almost totally obliterated" was dead on. But was it appropriate for a brochure intended to appeal to Western tourists, potentially Americans?

Just as I considered rewriting the text to soften the blow, Souksan pumped up the volume on the computer's speakers. Certainly the most useful feature of any computer at the NTA was the CD player, which provided endless entertainment for the entire staff. The next song was "Heal the World," by Michael Jackson.

"Ha! This is American song, no?" said Souksan. "Very good."

Perhaps Souksan thought nothing of it, but for me the irony inherent in this situation was overwhelming. It captured in a single moment the contradictions I often felt living as an American in Laos. What did the Lao I knew really think of me? Were we bitter, historical enemies or natural friends? When he listened to Jackson, did Souksan think at all about America's role in his country's history? Was America really "very good," all unimaginable wealth, pop music, and designer clothes, or did he silently despise the US for the problems it had caused. I'd had nothing to do with the war in Laos. But I was an American, after all, and I had benefited from that fact. Wasn't I partly responsible for the past as well? And wasn't I just another quiet American, a direct descendent of Graham Greene's fresh-faced Harvard man, convinced that I knew what was right? It wasn't guilt, exactly, that I felt as I heard Michael Jackson sing, but a nagging discomfort about my role at the NTA and in Laos in general.

I decided to leave the text untouched.

Despite our deep involvement in the domestic affairs of Laos in the past, and our government's unabashed interference in the course of its history, Americans know little about the landlocked Southeast Asian nation. When the Indochina War ended in 1975, 564 American soldiers were reported missing in action in Laos; of these, only 122 have been accounted for, while 442 remain "missing." Not a few families across America spend at least a part of each day wondering if their sons, brothers, or nephews are still alive in the remote hills of Southeast Asia.

These days, more than 200,000 Lao and Hmong now call the US home. Yet, most Americans have no idea where Laos is. "Lagos? Isn't that somewhere in Africa?" my classmates and neighbors had asked me before I left. When a friend attempted to send a letter to "Vientiane, Laos" through the US Postal Service, she was told that no such place existed. She addressed the letter to Vietnam instead, and it somehow arrived. In some ways, the "secret war" remains as secret in America today as it was when the White House orchestrated the bombing campaign in Xieng Khouang.

One afternoon, scouring the shelves at the Centre de Langue Française, I came across one of a handful of English texts in the library: the transcript of a confidential October 1969 US Senate Foreign Relations Committee hearing on America's security agreements and commitments in Laos. In October 1969, the American public had no idea that the US military was conducting operations in Laos. Officially, of course, it wasn't: even as it poured millions of dollars of military aid into the Royal Lao Army and supported bombing raids over the Plain of Jars, the US—just like the North Vietnamese—maintained publicly that it was upholding the neutrality of Laos. As a result of this Senate hearing, legislators on the committee were now aware that this was essentially a lie. Some were not impressed. One heated exchange between Senator William Fulbright and William Sullivan, deputy assistant secretary of state for East Asia and the Pacific at the time, was particularly telling. After Sullivan had admitted the deep, yet secret involvement of the US in Laos, Senator Fulbright asked, "Doesn't this ever strike you as sort of an absurdity? They [the North Vietnamese] are pretending they are not there, and we are pretending we are not there."

What Fulbright regarded as "absurd" provided the basis for just about the only American film about Laos ever made. *Air America* is an action comedy based on Christopher Robbins' quite serious book of the same name. It is partly fictional, but for pure comedy it cannot compete with the truth of the history of American involvement in Laos. Starring Hollywood hunks Mel Gibson and Robert Downey, Jr., it takes a decidedly light-hearted approach to the American military effort in Laos. The film opens with shots of USAID rice donations crashing through the roofs of rural bamboo huts spliced with actual footage of President Nixon denying any American presence in Laos. A pig falls from the sky into a hilltribe village, squealing as it tumbles to the earth.

"There is no war in Laos," an army recruiter assures Downey in Los Angeles before he is shipped off to Long Chieng, US military HQ in Laos and a town that wasn't even on the map. Later, a CIA man tells him that, "A secret war is the way to go. . . . We can't lose." The hopelessly corrupt General Song, the film's fictitious Royal Lao Army leader, dreams of operating his own Holiday Inn in California once the war is over, although he need not worry— his share of the profits from the illegal opium trade in Northern Laos will ensure him a comfortable retirement. As they finish up their daily flights over the Plain of Jars, the Air America pilots call ahead to an Italian restaurant in Vientiane. Mel Gibson makes a 9:30 reservation and orders the lobster special before finding himself suddenly under fire from the communists. The words he chooses to describe his own situation aptly sum up the United States' situation at the time: "I'm VSF."

Very Severely Fucked.

————————

The morning after my encounter with Souksan and Michael Jackson, I paid another visit to my friend Joe. That week, two old acquaintances of his happened to be visiting from the States. Jack had been in Laos during the war as an officer with USAID, working on water and electricity projects in villages throughout the country. Gary had worked for the CIA and had been stationed in remote military posts in the northern provinces. I was excited by the chance to talk to these two men about their experiences during the war. Their very presence made a period in history that I had only read about in books so tangible, so real.

Over scrambled eggs, bacon, toast, and coffee, we talked about the legacy of the Indochina War. Jack and Gary were friendly and open, happy to be back in a country and surrounded by a people they clearly loved. But discussing the war wasn't easy, as we approached the topic from such different perspectives. We couldn't escape the vast generation gap that separated guys like them from Americans my age. Even though they had lived through Vietnam, and had experienced first-hand the flagrantly misguided activities in which our government had engaged, they seemed far less cynical about it all than I was. Perhaps our failure to see eye to eye had to do purely with age. While my classmates and I had grown up in the aftermath of the Vietnam debacle, these guys had been raised in the years after the glory of World War II, when America had been perceived around the globe as invincible.

While I sensed that a part of Jack and Gary remained convinced that the US could do no wrong, many young Americans assume it rarely does anything right. They just cannot understand how any American could have believed in what our military was trying to accomplish in Laos and Vietnam. With the benefit of hindsight, my generation is quick to dismiss the conflict out of hand as having been a waste of time, money, effort, and lives. The disastrous consequences of the Vietnam War, both abroad and at home, have been seared into our collective memory. We are not even surprised when our government is accused of having engaged in shockingly illegal activities in the past.

In the weeks before I left for Laos, the so-called "Tailwind" controversy had erupted in the media establishment. CNN produced an incendiary story, narrated by celebrity journalist Peter Arnett, which accused the US of using nerve gas against its own troops in Laos. The piece claimed that the military had targeted American soldiers attempting to defect, and that the US government had worked assiduously to cover up its actions in the decades since. Under a deluge of criticism from the military and from some in the media, the network eventually pulled the story and issued an apology. The main reporter was fired and Arnett distanced himself from the report, even though he had narrated the whole thing. The truth remained in question.

I had first heard about the CNN story in my brother's apartment in Boston while we sat in his kitchen and listened to a daily talk show on the local National Public Radio station. As I digested the information, I found myself believing the accusations; they did not seem entirely out of the question. After hearing both sides, my brother said, "What's the big deal? Of course they did it."

His comments had been slightly tongue in cheek, of course, but they pointed to the ease with which Americans of my generation are able to condemn our government.

That makes folks like Jack and Gary angry.

"So you think the Tailwind story isn't true?" I asked.

"Look, I *know* it's not true," said Gary. "I was there, and there's just no way it could have happened."

Jack questioned the motives of the veterans who had allegedly contributed to the story. "You know, during Vietnam, only a quarter of all US troops stationed in Indochina ever saw any action." Most of them remained in the cities, behind the secure walls of American compounds, surrounded by swimming pools, "entertainment" facilities, and supermarkets stocked with imported American goods. Very few indeed were out in the jungle under attack from Vietcong guerrillas, or attempting to defect from the military.

According to Jack and Gary, during the Vietnam War, Vientiane was a particularly rowdy place to be. Between 1962 and 1972, the

US spent more than 500 million dollars to prop up the Royal Lao Government in Vientiane. The capital was crawling with American advisors and their dependents; at the height of US involvement in Lao affairs, the international school was educating nearly 700 students. Vientiane boomed as the economy expanded with wartime aid. Western hippies and CIA operatives alike drank the nights away in the city's new bars and nightclubs, and Lao officials built ostentatious villas on the outskirts of town. The streets were jammed with imported Fords, Chevrolets, and Mercedes.

And the movie theaters! While today there isn't one cinema in all of Laos, during the war there were *four* in Vientiane alone, two down in Savannakhet, and even one way up north in Houei Xai, a mere wisp of a town on the border with Thailand. A surplus of American aid meant that the seedier side of life in Vientiane also flourished. Jack and Gary confirmed travel writer Paul Theroux's assessment of the city during his brief wartime visit: "The brothels are cleaner than the hotels, marijuana is cheaper than pipe tobacco, and opium easier to find than a cold glass of beer."

Back in Washington, Senator Fulbright and other representatives who were privy to confidential information about Laos wanted to make their colleagues and the American public aware of the situation. During the same 1969 Senate hearing on Laos, Fulbright said as much: "If I could get up on the floor and say—which I may do one of these days—what you have told us of how ridiculous this is, a lot of my colleagues would say, for goodness sakes, this is nonsense, throwing [millions] a year pretty nearly down a rat hole." But he remained silent, and the war dragged on.

The Americans ran Vientiane back then—but they ran it into the ground. Eventually, the party came to an end with the communist victory in w 1975. The US had decisively lost the battle.

But that's not to say we didn't win the war.

Just down the street from my house, there lived a family I got to know pretty well over the time I lived in Laos. I'd say Bing was about 35. She lived in a simple one-room house along with her four children, who ranged in age from four to 14, and her younger sister. Her husband had passed away long ago, and her sister had never married. Now, Bing was the head of the family. During the day, they converted the house into a small clothing factory, and the family worked to produce an array of colorful shirts and skirts. The small black-and-white television in the corner of the room was usually on. The children were kept busy measuring cloth, cutting material, and sewing the fabric together. None seemed to go to school on a regular basis. Once a week, Bing would take the finished clothing to the Morning Market to sell as much as she could.

For a while, I dropped by Bing's house almost every day, either before work or just after I had come home. I would sit on her floor and happily accept a glass of cool water from one of the kids. If I was really lucky, an iced coffee. Iced coffee in Laos is a heavenly experience. Strong coffee mixed with sweetened condensed milk, and unsweetened condensed milk and sugar, is poured over ice and served in a plastic bag with a straw. The result blows away anything you might buy at Starbucks, and of course costs only a fraction of the price. In Vientiane, it became an addiction.

"How's business?" I would ask. In response, Bing invariably launched into her latest story about the trials of life in Vientiane. She was very vocal, and liked to criticize everything about her country: the roads, the people, even the government. Whenever she wanted to criticize the Party, Bing would make a discreet reference to the current leadership by waving her hand in the direction of the Presidential Palace on Lan Xang Avenue.

Bing was as forceful physically as she was with her words, and often, after telling a particularly bawdy joke, she would give me a slap on the knee that left me in pain for the rest of my visit. Her kids usually kept quiet, but would occasionally giggle at something Bing would say about me (this was particularly funny for them if I failed to understand what she was talking about). I don't think they ever quite got used to the idea of a *falang* sitting in their home.

She was always upbeat, but she had much more on her mind than clothes: she was trying to obtain a visa to visit her brother in the United States. He lived in Wichita, Kansas. When the US had pulled out after the war, hundreds of thousands of Lao—ultimately more than ten percent of the population—fearing the new regime, fled the country. Families were separated, marriages disrupted. And most of the refugees, like Bing's brother, ended up in the States.

"But why Kansas?" Bing wondered aloud as I was thinking the same thing. "Why not California? That sounds like a nice place to me. It's warm. Or how about Hawaii? I saw it on TV once."

In the twenty years or so since he had left, Bing had received only two letters from her brother. She had no idea what he did, what it was like where he lived, or if his children were healthy. For Bing, he was "missing in action," a casualty of the war, and she just wanted to see him again. But in order for a simple visit, she needed to submit a flurry of documents to the American Embassy: a request for permission to enter the country; her brother's W-2 tax forms; letters from her brother and his employer stating that he is in good standing; the bank statements of everyone involved.

Bing couldn't speak a word of English, and during my visits I tried to help her understand the visa application process by translating these documents loosely into Lao. As I leafed through the papers, I learned that her brother worked as a security guard at a plastics factory in Arkansas City, Kansas. He had 400 dollars in the bank, which he used to support his six children in Kansas. Two had been born in Laos, another two in Thailand, and a final pair in the United States.

"Why do they make this so difficult?" Bing often asked.

I would explain that the embassy suspected she might never come back to Laos.

It wasn't much in the US, but 400 dollars was probably more money than Bing had ever seen at one time.

She assured me that she would never want to live in America. "It's too cold over there, and it snows! I can't deal with snow!"

Bing was a victim of a war that continues to wound. Her situation made me angry. The US effort had led to the split in her family. I wanted to help her, to march into the consul's office and convince him to take her. But I knew that that would do more harm than good. I also knew that the embassy's fear of surreptitious immigration was hardly unwarranted. The desire for family reunification and the hope for a better life in America fueled an insatiable demand for visas—each time I went past the embassy, a line of applicants stretched out onto the street—and only a handful were granted every year.

All things considered, Bing's chances didn't look great.

Luckily, communication between Lao families and their relatives in the US had become much easier in recent years. The government no longer interfered with international financial contributions, and many families in Vientiane depended for their survival on the checks they received from relatives overseas. Former "traitors" were even allowed to come back and visit, and Bing hoped her brother would one day be able to make the long trip across the Pacific instead. Given her situation, it was the best hope she had of seeing him before it was too late.

———————

Eventually it came time for me to make a trip back to America, a place about which, it strikes me now, I thought of far more intensely and critically while living Laos than I ever had back home. What Ming had said about herself and China held true for me and the States, as well: it was from afar that I had the best view of the place that, according to my passport, at least, was home.

As I waited for my flight in the departure lounge at the Vientiane International Airport, I gazed out the window and onto the runway below. The familiar sight of a man ambling across the strip, shielded by a large straw hat and pushing his bicycle, came into view. Inside, a teenage boy stood in the middle of the room, surrounded by his family. His feet shifted back and forth, and he looked at the floor. This boy's features were clearly Lao, but the way he carried himself gave it away: he was an American. I hadn't seen this typical Western teenage behavior—the awkwardness of adolescence combined with an intense pride—since I'd arrived in Vientiane. He was decked out in baggy pants and a baseball hat slung back to front. Head shaved, he sported two loop earrings. He was heading home to America on his own after a visit with his relatives in Vientiane. He seemed out of place: what did he have in common with these people anymore? He barely knew the language, and probably missed his friends in the US. When it came time for him to go, the family gave the boy a cheerful send-off.

One person in the group, however, wasn't smiling. The boy's elder sister, I noticed, was fighting the urge to cry. She held back tears as he made his way through the customs checkpoint. Finally, she couldn't take it any longer, and, looking back just as I stepped out into the scorching heat and onto the runway, I noticed a teardrop rolling down her cheek. No amount of foreign currency arriving in the mail from the US each month could compensate for a lost brother.

Part II

Amarillo

You should not dream of the ten pieces of gold on the other side of the lake, but rather appreciate the five pieces in your hands.
Lao Proverb.

During the summer between my two years in Laos, I went home. I decided to return not so much because I missed the trappings of American life; to be sure, the thought of fresh bagels and chocolate-chip ice-cream crossed my mind every now and then, but never for long. I went home because I felt the need to get away from Laos. By the end of my first year in Vientiane, I was comfortable there—almost too comfortable, I thought. Laos' isolation had gradually led me to feel disconnected from the rest of the world. The goings-on of a capital city of only a few hundred thousand—a large village, really—in a country most people never thought about, had suddenly become the center of my universe. Current events in the US and Europe, even in neighboring Thailand, seemed far away indeed. What did they have to do with my life in Vientiane? I had seen other expats, seduced by the ease of living in Laos, turn their backs on the outside world as well, only to find themselves stuck in Vientiane, unable to leave. I wanted to avoid such a fate.

Of course, there were more basic needs driving my desire to return. I hadn't seen a movie or a concert in nearly a year, and I was ready for some real entertainment. When you find yourself singing along to the hits of barely pubescent pop groups during rare glimpses of MTV Southeast Asia, you know it's time. When you start to think that the Backstreet Boys really deserved the devotion they received from teenage girls the world over, it's time to go home.

After arriving in the States, I spent a few days in bed, recovering from jet lag. Once fully awake, I decided to drive across the country, from my parents' home outside Washington, D.C. to San Francisco. Along the way, I stopped to see virtually every film released in America that summer. I caught as many live music and theater performances I possibly could, from New York to Columbia, South Carolina, and from Santa Barbara to Chicago. I walked under the Spanish moss in Savannah and over the Brooklyn Bridge. I sat at the foot of Mount Rushmore and on the beaches of Rhode Island. And, just to make sure they knew I hadn't fallen off the face of the earth, I visited old friends, wherever they were.

But the most important stop I made during my drive across the country was a visit to some folks I'd never met before. They lived in Amarillo, Texas.

Back in Vientiane, the most dedicated student in any of my English classes was, without a doubt, Kham. Most of my colleagues I had to cajole into coming to class, but not Kham. Every lesson, without fail, he showed up—worn, black leather briefcase in hand, ready to learn—ten minutes before class had even begun. If they came, many of his classmates would arrive ten minutes before the *end* of class. And Kham didn't even work at the NTA. During the day, he worked for the government as a tour guide at Laos' National Ethnic Culture Park, just outside Vientiane. Twice a week, he dutifully drove his motorbike twenty kilometers into town, through rice fields and past the gigantic steel vats of the Beer Lao brewery, for his English lessons at the NTA.

After class, he would head home for a nap and dinner before he set out again for his night job: singing at the Paradise nightclub downtown. The Paradise was a dive. The seats were sticky, the clientele seedy. But Kham was quite a crooner, and he delighted guests until late into the evening with his effortless performances of traditional Lao ballads. He always performed in a spotless white suit and pink shirt, and shared the stage with an aging beauty stuffed into a sequined skirt and stilettos. Every thirty minutes or so, the singers would take a break, the Thai pop songs would come on, and Kham and I would share a beer.

If ever Kham was unable to make it to English class, he would call me at home to let me know. In return, if I was unable to teach, I'd call him at the Culture Park—or stop by the Paradise—to make sure he knew. In the Lao PDR, that kind of co-operation was something truly revolutionary.

Kham often came to class in the latest American fashions. He wore brand new T-shirts with "USA" splashed across the back, faded Bugle Boy jeans, and Nike cross-trainers. One afternoon, I asked him how he possibly found such gear in Laos. He explained that almost every month a package from the States arrived in his mailbox. Sometimes it contained US dollars, sometimes a few items of new clothing. They were sent by his elder brother, who had left Laos more than twenty years before to make a life for himself in America. Kham hadn't seen him since.

When his brother had left in 1978, Kham decided to stay behind. "It's good for a family to have sons," he told me. "They can help the parents." But over the years, Kham had diligently kept in touch with his brother. The letter he planned to send to the US later that afternoon contained some important news. It read, in English, "I have a son now. Like you, the first child is a son, the same as our family forever."

As I checked his letter for grammatical errors, Kham explained that his wife had recently given birth to a baby boy. Only a few months before, his brother's wife had had the same good fortune. In every generation of his family, in fact, for as long as Kham could remember, the first-born child had been a boy. He was hopeful that one day he would meet his nephew—or at least have the chance to see his photograph.

On my last day at work before the summer, Kham brought his brother's address and phone number to class. The information on the yellow Post-it note was minimal: Robert Thipaphay, Emily Street, Amarillo, Texas. "'Thipaphay' means 'Apologize to Mother,'" Kham said. "He took it before he left for America."

Just before the end of class, I made a promise to Kham: during my trip home, I'd pay a visit to his brother, and I'd return to Vientiane with a photograph of his nephew.

———

The Big Texan Steak Ranch & Opry is located at Exit 16 off Route 40 West, an interstate that leads directly from Dallas to the small city of Amarillo in the Texas panhandle. The Big Texan is "world famous" (I learned only after I'd arrived, having pulled off the highway to use the facilities) for its truly Texas-sized challenge: eat a 72-ounce steak and "all the trimmings"—salad, bread, potato, and shrimp cocktail—in an hour or less, and you get the meal for free. Over the years, 35,000 customers have accepted the challenge; only 5,500 have succeeded. Posted on the wall near the hostess' counter was a roster of recent successful contenders. The previous night's winner? "Jan," from Copenhagen. When I'd first learned that Robert lived in Amarillo, the notion of a Lao man and his family residing in the Texas panhandle had struck me as absurd. This brief visit to the Big Texan made it seem no more likely.

But as I continued through Western Texas, the images that flew past my windshield began to remind me of the landscape I'd seen during my travels in Laos. The cattle fields on either side of Route 40 leading into Amarillo were dry and harsh—much like the earth lining the route from Vientiane to Pakse in Southern Laos. Both places seemed barren and arid, even scarred. A recent Lao immigrant might feel at home, I thought, in this empty land of absent cowboys, retired ranchers, and die-hard Republicans.

When I pulled up in front of the house on Emily Street on an early Saturday evening in July, the neighborhood was deserted and a strange calm pervaded the air. I rang the doorbell, but as no one was home, I decided to take a walk down the street. Robert lived in a neighborhood of identical one-story houses, neatly lined up in rows. Each came with a garage and modest front yard where the grass struggled to survive the Texas heat. His was a community on the edge of nowhere: a development of modest brick homes where only a few years before there had been a sprawling cattle ranch. Amarillo had a population of only 170,000, but it was growing fast; 76% was white, 14% was Hispanic, and less than 2% was Asian. Suddenly the silence of the neighborhood was broken when a group of Spanish-speaking Americans drove past in a beat-up Chevy Citation, blasting the joyous music of their ascendant Latino culture into the balmy evening air.

As I made my way back to Robert's house, I saw a second-hand BMW sedan pull into the driveway. An Asian man in his late fifties emerged from the driver's seat. He wore faded blue jeans, a belt with a large silver buckle, and clean white sneakers. Could this be him?

"*Sabaidee!*" I called, using the greeting that crossed my lips countless times a day in Vientiane, but which I hadn't uttered in weeks. What in Laos had come so naturally, just the sort of thing you'd say to an acquaintance on the street, seemed out of place here in Amarillo.

"*Sabaidee,*" the man replied, his hand outstretched. "You must be Brett." Soon, a woman, evidently his wife, joined us. She was demure, soft-spoken, and, clutching her handbag, always remained just a step behind her husband. Her smile as she greeted me was disarming. These two, I soon learned, were Dan and Sally, Robert's parents-in-law.

Inside, Sally sat me down on the sofa in the living room, offered a glass of sweet iced tea, and nearly buried me under an avalanche of photos. Album upon album of pictures helped me to identify the three couples living together in this small house: Dan and Sally; their first daughter and her husband; and their second daughter, and her husband, Robert. The star of the most recent albums, however, was by far the youngest member of the household: Robert's newborn son, Billy.

"This is Billy," gushed Sally. "He's so smart."

The child was beautiful, smiling broadly in every photograph, always the center of everyone's attention. As Sally tidied up, Dan collapsed on the sofa next to me and switched on the television. The photo albums guided me through the family's early years in America, starry-eyed first visits to Las Vegas and Disneyland, car purchases and high school graduations, all the way back to the early days in Laos. When I began to examine the black-and-white prints of Pakse before the Indochina War, Dan's attention drifted away from the screen and he began to tell me his story.

Dan was a close relative of Prince Boun Oum of Champassak, the leader of the southernmost of Laos' three pre-independence kingdoms. After World War II, Laos was declared a constitutional monarchy within the French union, and King Sisavangvong of Luang Prabang was appointed head of state. As a result, the kingdom of Champassak was rendered virtually powerless. Prince Boun Oum never officially succeeded his father as king of Champassak, but he did become the region's most important single spiritual force. He also remained an influential right-wing political leader in Laos until the communist victory in 1975.

Thought by the Lao to be *saksit*—sacred, or holy—Boun Oum was said to have the power to change form at will—into a bird to fly, say, or a fish to swim under water—and to expel evil spirits from the kingdom. He played a key religious role as the high priest of all major festivals in the south, particularly the annual celebration held in February at the glorious Wat Phu in Champassak, a decaying Khmer temple complex that pre-dates even Cambodia's Angkor Wat.

Before the revolution, Dan's family was one of the most powerful in Laos. As its leader, Boun Oum was a major player in Laos' wartime politics, and he ultimately served as the nation's prime minister in the early 1960s. He retired officially from politics in 1962, but continued to exert tremendous influence behind the scenes until the end of the war. He opened a casino in Pakse, Champassak's capital, and spent his last years in Laos working to complete a grand palace, the fifty-odd rooms of which were built to accommodate his many girlfriends. Unfinished when he escaped to Paris—where he ultimately died in exile in 1980—the building today houses the Thai-owned and operated Champassak Palace Hotel, where I had once stayed during an office trip down south.

Dan, now in his late fifties, grew up in Pakse. A bright student, he was able to attend military schools under the Americans and the French, both in Laos and in Paris. He eventually rose to become an officer in the Royal Lao Army. A page in one of the family albums is dedicated to pictures of him and his brother in uniform, seated on military motorcycles and visibly proud of their role in defending the nation against the communist "rebels." As Dan pointed to one photograph, I noticed that the bulky ring on his index finger bore the familiar seal of the pre-war Royal Lao Government, a three-headed elephant. Each head signified one of the three ancient kingdoms: Luang Prabang, Vientiane, and Champassak.

Sally spent her childhood in Pakse as well. She studied nursing in Paris and, on her return to Laos, began working in an American-built hospital in Pakse. During the war, Dan was treated for combat wounds in the same hospital, and it was there that he first met Sally. "She took care of me in the hospital, just like she takes care of us today." They fell in love, married, and soon had two daughters and a son. The son, the youngest, would not meet his father until he was a sophomore in a Texas high school.

In 1975, Dan was sent to a re-education camp in Northern Huapanh, one of the least accessible of Laos' provinces. Facing a bleak future as the wife of an official in the former regime, Sally decided to take the children across the border into Thailand. With the help of a Catholic sponsor, they moved on to America, where they were able to join Sally's brother in Houston. She moved the family up to Amarillo after finding a job there with the city government as a refugee healthcare adviser. Among other things, she helped immigrants—from Laos and Vietnam, and more recently from places like Bosnia and Kosovo—navigate through the maze of paperwork required to obtain employment, education, and healthcare in the US. When Sally and the family had first arrived in Amarillo, they had been among only a handful of Lao residents. By the time I visited, the Lao community had expanded enough to support a Lao food market and Wat Lao Buddharam, a temple just off Fritch Highway.

Even without a father at home, the three children moved smoothly through the American public school system. Sally was a demanding mother, setting high standards and enforcing strict rules. Beth's official graduation portrait from Amarillo High—a vast concrete and brick structure I had driven by on my way to Emily Street—hung on the living room wall. Adorned with bright red ribbons and a National Honor Society certificate, the framed portrait was a testament to Sally's remarkable success in single-handedly raising her children in a foreign land.

———————

"They tried to wash my brain. That's why I'm crazy sometimes."

Driving along the multi-lane highways of Amarillo to a Thai restaurant for dinner, Dan apologized for taking a wrong turn. He rarely talked about the seven years he spent in the *samana* in Huapanh. When he did, it was often as an aside, or in a blasé, joking manner. At the camp, Dan had performed menial and often meaningless physical tasks, sat through endless seminars on socialist ideology and, as he put it, did his best to resist the daily anti-capitalist indoctrination. Eventually he worked as a bus driver and interpreter for army supply runs between Northern Laos and Vietnam. He spoke French, Vietnamese, and even a little Russian, which was helpful—the newly arrived Soviet advisers certainly hadn't learned to speak any Lao.

Only after he was released from the camp and sent back to Vientiane did Dan learn that Sally had left for the States years before. He wasn't surprised or disappointed, but simply anxious to rejoin his wife and children. "I had to follow my family," he explained, "so I crossed the Mekong." He lived in a refugee camp in Northern Thailand for another two years before receiving his own visa to enter the US. By the time Dan arrived in Texas, able to speak only a few words of English, his wife was comfortably settled into life in Amarillo. His children had long left their past in Laos behind, and embraced America. After so many years apart, Dan barely recognized his own family. The reunion was awkward, and Dan's belated transition to American life far from smooth, but in the end things worked out. In a way.

"We eat out almost every night these days—no time to cook," Dan told me. I could see why. To make ends meet, he and Sally worked extremely long hours; the chance to spend a Saturday evening together with them both was rare indeed. Until the week before my visit, Dan had been working Monday through Sunday, days and nights. He was a guard for a local security corporation, and, just as he had in the old days in Laos, he wore a uniform and carried a firearm to work everyday. "The priest comes to my house sometimes; asks why we don't go to the church," said Dan. "No time, I speak him. No time. And look, too many people go to church every week, but leave their husbands, run around. The most important thing is to stay together."

Sally murmured agreement from the back seat: "Together."

Inside the restaurant, Sally seemed weary. Her hair was slightly askew, and the emerging lines on her face revealed the hard work she had put into raising three children alone in a foreign country. Life in Amarillo was a far cry indeed from her aristocratic upbringing in Pakse. When she'd arrived in Houston, she barely knew how to cook, and had never driven a car. "For the first time, there were no servants to drive us, to cook and clean." For both Dan and Sally, the shock of the fall in status was great. On Emily Street, the second-hand BMW in the driveway and the living room's home entertainment system—complete with six remote controls and a set of speakers taller than I—were tangible reminders of the difficulty of letting go of their memories of an upper-class lifestyle. "With everyone's salary, we have a pretty good income," Dan explained. "But we spend it all."

Dan and Sally had returned to Laos for a brief visit the previous winter. At the shabby airport in Vientiane, Dan told me, the immigration official on duty had immediately recognized his surname as a sign of royalty. But Dan decided that he wouldn't hide his past. "Yes, I fought in the Royal Lao Army," Dan had told him. "I worked for the Americans. I am American. So what do you want to do?" The officer had been reluctant, but eventually let Dan through without incident. Now that it was Lao government policy to allow most émigrés back, the official had had no choice.

A number of Dan's Lao friends in Amarillo had also served in the Royal Lao Army, and they refused to believe that it was even possible to return while the communists were still in power. "'Aren't you scared?' they asked me before I went back," said Dan. "Some are still fighting the war. They talk about taking over, about sending money for fighting. But I don't get involved." In fact, Sally dreamed of saving enough money to spend a few months of every year in

Laos after she and her husband eventually retired. Her sister lived in Vientiane, and had even reserved a room in her house for Dan and Sally.

"Why don't you move back for good?" I asked her as we were driving home after dinner.

"I've lived in Amarillo for 21 years," explained Sally. "It's like my home, you know."

"We work hard," Dan added. "But we still love America. You know, here, we have freedom."

Dan sounded convinced, but I wasn't so sure. Yes, they had freedom, but at what price? His statement sounded suspiciously like a bit of pro-American rhetoric offered just for my benefit. But what did Dan and his wife really think of me? The only connection I had to their family was my friendship with their son-in-law's brother, a man they'd never even met. And yet they'd welcomed me into their home so openly and with such apparent ease, as if I'd been an old friend. Were they happy to host a random American who happened to have lived in Laos? Or did they consider it a burden, yet another encroachment on their precious free time? I wondered if they appreciated their new lives in the US as much as they let on. Perhaps in my presence they felt *obliged* to appreciate America—in the same way that they felt obliged to the Catholic sponsors who had helped them to come to Texas in the first place. As I mulled over whether or not to voice any of my confusion, I heard Sally echo her husband from the back seat.

"Freedom," she said.

***

It was well past midnight before I first met Robert, Kham's brother and the man I had come all this way to find. He walked into the living room, where I was once again leafing through old photographs, this time on my own, and introduced himself with a firm handshake. Robert was strong, and his muscles bulged through his work uniform of white jeans and a white T-shirt. He was a healthy man in his mid-thirties, but he looked exhausted.

Like many other Lao and Vietnamese living in the area, Robert worked for IBP, a beef processing plant and the second largest employer in Amarillo. When I had driven by IBP on Route 40, the rancid odor of the meat had penetrated the car. According to Robert, it wasn't that comfortable inside the plant either. "It's really cold in there, like 35 degrees sometimes," he told me after he had taken a shower and changed. "That's, like, freezing!"

At the plant, Robert worked near the end of the line. First, the cattle—thousands per day during summer—were skinned, gutted, cleaned, and sawed into pieces. Then, agricultural officials inspected and stamped each individual piece, marking grade level and ensuring safety. Finally, it was time for Robert to punch the assigned government code and categorization of every piece of meat into his computer.

"I've been working overtime lately," he said, "'cause a lot of people, the economy is so good, they quit for another job."

But Robert never refused the extra work, thinking of the payments on his new Jeep Cherokee and of Billy's future education. He and Beth wanted to send their son to a private Catholic school, which would cost a few hundred dollars a month, an enormous investment for the family. They had enough to get by, but not much beyond that.

Robert had worked hard all day at the plant, but he wasn't too tired to go out this Saturday night. He kissed Billy good night and we piled into the Jeep and drove over to a friend's house for a party. Robert seemed relieved to be leaving his son, wife, and parents-in-law behind, at least for the evening. "So much responsibility. I have to work for everyone now."

I thought immediately of the money and clothing Robert regularly sent to Kham back in Vientiane.

In Robert's friend's backyard, Lao men sat around drinking beer and chewing on slices of grilled pork fat. I was the only white guy, but I was right at home; it felt just like a typical Saturday evening in Vientiane. I sat down, opened a Heineken—Beer Lao wasn't yet available in Texas—and listened. Not a word of English was spoken as the men discussed the work week, argued about the true age of a Thai singer who had performed at the community center the other night, and commiserated about the trials of life in Texas. They seemed happy to be among the people they knew best, free from the daily struggle with a language and culture that wasn't their own.

Every once in a while, the men would sigh and reminisce about Laos—even those who, having lived in America most of their lives, could barely remember the place. News of the Lao government's recent economic liberalization program had convinced many of these men that the real golden opportunities lay back in Vientiane. Life over there just had to be better than this, they thought. As I listened, I didn't try and convince them otherwise. But I knew that they were really speaking of an imagined Laos, a romantic illusion of their homeland.

When I asked for the toilet, Robert grinned and gestured to the shadows just behind the wooden fence at the back of the house. I made my way through the large and slowly expanding pile of junk that sat in the backyard: corrugated metal and timber, cans and bottles left over from previous nights of revelry, miscellaneous car parts, a discarded weightlifting set. As I stood in the dark, unpaved alley behind the house, I glanced over my shoulder. After all, public urination was a crime in most municipalities in America. I sensed the depth of my own nostalgia for Laos, where such concerns would never have crossed my mind. From the perspective of the mundane workaday world of Amarillo, with all its rules and regulations, life in Laos seemed blissful, almost impossibly comfortable.

When I sat back down again, I met Jamie, who had lived in Amarillo for nearly twenty years, ever since he left Laos with his family at the age of age five. These days, he was thinking of going back. "I wanna move back to Laos, you know. Start a business. Make some money, you know. Life is easy over there."

Life is easy: that's just what my colleagues and friends in Vientiane had so often insisted about life in *America*. Their dreams of one day moving to the US to make it big sounded oddly familiar to Jamie's grand plan. Like Robert, Jamie worked at the meat plant, hosing down the freshly slaughtered cows. In his free time, he liked to gamble. "One night, I lost 5,000 dollars," he boasted to me in front of his friends. "Bet on four football teams, and they all lost!"

While the men relaxed outside, their wives and daughters were gathered in the kitchen. According to Robert, they were preparing for the traditional ceremony that would be held the following morning to welcome a pair of monks visiting from Laos. The floral votive arrangements were identical to those I had seen during the boat-racing festival on the Mekong so many months before, though crisp dollar bills replaced the 100-kip notes. In the driveway up front, a group of Lao-American teenagers had gathered to hang out. I had heard them talking when we'd first pulled up to the house in Robert's Jeep. They discussed the latest gossip, compared new clothing, and complained about school. No one talked about Laos. Every now and then, one of them floated into the backyard, and two worlds seemed to collide; rarely conversant in Lao, these teenagers precariously balanced their identities as Americans with their connection to the Lao traditions being practiced around them. A plump boy of about 13 drifted in and out of the group of men throughout the evening, munching on potato chips. He fulfilled his traditional obligation to serve his elders ("Get me a beer, will you?") with evident distaste. His acne and extra pounds demonstrated, I thought, his full assimilation into American society.

When I noticed that Robert had begun to yawn, I suggested that we call it a night. He quickly agreed. As we prepared to leave, the gambling began. Dollar bills were passed quickly between hands and on and off the Lao astrological board game. The rules were simple: roll the dice, and predict the sign on which it would land. Would it be the rabbit? Or the snake? Jamie took a swig of his Colt 45 malt liquor and keenly observed the board. I imagined that he had a lot riding on this game. It was three o'clock on Sunday morning in Amarillo, and the work week was finally over.

———

Much later that same morning, Robert, his wife Beth, Billy, and I drove to Amarillo's popular Golden China restaurant for the all-you-can-eat lunch special. "A lot of people come here after church," Beth told me after we'd taken our seats at one of the few free tables. I glanced around and saw that, indeed, many families were in their Sunday best. Robert and I had only recently woken up. While Robert helped himself to the buffet, Beth told me about her job at Amarillos's public health department, which provided free medical advice, birth control, and baby formula to single mothers in need. She enjoyed her work, but was not entirely convinced the city was doing the right thing for these women.

151

"You know, Brett, I think a lot of the women lie," she said. "They have really nice cars and everything. They say they aren't married, but they are. I don't understand these women—a 12-year-old came in yesterday, pregnant. We have a lot of Spanish, you know; they don't believe in birth control. Ten, sometimes a dozen children, all from different fathers." Across the dining room, a small child screamed and threw a fistful of *moo shoo* pork in our direction.

Not all the Lao-American students in Amarillo were as successful as Beth had been. She told me that the city was struggling with the scourge of teenage gangs; Lao and Vietnamese, Hispanic, and African American, they seemed to split along strictly ethnic lines. Fortunately, there had been little violence so far. Mostly, the kids hung out, drank, dabbled in drugs—and produced unwanted children. Beth attributed much of the trouble to a lack of parental supervision and attention. With both parents working non-stop, often nights, to make it in a new country, it was no wonder that some Lao kids simply fell through the cracks.

Back in Vientiane, it had often seemed that Kham, Bing, and my other Lao friends could talk of little else but coming to America. It remained in their minds the promised land, a place of untold opportunity and freedom. But in Amarillo, the constant preoccupation of Robert and his wife was just the reverse. When I asked about Robert's thoughts about the future, he said, "I want to save enough money to go to Laos. It is my dream." For he knew first-hand what his relatives back in his homeland refused to believe: life in America wasn't easy at all. Sure, you made more dollars, but they seemed to disappear before you even had a chance to put them in the bank. Living in the US meant working overtime just to pay for health insurance, monthly car installments, a mortgage—a myriad concerns that the average Lao simply did not face.

And there was another thing, too: "Here in America, you have all the material things," Robert said. "Everything you want. But it's not the same *feeling* as in Laos."

Beth sensed the spiritual emptiness of her American life as well, and longed for the chance to go back to her homeland. She was desperate to visit a place she hadn't seen since she was nine. If and when she did get the chance to return, I thought to myself, she would be in for quite a surprise. Judging from her unceasing stream of queries about life in Laos, she would need to prepare herself before she went. "Do they have 'all-you-can-eat' over there?" she asked. "How are the burgers? I heard they were dry, not like here. Do they have donuts?"

After lunch at the Golden China, we did what all the other families in Amarillo did on Sunday afternoons: we went to the mall. "Billy likes to shop," Beth told me. At ten months old, Billy could barely crawl, but already he liked to shop. The mall was bursting at the seams with customers on this July afternoon, and there wasn't another white face in the crowd. I hardly heard a word of English through the polyglot din of Spanish, Vietnamese, and Lao.

In the food court, Robert ordered a Coke, the largest size possible. Beth chuckled before saying, almost to herself, "I bet you can't ask them to 'supersize' it over there, huh?"

I wandered with Robert and his family in and out of the crowded shops, past the latest fashions in outlets like Britches and The Gap. We strolled up and down the aisles of a giant toy store, and I watched Billy's eyes widen at the innumerable choices before him. The mall was the key to the American dream. It was the one place where people from around the world, of disparate races, religions, and cultural backgrounds, could come together to purchase their own part of America—a new pair of sneakers, perhaps, or the latest DVD player. In 1998, the average American consumer spent 1,508 dollars on clothing alone. That same year, the average annual income in Laos was less than 400. Robert worked hard, earned money, and decided how to spend it, and therein lay the power of America. The freedom to supersize.

The lens of my disposable camera framed an image of Robert carrying Billy triumphantly on his shoulders through the mall. I saw a proud American father, confident that he owned at least a small piece of the American dream. I snapped the shutter and, satisfied, put the camera away. This was the photo I'd give to Kham when I returned to Vientiane.

Up North

When I came into work again after the summer, it felt as if I'd never left. Back at the NTA, nothing had changed. General Cheng was still in charge, Mon was still wondering whether or not to leave, and the computers were still crashing every few minutes. None of my colleagues seemed to have noticed that I'd been away. Some things in Vientiane had changed, of course. The traffic had increased, as had the number of teenage boys with long hair and girls in jeans. And the capital had a brand new airport, courtesy of the Japanese government. The gleaming international terminal had sliding glass doors, elevators, and a snack bar. All we needed now were the tourists.

One afternoon soon after I returned, Khit, General Cheng's gun-toting right-hand man, told me that he and a few other NTA staff members would be taking a trip up to Sainyabuli province in the northwest. The purpose of the trip would be to survey the province for potential tourist attractions. The General wanted to know if I'd like to come along. Khit had given me as little advance warning as possible: they'd be leaving the following morning. But I jumped at the chance, determined to see more of the country I was helping to promote.

I rushed home after work and packed, informed my neighbors that I'd be away for a few days, and let my friends know where I'd be in case of an emergency. My colleagues and I would be traveling on Route 13, and some of my friends wondered aloud whether it was worth the risk.

Laos may once have been the Kingdom of the Million Elephants, but when I lived there, the country only had one major road. The French completed the southern portion of Route Coloniale 13 back in 1930, when Laos was still firmly part of Indochine and on the receiving end of France's grand *mission civilisatrice*. In the early 1940s, construction on the section from Vientiane to Luang Prabang was finally begun. But the road wasn't actually completed until another five decades had passed, when the final stretch from the unremarkable town of Kasi north to Luang Prabang was paved in 1997. For years, this short section of the road had been a constant source of trouble for the communist government.

In 1995, anti-communist rebels attacked a convoy on the road, injuring two French tourists and killing four Lao. In June of 1996, bandits hijacked a Swedish aid agency vehicle in the same area. Later that same year, a van belonging to a Vientiane-based tour operator was attacked near Kasi. Four passengers were killed, including the company's owner, Claude Vincent, a Frenchman and, at the time, a major figure in Laos' nascent tourism industry. Vincent had lived in the country for most of his life, as his father had been a teacher at the Lycée Vientiane before the revolution. In the capital, Vincent was considered something of an honorary citizen, and his passing was mourned by much of the community. When the road between Kasi and Luang Prabang was finally paved and secured in 1997, the government claimed that the banditry problem had been solved. For the first time in history, Laos' two most important cities were connected by a safe and passable road.

Or so it seemed. Route 13 remained off-limits to all employees of UN agencies and foreign embassies. These same institutions had also declared the national airline, Lao Aviation, unsafe, so it was essentially impossible for most expats to travel north of Vientiane without getting someone in trouble. Development aid workers, already reluctant to leave behind the comforts of the capital—with its Italian restaurants, imported Camembert, and air-conditioning—had even less motivation to get out of Vientiane.

UNDP employees working on provincial aid projects hadn't even seen the areas they were charged with developing; their knowledge was limited to what they read in the project documents and feasibility studies that lined their office bookshelves. No one really had any idea what was going on outside of the capital. Every so often, reports of bandit attacks and gruesome traffic accidents would trickle down the Mekong from the northern provinces and onto the Vientiane grapevine.

In the absence of any reliable information from the state media, and without a free press to turn to, foreign residents in the capital found themselves chasing desperately after these small drops of information. Living in Vientiane, we were cut off from current affairs not only in the rest of the world, but in the rest of the country as well. A rancher in Amarillo had a better chance of being informed about goings-on in Northern Laos than did the average Vientiane resident. The capital's news vacuum allowed us to go about our lives as normal, blissfully unaware that innocent citizens were being killed elsewhere in the country. Often, Party officials were among the last to know; even in 1999, entire swathes of the country remained outside the grasp of the central government's control.

The only way to get to some of Laos' most remote provinces was by helicopter, which wasn't always an inviting prospect. A few years before, the Lao Women's Union had organized a sightseeing trip for a group of ambassadors' wives up to Huapanh, where Dan had been sent for re-education. Huapanh had been the cradle of the Lao communist movement, and when the Pathet Lao took over, there had even been talk of establishing a new national capital in the province. But today, the only reliable route to Huapanh was by helicopter—no regular air service was available, and the roads in the northeast remained barely passable. So the wives were piled into a Chinese-issue Lao People's Army helicopter and sent on their way. The trip went smoothly enough until they approached Huapanh's makeshift airport and found themselves in a fog so thick that the runway wasn't even visible. As the pilot circled, waiting for an opening, rumor spread among the wives that the gas was about to run out. Panic hit. The Union officials appealed for calm, but the women were hysterical. Some began to scream. Eventually, the pilot gave up, turned around, and flew back to Vientiane. Better luck next time, the wives were told.

As I wasn't associated with the UN or any other legitimate outfit, the only restriction on my travel was my calculation of the risk involved. Having spent the summer on the highways of the US, cowering in the shadows of the 18-wheeler trucks that regularly hurtled past my small sedan, I figured Route 13 couldn't be so bad.

The day before we left for Sainyabuli, Khit had told me that the NTA van would swing by my house at six o'clock in the morning to pick me up. I woke up just in time to leave at this ungodly hour— I didn't want to miss the van. Who knew when I'd have another opportunity to travel north? I sat outside my front door and watched as an elderly man from my village took advantage of the cool early morning breeze to perform his daily exercises inside the grounds of the temple across the street, and waited. Six o'clock came and went. I paced back and forth in my living room, and waited. Seven o'clock came and went. I walked out to the main road to make sure the NTA crew hadn't missed the turn, and waited some more. . . .

Finally, at 7:45, my blessed chariot arrived, barreling down the small alley that passed for my street. Without further ado, we set off north.

Once you pass Vientiane's airport, any signs of urban life quickly disappear, and all that can be seen for miles around are large expanses of green. As soon as we hit Route 13, our driver, Noxay, put the pedal to the metal. Noxay was a quiet man but absolutely ruthless behind the wheel; he stopped for nothing and no one. Whenever a child, cow, dog, or chicken so much as approached the center of the road, he blew his horn and raced on through. Oblivious to the chaos outside, Khit popped a tape of his favorite Lao comedy performance into the car stereo.

This sketch involved only a single joke, but it managed to sustain the comedians for hours and to send my colleagues into hysterics. It consisted of a dialogue between two characters, a Lao man and a visiting foreigner, a *falang*, who spoke broken Lao in an absurdly nasal voice. The hilarity resulted from the tendency of the foreigner to mix up the pronunciation of the words *meuai*—"tired," and *moi*—"pubic hair." You see, in Lao, the word *lai* means both "very" and "a lot." So if you don't watch out, you might end up saying something truly uproarious like "I have a lot of pubic hair" when what you meant to say was "I am very tired." This joke re-surfaced as a constant refrain throughout our trip, only increasing my desire to say that I was very tired.

In the van, I managed to tune out Laos' own Two Ronnies and turn my attention to the extraordinary scenery. As the road climbed up into the mountains, an occasional limestone karst would jut unexpectedly out of the landscape. Forested hills sheltered small village communities whose way of life seemed to have remained unchanged since well before the French first laid the groundwork for Route 13. This was a fragile environment, and I could feel the specter of development encroaching on its pristine beauty. But not just yet. Today there were only a handful of vehicles on the road: rickety trucks transporting goods, and large passenger pick-ups to which wooden benches had been precariously attached.

As I was shifting in my own comfortably padded seat to get a better view of the countryside, I felt something sharp and metal dig into my ankle. I checked under the seat and found a Lao People's Army AK-47 resting on the floor near my feet. Khit noticed my surprise from the front seat and gave me a silent wink. This wasn't the last weapon I'd see on Route 13.

Just then, the van abruptly slowed down. Up ahead, a soldier standing by the side of the road had signaled for us to stop. He was dressed in a basic green uniform, torn at the seams, and wore sandals rather than proper boots. A rifle was slung over his shoulder, but he seemed very young. As we approached, I grew worried; he looked more like my idea of a bandit than a member of the Lao People's Army. What did he want with us? Khit and Noxay, on the other hand, weren't the least bit fazed. After we stopped, they warmly greeted the soldier and pulled him into the van! The man gave me a quick nod and a polite smile, and took a seat. Stranded without any means of transportation, he had just needed a ride up Route 13.

All along the road, in fact, soldiers were policing the troubled route. When the second soldier flagged us down, though, I remained wary. I worried about my immigration status; my visa had run out the week before, and my passport was stuck in Vientiane, hopefully in the hands of a well-intentioned Foreign Affairs bureaucrat. What if this soldier asked for my papers? But I had nothing to fear. We gave him a ride as well, and he barely noticed me sitting quietly in the back corner of the van. By the time we picked up the third hitchhiking soldier, all I had to worry about was holding on to my place in the van.

Whenever we encountered a soldier along the way to Sainyabuli, even if he didn't flag us down, Noxay and Khit would invariably stop, offer words of encouragement, and hand out a few packs of cigarettes. Was their magnanimity a manifestation of Lao patriotism of the most genuine sort? I wondered. Or was it a result of the strong military connection between General Cheng at the NTA and the Lao People's Army? In the end, I decided it was simply a way for my colleagues to smooth the path to our destination. Considering what we all knew about possible bandit attacks and the crumbling condition of the pavement beneath us, we certainly didn't need any more unexpected bumps along the way.

By the time noon rolled around, we were hungry. But not many people lived along Route 13, and finding a place for lunch was an almost insurmountable challenge. The few restaurants we encountered along the road were either closed or had simply run out of food. Eventually we came to a small shack just beside a waterfall that acted as the shower, swimming pool, and communal sink for nearby villagers. Inside, a woman of at least seventy and her daughter relaxed on the bamboo mats that lined the floor. They were happy to offer us a meal, but they weren't about to prepare it for us. It was long past lunchtime, and they were finished working. "*Baw pen nyang*," we said. "No problem." Khit simply commandeered the kitchen and set about preparing a marvelous meal of *tam mak hong*, a spicy papaya salad, omelets, and fresh sticky rice.

As we devoured this small feast, our talk unexpectedly veered into the realm of the political. Most conversations in Laos stuck strictly to the mundane; politics was an area you never ventured into. But there were ways to get people to express their thoughts on the matter. This time, when I attempted to use the official Lao term for "socialism" in a sentence, I unintentionally confounded my colleagues. They didn't know what I was talking about. When I whipped out my handy Lao-English dictionary and vocabulary notebook, a simple Lao-language lesson evolved into a discussion of the central concepts in modern political life. Communism, capitalism, socialism, democracy—what did they all really mean?

"What is capitalism?" I asked.

"It means rich, like America!" Khit responded.

"And what about communism?"

"Oh, that means poor, very poor."

Khit's equation of communism with dire poverty struck me as interesting. Wasn't the government committed, at least on paper, to bettering the lives of its citizens through the socialist experiment? Was Khit, a member of the Party and an officer in the army—arguing that Laos was consigned to a future of poverty under the communist system? I wondered what his boss, General Cheng, would think of that. Wisely, I decided not to pursue this line of questioning, and instead continued to munch away. If you ask too many questions, people quickly stop talking.

———

The banditry problem along Route 13 might have been solved, but that didn't mean a trip on the road was risk-free. Route 13 was an endless series of sharp curves twisting through the mountains of Central and Northern Laos. This was a two-way road with only one lane, and it was often impossible to see who was coming around the bend from the opposite direction. After we had finished lunch and were back on the road, we picked up a soldier who had heard from a number of vehicles traveling south that there had been a serious accident up ahead. He needed to see the crash for himself, but had no means to reach it.

At the site of the accident, we came upon a huge truck turned completely on its side. Cartons of cigarettes, the truck's cargo, littered the road. A demolished motorbike lay in the center of the road. Any human victims were nowhere to be seen. We stopped to gawk, take photographs, murmur our disbelief, commiserate with the responsible soldier—and "shoot the rabbit," the Lao euphemism for relieving oneself in the bush. Presently, the soldier, doubling as a policeman, wrote up his official report. A report? I wanted to ask. What could possibly be the point? It probably wouldn't even be filed for weeks. But I knew that the soldier was just doing the best he could with next to nothing. His predicament mirrored that facing most police officials in Laos, who had neither the resources nor the motivation to effectively control crime. When motorbikes were stolen in Vientiane, the police were often the last to know. Citizens knew that reporting crimes was almost always a waste of time— all that would come of it was an official report.

We left the soldier alone at the site and got back on the road. Soon enough, the signposts announced that we were approaching the vicinity of Kasi, the sight of so many a fabled bandit attack. I instinctively slouched in my seat and prepared for the worst. I usually take official travel advisory warnings lightly; surely it's more dangerous to drive on the Beltway in suburban Virginia than to travel most places in the world. But now, as Kasi neared, I wondered if perhaps I'd been too cavalier; my encounter with Laos' finest had hardly increased my faith in the security of the road. What if something did happen? Would anyone in Vientiane, let alone back home in America, ever even find out? Was my fate to be decided here, in this no-name roadside town in Northern Laos? By the time I calmed down again, Kasi was long gone. We soon reached Luang Prabang, and Route 13 came to an end.

At the former royal capital, without so much as a break in this recently designated World Heritage Site, we turned on to a far smaller road that veered west and ended abruptly at the Mekong. Bridges had not yet reached this part of the world. On the eastern bank of the river we encountered a small ferry that would take us across. Though there were no cars in sight, the listless ferry operator insisted that we wait until the boat was completely full before making the one-minute journey to the other side.

On the western bank, Khit informed me that we had arrived in Sainyabuli. Like any good student, I had done my reading, and knew that the province had a population of about 300,000 and lay between Thailand to the west and Vientiane and Luang Prabang to the east. It was Laos' "rice basket," producing indispensable crops like cotton, peanuts, and tamarind. Though it shared a border with six different Thai provinces, Sainyabuli was considered one of the most remote provinces in Laos.

Remote, yes, but Sainyabuli had never been the most peaceful of provinces. The frontier with Thailand had been a perpetual trouble spot for the Lao government, and in 1987 a dispute over the location of the border exploded into a full-fledged military conflict between the two nations. The Lao pointed to a 1960 American map claiming that the border followed one part of the Nam Heuang River, an offshoot of the Mekong, while the Thais cited a 1908 French map identifying a different branch as the border. When Lao troops arrived in the disputed territory—an area of 77 square kilometers—the Thais responded with air strikes. More than 100 Thai and Lao soldiers died in the ensuing battle, which ended when a compromise border was fixed in 1988.

Sainyabuli was also a base for an insurgency group named Chao Fa, or "Lords of the Sky." The insurgents belonged to the Hmong minority, members of which had fought against the communists with the backing of the CIA during the Vietnam War. Twenty years later, some were still fighting. With anti-government groups roaming its hills, and problems like illegal drugs and timber smuggling plaguing its borders, it's no wonder the Lao government considered the province insecure.

Foreigners weren't exactly encouraged to visit Sainyabuli. That's not to say that visitors were clamoring to get in; Sainyabuli didn't have much to offer the average tourist. The ancient Khmer empire had never reached the province, so no ruins were left behind. It was never a cultural or political center under the Lan Xang Kingdom. And the French seemed to have forgotten that Sainyabuli even existed—no Route Coloniale led here. At the NTA, when I had been asked to write a brochure about Sainyabuli, I'd been at a loss. Turning to my colleagues for assistance, I was met with blank stares. "Sainyabuli. . . ? I'm sorry, Mr. Brett, I can't help. I've never been."

But what Sainyabuli did have was some of the country's most extraordinary natural beauty. A 100-square-kilometer National Biodiversity Conversation Area sat at the western edge of the province. According to international environmental groups based in Vientiane, the area contained such rare animals as rhino, gibbon, and tigers. Of course, none of this unsullied nature was accessible to the average visitor, but it was nice to know it was there. As we made our way along the empty road leading into the provincial capital, I noticed a vast rocky limestone outcrop in the distance, the façade of which vaguely resembled a pair of walking elephants. This was Sainyabuli's famous Pha Xang, or Elephant Cliffs. The province was said to be home to more elephants than any other in Laos. Did these two towering images count?

The capital of Sainyabuli was a ghost of a town on the banks of small tributary of the Mekong. It was home to only one proper restaurant, perhaps two guesthouses, a post office, and a nightclub. Only in Laos would a place like this be considered a provincial capital. The only other out-of-town visitors seemed to be a group of soldiers from the surrounding countryside, happy to be in the "city" for a break from their policing duties out in the sticks. There were no foreign tourists to be found.

My colleagues and I stayed in Sainyabuli's recently constructed government hotel, which was off-limits to the general public. The hotel was open only to the official delegations from Vientiane that occasionally drifted through and needed a place to stay. The white marble floors and shiny new plastic sofas in the lobby could not disguise the fact that this was merely a skeleton of a hostelry. If the place had regular employees, I never encountered any of them. Upon arrival we were left to fend for ourselves. There were no towels, no toilet paper, no electricity, and no running water. I shared a room with Khit, and as we unpacked, he proudly displayed his ubiquitous handgun. At least I'd be safe, I thought.

———

At noon the next day, we drove a few kilometers outside of town to one of Sainyabuli's genuine attractions, Tad Jaew Waterfall. The falls, about thirty meters high, sat at a bend in the Mekong that afforded one of the most spectacular views of the river in Laos. The spray from the cascading water provided some welcome relief on this hot day. After we had finished admiring the landscape, we sat down for a picnic lunch prepared by the Sainyabuli provincial office.

Soon enough, we were joined by none other than General Cheng. The peripatetic general had a habit of popping up at official functions around the country at the very last moment. As he never actually traveled with the NTA staff, it was often a mystery to me how he arrived. But, regardless of how remote the location, he never failed to show up. It was no wonder he never had time for our English lessons back in Vientiane. This time, I noticed his personal four-wheel-drive parked off in the distance. His driver, Oudom, was busy washing off the dust and mud from the car with water from a nearby stream.

Our host at the lunch was a well-fed man, clearly of some stature, who turned out to be the vice-governor of the province. As if by magic, he produced a case of French red wine, which he began to pour as his staff laid out a lavish meal of fresh fish, stir-fried vegetables, and sticky rice. It was clear to me that the NTA would not have been received with nearly so much fanfare if General Cheng hadn't been the chairman. He may not have been much of a manager, but Cheng did lend a certain prestige to the idea of tourism development. Whether he was driven by the prospect of personal gain or by the desire to help his province develop, the vice-governor tried his best to impress.

As we ate, we were entertained by another Vientiane official who had somehow made his way up to Sainyabuli: the inimitable Ounkham, a singer and songwriter who had worked for the Pathet Lao since before the revolution, and was a legend among Party members. In the early days of the Lao PDR, he had written songs for the Ministry of Information and Culture to help cultivate in the populace a spirit of patriotism for the new regime. Today, he continued to compose music for the government; it was Ounkham, in fact, who had written the tune I'd come to know so well, the theme song for Visit Laos Year 1999–2000.

Ounkham was a jovial character, and his face glowed with excitement as he downed yet another glass of wine and broke into song. His voice was beautiful, almost ethereal. As General Cheng and the vice-governor clapped in time with the familiar tune, Ounkham sang a cappella of the glories of Lan Xang, the beauty of Laos' provinces, and the power of the Pathet Lao—all in one breath:

Laos from North to South has many wonderful things to see:
Mountains, water, and wind.
Forests with abundant unspoiled nature,
The sound of waterfalls falling on rocks.

That night, back in the big city, a few of us went out to the Sainyabuli nightclub. It didn't take long to get there, as the place was right next door to the Sainyabuli Hotel. It was housed in a small wooden building that had inexplicably been decorated with Christmas lights, and brought to mind one of those ranch-and-steakhouse tourist traps in the Rocky Mountains. Inside, it was filled to capacity. A lone female singer had just taken the stage, and she began to grapple with a set of Thai imports, traditional Lao songs, and distant approximations of Western pop hits. At first she seemed uncomfortable, but the crowd soon put her at ease; she was just about the only entertainment for miles around, and they were easy to please. When she embarked upon a particularly upbeat version of Celine Dion's "My Heart Will Go On," I hit the dance floor.

Dancing in Laos was an odd affair indeed, a confused melange of three entirely distinct traditions. There was the traditional Lao *lam vong*, which involved very little movement save for the graceful twisting of the wrist and hands. Then there was the relatively fast-paced Thai-style disco, during which the crowd would jump up and down and swing their arms about, each according his own personal rhythm. Finally, there were the slow dances, or *saloh*. The *saloh* were painfully reminiscent of seventh-grade co-ed dances in the school gym, when boys shuffled their feet next to girls who towered over them and, braces glistening in the light of the revolving disco ball, patiently waited for the song to end.

At the Sainyabuli, when a *saloh* began, men and women silently paired up, held one another at a comfortable distance, and avoided eye contact at all cost. As soon as the song was over, the partners gave each other a polite *nop* and excused themselves from the floor, disappearing into the shadows as quickly as possible. Romance was completely missing from this picture.

Sex lingered heavily in the air in most Lao nightclubs. It hung in the double entendres that peppered conversation, the knowing winks young men threw to the women across the room, the intentional brush of a girl's hand against my thigh. But it was nowhere to be found on the dance floor. These people talked about sex all the time but, to see them dance, you'd wonder if they were actually capable of doing it.

As I surveyed the men and women dancing—not a difficult task as most were about a foot shorter than I—and pondered this question, an older woman suddenly jerked me out of my reverie. With a grin she yanked me over to where her girlfriends were dancing in a circle, and pushed me into the center. I soon found myself dancing face-to-face with the most glamorous woman in the house. I must admit I'd noticed her the moment she'd walked in the door. She wore a slinky dress that was coated in gold sequins and hugged her body, and a pair of dangerously high stiletto heels. Her face was caked with heavy make-up, her hair highlighted with blond streaks. This girl was definitely not from Sainyabuli.

"So, where are you from?" she shouted to me over the blasting music, in perfect American English.

Say what? It had been days since I'd heard a word of English, and my shock was further compounded by the fact that this young woman spoke with a thick Southern accent.

"America," I replied, taken aback.

"Yeah, but where?"

"Washington, D.C. And you?"

"North Carolina."

"North Carolina?"

We tried to escape from the dance floor to talk, but the women surrounding us, tickled by the sight of one of their friends dancing with a foreigner, wouldn't let us leave. So, over the music, we continued our conversation. I learned that she was visiting Laos for the first time since emigrating to the US as a child in the late 1970s. For this southern belle from Charlotte, the return had been eye-opening.

"So how do you like Laos?" I asked.

"This place is really undeveloped. I was really surprised."

"Don't you find it beautiful?"

"I guess so. But I'm bored. There's nothing to do."

She was clearly underwhelmed by her return to her native land, and nothing I could say could convince her otherwise. Luckily, she'd be heading back to the US in a few days.

After saying good-night to the restless North Carolinian, I went to use the facilities out back. Crouching over the hole in the ground that served as the Sainyabuli's only working toilet, I imagined how happy she'd be to return to the comforts of Charlotte.

On the way back inside, I noticed Khit and Oudon, who worked in the NTA finance section, heading in the direction of the hotel. Oudon was a walking ATM, ever armed with a briefcase stuffed with freshly printed stacks of kip. I rushed after them, glad to see that they were calling it a night. I'd begun to tire of the Sainyabuli, and was exhausted. Just then, however, Noxay appeared beside us in the NTA van, and Oudon and Khit pulled me inside. Evidently, this night wasn't over yet.

"Are you tired?" Khit asked.

"Yes, I'm very tired," I replied, forgetting myself for a moment.

"Ha! He has a lot of pubic hair! Did you hear that, guys?"

We were soon speeding down Sainyabuli's Main Street and out into the empty countryside. How Noxay was able to find his way was beyond me, as nothing but darkness surrounded us. Eventually, he took a sharp right and we pulled up to a small wooden shack—the only light for miles around—and entered what appeared to be a makeshift watering hole. Inside, the few remaining guests were quietly drinking themselves into oblivion. A man with unusually long hair and a bright orange blazer stood in the corner before an electric keyboard and, head down, crooned into a microphone. He seemed to have been standing in the same spot for years. Not once during our visit did he look up. After so long, what was there for him to see?

We sat down and Oudon ordered a few beers and some fried pigskin, a traditional Lao "drinking snack." After the drinks arrived, a woman emerged from behind the bar, sidled up to me, and began to pour my beer. Once, perhaps, this woman had been beautiful. But tonight she seemed weary of the world—though the appearance of an American in her nightclub had sparked her interest. She began to run her fingers through my hair and comment on my "beautiful white skin." Before I knew it, she had set about seducing me. "*Koi mak chao lai*. I like you a lot," she cooed. "*Chao ngam lai*. You are so beautiful."

Oudon, Khit, and Noxay lost no time in negotiating, on my behalf, a price for the night with her. But where would we stay? I wondered aloud. No problem, according to Oudon, I could just take her back to the hotel . . . where the rest of the NTA staff was sleeping.

I demurred, but not after finding out her asking price. For me? Ten dollars for the night.

The truth was, prostitution was rampant in Laos, and cheap. Lao men regularly visited brothels, both before and during marriage. In places like Sainyabuli, drinking and screwing were the main leisure activities; there wasn't much else to do. NGOs in Vientiane feared that prostitution would lead to an explosion in AIDS cases in Laos, as the HIV virus spread through unprotected sex in the provinces. One group had developed a condom—Number One brand—for production and distribution in the country. But in its AIDS-prevention material, the government liked to associate the problem with international visitors, labeling the disease a foreign import. A UN-funded project at the NTA had even been established in order to address the problem of unprotected sex in the tourism sector. But nasty *falang* men looking for a good time weren't the problem.

What would my colleagues really have thought had I accepted their offer of a night with the girl at the bar? It wasn't clear that their enthusiasm for my enjoyment was sincere. Perhaps they were simply testing me to make sure I didn't slip up. I found myself in a strange position at the NTA: certainly I had nothing to worry about regarding my long-term future within the Lao government—I had none—but at the same time, I was constrained by my position as a foreigner. My ability to stay in Laos for as long as I liked depended on the NTA, which had to initiate the process each time I renewed my visa. Without the support of my sponsors at the office, including General Cheng, I would have to leave the country, so I was particularly careful about my behavior around my colleagues. The NTA rumor mill was notorious, and had I slept with this woman, everyone at the office would have known about it within hours.

But more important than all this, what would I have thought of myself? This was the closest I had ever come to paying for sex, something I had never imagined I would do. Until then, prostitution had been something I'd thought about only hypothetically. It was an idea confined to the realm of fiction, far from the reality of my life. When confronted with it directly, however—with her skin and her breath so tangible—the act seemed eminently possible. A few more drinks, and perhaps I would have said yes. Eventually, Oudon, Noxay, and I stood up to leave. Khit, on the other hand, decided to stay behind. As we made our way out the door, the Sinatra of Sainyabuli nodded his head. But still he didn't look up.

Back at the Sainyabuli nightclub, I collapsed into a seat at a table in a dark corner, only to find myself sitting next to the vice-governor. He brandished a bottle of Johnnie Walker and demanded that I partake, while a woman approached the table from behind the bar and sat down beside me. In short spurts of English, the vice-governor ordered me to have fun. "You turn left, and she turn right. I appoint her your partner! Ha!" After one awkward *saloh* dance, free as usual from the slightest bit of sexual innuendo, I didn't see much more of my designated "partner." Maybe she had been frightened off by my *falang* strangeness.

Just then, Khit glided in, a smug grin plastered on his face. As he began to dance provocatively around the floor, I thought of his wife and son back in Vientiane, whom I'd met on a number of occasions. Khit, like most Lao men I knew, was a mess of contradictions. On the one hand, he was tremendously kind, physically close with other men, and at times even quite feminine. On the other, he was crude, obnoxious, and fiercely sexist, obsessed with proving just how much he could drink and how many women he could lay. It seemed he wasn't yet done for the night.

In Sainyabuli, the provincial government had imposed a strict midnight curfew. And since the city's generator stopped running at exactly midnight, it wasn't difficult to enforce. As soon as the clock struck 12:00, the club cleared out. With nowhere else to go, people went home. On my way back to the hotel, I ran into Ounkham, who had once again appeared out of nowhere. We stumbled back to the hotel, singing about the beauty of the Lao countryside:

In the land of frangipani,
Luang Prabang is a world famous city.
The Plain of Jars of the Jeuang People,
The ancient heritage of Xieng Khouang.

Ounkham wielded his cigarette lighter to lead the way up the stairs of the majestic Sainyabuli Hotel. He held it near the door to my room just long enough for me to fumble with my key and get inside. The light from the moon shone through the window and fell on my bed.

My roommate Khit was nowhere to be found.

Lonely in Laos

When I first arrived in Laos, the only available tourist guidebook about the country was the Lonely Planet. For the backpacker (not, lest we offend, the "tourist") whose goal was to spend as little money as humanly possible, *Le Lonely* was indispensable. As a result, its author had acquired an almost god-like power over the tourism industry in Laos. Single-handedly, he could determine the fortunes of a restaurant or guesthouse. For any aspiring restaurateur or hotelier, a mention in Lonely Planet was the key to survival in Laos' quickly developing tourism industry; if you didn't make the book, you hadn't a chance.

In fact, with the stroke of a pen, this writer had put an entire village on the map:

Vang Vieng had the good fortune to be located at a bend in the Nam Song River just 160 kilometers north of Vientiane. Here, the breathtaking limestone karsts concealed a vast network of caves to be explored. In 1998, the town boasted a handful of guesthouses and two restaurants. A few travelers would trickle down from Luang Prabang on their way to Vientiane, or vice versa, but not many. In the town itself, people moved around slowly on foot or by bicycle. By dusk every night, the place was dead. Once Vang Vieng was mentioned in Lonely Planet, however, it was converted overnight into a backpacker's mecca. Throughout Southeast Asia and beyond, travelers knew about the wonders of the town and its environs— where, soon enough, the food wasn't the only thing that was cheap. Curiosity fueled an explosion in the town's tourism industry.

By the time I last visited Vang Vieng, nearly every house had been converted into a guesthouse or restaurant, each offering the same services: banana pancakes in the morning, and tours of the nearby caves in the afternoon. There appeared to be more tourists in Vang Vieng than actual residents, traipsing around town in their tank tops and cut-off jeans, dreadlocks and matted beards, guitars hanging from the straps of their backpacks. The sweet smell of marijuana smoke lingered in the air around them, and Lao teenagers would hang out on the street until midnight, singing along with garbled versions of "Blowin' in the Wind." Honda Dreams were everywhere; the town had been turned on its head.

The Lonely Planet author didn't have much regard for the NTA: "The LNTA's top officials organize endless meetings and seminars to discuss the future of tourism in Laos but in actual fact they wield very little power and as a governing body the office is ineffectual," he wrote. "The bottom line is that you're better off going just about anywhere else in Vientiane but the LNTA if you're seeking accurate, up-to-date information on travel in Laos."

I would have loved to have taken offense at this harsh assessment of my office, but, alas, it was largely true. The folks at the NTA were usually the last to know about the wholesale transformation of towns like Vang Vieng, underway all over Laos.

Sometimes, in fact, I wished that travelers would heed the Lonely Planet's advice regarding the NTA. While they seemed to slavishly follow every other instruction in the guidebook regarding where to go and what to see, many travelers would persist in stopping by the office. They would come in to ask for everything from maps of the city to Beer Lao T-shirts; from advice about road safety to bus schedules. One day, a blond Swedish backpacker, as friendly and handsome as he was filthy, straggled in off the street. It was clear that he had quite a problem: he had lost his girlfriend. Not his backpack. Not his passport. His girlfriend. As my colleagues and I tried our best to stifle our laughter, we listened as he explained how this could have happened. The two had last been traveling together in Thailand, where they had split up. He headed for Japan, while she went up to Luang Prabang. According to the plan, they were to meet in Vientiane, but she was nowhere to be found. Had anyone at the NTA seen her? We dutifully put her passport photo on file, and notified the new "tourist police" office upstairs. The Swede went on his way and traveled up to Luang Prabang himself. By the time he passed by the NTA again, a week later, there still had been no word about his girlfriend. We could do little to cure his loneliness.

I had difficulty relating to the travelers I met in Laos. Even though most were about my age and from the West, I usually felt a far stronger connection to Lao friends like Bing and Kham. I was hardly a permanent resident, but neither was I merely passing through. I had made an investment in Vientiane, however haphazard and unplanned, and to me it felt like home.

For most backpackers, Laos was simply another stop along the way; a laid-back destination with cheap accommodation and good beer. When travelers would ask me, "So what should I do in Vientiane? I have just one day—what should I see?" I had no idea where to begin. What did I do in Vientiane each day, anyway? Despite my best efforts at the NTA, I didn't really consider Vientiane a tourist destination. It was where I lived.

There was one way I could get a sense of what tourists felt about Laos without actually talking to them. As part of Mr. Kawabata's consulting program, the Statistics Unit had begun surveying travelers at the airport and at the border crossing with Thailand. Each morning and afternoon, Seng, Mani, and anyone else who could be cajoled into participating would pile into the NTA van and head off to hand out written questionnaires for tourists to complete. I wiled away many an hour sifting through the old surveys that had piled up in the corner of the Statistics Unit, reading the comments.

Most of what the tourists had to say was overwhelmingly positive: "Laos is a beautiful country with very gracious people," one wrote. According to a Belgian visitor, "Laos is nice and friendly." Complaints tended to be minor: "Laos is good country and people are very good. Culture is amazing. Only cleanliness is not good," wrote one Pakistani tourist. His compatriot added, "Lao PDR is very good. Country and people too. But in Lao is cleaning problem."

Transportation problems were among the most frequent complaints: "I think domestic airplane is not safety," wrote a Japanese. "Kind people but very dirty roads."

"It was difficult to go for a walk because the road was under water."

The tourists had some very helpful suggestions: "An ATM would help a lot." (Tell me about it.) "I will like your city or government to have a business transaction with Nigerians."

An American was typically take-charge: "Get better planes for domestic Lao Aviation flights." Did they realize that we rarely even had toilet paper at the office?

Some visitors had clearly been unimpressed. One German wrote, "The Lao are the laziest people in all of Asia." Well!

A tourist from Singapore wrote, "Access road to guesthouse is dirty and very smelly. Also too many chickens around that call from four in the morning."

My favorite comment? "I want to eat Lao Food!"

That Luang

It was late November, and Vientiane hadn't seen a drop of rain for weeks. Almost overnight, it seemed, the temperature in the capital had taken a dramatic dive. Sure, it was still as mild as an early spring day in New York, but for Laos, this was freezing. The rainy season was over, and winter had officially arrived.

When "winter" hit Vientiane, people reacted as if hell itself had frozen over. While I strolled about in my usual light summer wear, everyone else was dressed as if for a snowstorm. In the early mornings, whole families made the journey to school and work on a single motorbike, huddled together to protect against the wind, bundled up in heavy down jackets and hand-made woolen hats. There was a rush on used clothing at the outdoor markets. In only a matter of days, the entire city had come down with a cold. Outside my window, passers-by sneezed and used their bare hands to blow their noses onto the street. In this cold, who had time for tissues?

At the office, too, everyone's nose was running. A continual chorus of sniffles provided the background to our work, as it was considered highly impolite to blow one's nose within a closed public place. My co-workers' energy had dissipated, dipping to a level as low as the temperature outside. Not a few times did I arrive at work in November only to find Mon passed out on the UNDP office couch or resting her head heavily on her desk. "*Koi ben wat*," she would tell me, looking up only briefly to acknowledge my presence. "I have a cold." I heard this phrase so often around town, it had come to sound like a mantra.

For me, on the other hand, winter in Vientiane offered something of a revelation: never before in Laos had I experienced such pleasant weather. In the evenings, I would stop by the vendor just up Chao Anou Road for a cup of hot, sweetened soy milk. Or I would come home and fix a cup of tea, curl up in my bed, and listen to the nocturnes of Chopin as I let the cool breeze blow gently in the open windows and over me. Pulling my blanket right up to the tip of my nose, I would sleep more soundly than I had in months. It was a far cry from the hot, stagnant air and sweaty sheets that normally plagued my nights. During these wintry retreats, nothing could disturb my slumber.

It wasn't without some hesitation, then, that I responded to the insistent call of my alarm clock at 5:30 on this November morning and hauled myself out of bed. Tiptoeing past my bedroom window on the way to the bathroom, I saw that the sun was just about to rise over the city, and I hurried to get dressed. Like thousands in Vientiane this morning, I'd have to rush if I was going to make it to That Luang, the Great Stupa, in time.

———————

Aside from the end of the rains, the drop in temperature and the ubiquitous sniffles around town, the most important signal that summer was really over in Vientiane was the arrival of the That Luang festival, the grandest of all the city's annual religious events. Every year, from the thirteenth through fifteenth days of the Buddhist calendar's twelfth month, That Luang was the focus of everyone's attention.

Lying just northeast of the city center, the Great Stupa is the symbol of the nation and certainly the most important monument in the country—it appears on Laos' national seal and on the logo of the NTA. The ground on which That Luang sits is itself sacred; according to legend, a breastbone of the Buddha was placed on the site by Indian missionaries in the third century B.C. Some in Vientiane would argue that the place was sacred long before then, as it had been inhabited by two *naga*. In any case, we know that a Khmer monastery was subsequently built there between the eleventh and thirteenth centuries.

As I rode out of the city center, the monument appeared on the horizon to the east. Behind it, the rising sun produced a striking silhouette of the majestic stupa. It was immediately clear to me why King Setthathirath had chosen this site for the construction of That Luang back in the mid-sixteenth century. He began work on the stupa in 1566, having just moved the capital of Lan Xang from Luang Prabang down to Vientiane. Ultimately, he presided over the construction of four additional temples, one on each side of That Luang. Today, only two remain: to the north, Wat That Luang Neua, the residence of the supreme patriarch of Lao Buddhism, and Wat That Luang Tai to the south. The entire stupa itself was covered in gold leaf, and when I arrived, the sun was already shining brilliantly on its surface, creating a warm glow that attracted worshippers from miles around.

I had forced myself out of bed this morning in order to witness the highlight of the annual festival: the sacred ceremony of *takbaat,* or offerings of the faithful to the monks. The *takbaat* was the primary obligation of Lao Buddhists, and their most important means of making merit.

In fact, the merit-making ceremony took place every morning throughout the year, in neighborhoods all over Laos. Monks walked single-file through the streets surrounding their temple and stopped outside nearby homes to collect alms of sticky rice or whatever food had been prepared from local worshippers, almost always women. During Buddhist festivals, however, the faithful gathered inside the temple grounds to make their offerings.

Well before dawn, worshippers dressed in their finest traditional clothing, had begun to gather at That Luang. The women wore silk blouses and colorful *sin*, while men were dressed in clean white shirts, blue pants, and checkered *pa biang*, the sash that is draped over the shoulder and across the chest.

When I reached the entrance to That Luang, the grounds were already filled with kneeling worshippers. The only space left was reserved for the very highest authorities, including the president and the prime minister, who would soon arrive to take part in the ceremony.

Those of us who had overslept, or just weren't high-ranking enough, settled for a spot outside the temple walls. The area in front of the stupa entrance surrounding a statue of King Setthathirath was already filled, so I made my way through the sea of faithful to the vast plaza beyond.

More than a thousand monks, representing every temple in Vientiane and others from around the country, lined the edge of the plaza. Clad in saffron robes, they sat quietly in front of rows of large bowls, ready to accept the offerings of the faithful. The festival had been organized by the government and the Buddhist clergy, with the participation of monks from all over Laos, and even a few from Thailand and Cambodia. Throughout the week, these monks stayed in the cloisters of That Luang and in the monastic quarters of other temples in Vientiane.

Eventually I spotted an empty space on the ground next to an elderly man and his wife. When they saw me approaching, they automatically shifted in order to make a place for me on their straw mat—a concrete expression, perhaps, of the inherent inclusiveness of Buddhism. While clearly I was no practicing Buddhist, the couple welcomed me without a second thought. Soon after I had removed my shoes and tried as best I could to fit onto the mat, the prayers began and the *takbaat* ceremony was underway.

The soothing monotone of the monk's voice, broadcast into the skies above the esplanade, washed over the devoted thousands below. The man and his wife seemed to know the ancient prayers by heart; as they paid homage to the Buddha and to the sacred stupa itself, they uttered the Pali words without thought. A group of young children seated on a neighboring mat weren't nearly as familiar with the prayers. They sat in forced silence, likely wondering when it would all be over.

Occasionally, the worshippers clasped their hands together and bowed in unison in the direction of That Luang. At the signal of the speaker, they poured a small amount of water on the ground, symbolizing the transferal of their merits to ancestors long departed. Once the prayers had ended, we rose to offer sticky rice, fruit, and sweets to as many of the monks and novices as we could. When we returned to the mat, I asked my companion why he and his wife had chosen this spot for their *takbaat*. Did the family have any connection to the monks nearby?

"Oh, no. Our family has just always sat here, for nearly 15 years," he replied. "These days, you know, the area inside the temple grounds is reserved for the Party leaders. We normal people sit out here."

"Has the celebration always been this big?"

"Oh, yes. Always."

"Even after the communist takeover in 1975?"

"Well, they tried to discourage religious activity for a while, mostly among Party members. But they realized they couldn't offer anything better. Religion was just the best way. So now everyone takes part in the festivals, even the Party leaders!"

After the offering ceremony was over, I bade farewell to my hosts and walked back to the entrance to That Luang. Finding it shut and guarded by an uncharacteristically stern policeman who seemed highly unlikely to succumb to the charms of a naïve foreigner, I made my way around the corner of the temple walls and slipped in through a side door. In Laos, I'd discovered long before, there was always a way around the rules. The grounds were now nearly empty, and as a few straggling worshippers made their way out of the stupa, I set about quietly exploring this great symbol of the Lao nation. . . .

Luckily, I had a guide. Browsing in an antique shop downtown one rainy afternoon months before, I had happened upon a few worn copies of an old, pre-revolutionary French-language periodical printed in Vientiane, the *Bulletin des Amis du Royaume Lao*. It had been years since anyone had looked at these copies of the long defunct *Bulletin*, buried as they were beneath a thick coating of dust in a dark corner of the shop. To me, however, they were treasures, filled with invaluable information about traditional Lao culture and religion. I bought them all.

In the October 1970 issue, in between advertisements for restaurants and boutiques that still existed in Vientiane—albeit under different names—I found a description of That Luang written by a key pre-revolutionary figure, Phagna Bong Souvannavong.

Born in 1906 in Vientiane to one of the city's most powerful and well-respected merchant families, Souvannavong had been a teacher at the Lycée Pavie in the 1920s. Subsequently, he had served in all sorts of capacities in the Royal Lao Government—once, as minister of education, public health, tourism, cults, fine arts, post and telecommunications. What a title! In pre-war Laos, a small country with a far smaller educated elite, this was the kind of portfolio capable leaders got stuck with. Souvannavong had a great interest in traditional Lao culture and religion, and he also occupied various leadership positions on national committees for Lao literature and art. He had a lot to say about That Luang:

"Since our childhood," Souvannavong wrote, "our parents have taught us to build stupas and to venerate them. This teaching has become an integral part of our lives, and it must be acknowledged that it would become obsolete if it were not among the most beautiful Lao traditions nor among our most pious Buddhist beliefs."

The Lao word *that*, or stupa, comes from the Pali word *dhatucetiya*, and signifies a monument containing relics of the body. Stupas originated in India just after Buddha passed away at the age of eighty; his disciples built the structures in order to protect his remains. As a result, the largest and most ancient *that*—like That Luang—are said to contain at least some relics of Buddha himself. Over the centuries, however, the term has come to include contemporary funeral monuments that contain the ashes of common folk. In Laos, I found *that* in all shapes and sizes. Recently, the Party had begun to co-opt the religious symbolism of the *that*, using them as commemorative monuments like the Memorial to the Unknown Soldier just west of That Luang.

That Luang itself consisted of three levels, and, according to Souvannavong, each represented a different stage along the path to Buddhist enlightenment. The lowest level signified the materialistic world of desires; the second, the world of appearances; and the highest, the world of nothingness—*nirvana*. On the third level, there were thirty miniature stupas. At the base of each was inscribed one of the ten *palami*, or Buddhist virtues of perfection: generosity in giving alms; morality; renunciation; wisdom; energy; patience; truth; resolution; compassion; and imperturbability. A tall order, indeed.

The Great Stupa also had the appearance of a large, open lotus blossom. In the symbolism of Lao Buddhism, the lotus represented the female organ of procreation. Thus, the petals on the second terrace of That Luang gave birth to the thirty miniature stupas, and ultimately to the tower at the very pinnacle, which represented the male.

The cloister surrounding the stupa contained a few decaying examples of classic Lao and Khmer sculpture. One of the broken statues I found lying on the ground was an image of the Khmer king, Jayavarman VII, who had constructed much of the Angkor complex in Cambodia. The image had been discovered in 1951 lying forgotten in the forests surrounding That Luang. The cloister walls were pierced by a series of tiny windows, added during the reign of Vientiane's King Anouvong in the early nineteenth century, as a defense against attack. They were of little use during subsequent Siamese and Chinese invasions of the city—not to mention an 1896 lightning strike—which left the Great Stupa in ruins.

The first restoration work on That Luang began in 1909, but serious reconstruction wasn't undertaken until the French oversaw a project in the early 1930s. Souvannavong, however, wasn't sure that the French restoration had been faithful to the original monument. According to Buddhist tradition, the world is divided into two distinct zones: the east is the zone of illumination, while the west is the zone of ignorance. As a result, important Buddhist images and monuments invariably faced the east. Originally, That Luang faced east as well, away from Vientiane, but the restoration authorities reversed the layout of the temple grounds. Today, the main entrance is through the western wall, and the doors face the city center. To the French, who had plans for a grand avenue leading from That Luang into town, it had just made more sense for the entrance to face Vientiane.

On all four of the stupa's sides sat a prayer pavilion. Inside of each structure I found an ancient stele on which was inscribed a Pali prayer in honor of That Luang. It read: "Homage to Buddha, who is Arhat [one who has considered the true nature of things and who has achieved nirvana] and who has reached enlightenment. They came from the east, five Arhat, the principal of which was Phra Maha Kassapa, and deposed the bones in this venerable stupa. I tilt my head to pray and to remain faithful forever."

As I made my way around the stupa, pondering the significance of these words, I realized that each pavilion contained a set of exactly 12 stairs—except for the one along the western edge. It had only 11, and provided no access to the first terrace. In their zeal to civilize, the French had made an obvious error. Souvannavong was right: the West was the zone of ignorance, after all.

Lost in exploration, I had failed to notice that I was now the only one left inside the temple. The sight of an approaching policeman jolted me out of my reverie and, before he had a chance to kick me out, I made a quick exit through the south side of the cloister. Just outside the doors, along the edge of the temple walls, women sat on the ground behind small stalls selling treats to the steady stream of celebrants. Wherever I looked I found delicacies like *ping-kai*, grilled chicken on wooden skewers, and *khaolaam*, sticky rice flavored with coconut milk and cooked in bamboo. I bought a stick of *khaolaam* and, munching on this incredibly tasty snack, strolled back over to the esplanade, where a trade fair held annually in conjunction with the That Luang festival was already in full swing.

Around the edge of the plaza, vast billboards extolling the virtues of brand-name products like Pepsodent, Pepsi, and Marlboro towered over the monks, who remained seated to accept offerings from latecomers. Private businesses, foreign governments, and international organizations had erected wooden booths to promote their products and programs. Scattered throughout the area, far less elaborate stalls sold imported products from Thailand, China, and

Vietnam. On their way home from the *takbaat* ceremony, revelers stocked up on plastic wallets, tennis shoes, T-shirts, and flip-flops. Families delighted in carnival games like bingo, darts, and a frighteningly rickety merry-go-round. Children ran through the streets shooting at one another with newly purchased cap guns. How far off the path to enlightenment were these kids veering? I wondered.

This was a religious festival, but to me it felt more like an old-fashioned state fair. Just past the daredevil motorbike extravaganza sponsored by Marlboro, I happened upon a small, dimly lit tent that turned out to be That Luang's very own House of the Weird. Inside, glass cases held two-headed cows and gigantic serpents embalmed in formaldehyde. A live five-footed pig lay on the ground, subject to continual pestering and prodding. When a severely overweight Thai tourist walked in, displacing half the crowd, he was treated like a freak himself, attracting more attention than the actual exhibit. People had come to That Luang to worship, yes, but also to gawk. The event was a perfect marriage of the sacred and profane, a deeply religious occasion that no one took too seriously.

Just as I was about to head home to recover from this uncommonly early morning activity, the sound of a gong reverberated through the loudspeakers. The crowd was being called to view the ceremonial *teekhee* 'hockey' game that was held on the grounds each year. Already, a procession of musicians, dancers, and city authorities carrying the sacred *teekhee* ball from inside That Luang to the plaza was underway. The ball, about 15 centimeters in diameter and made from bamboo roots, was guarded throughout the year by the elders of the village surrounding That Luang, and taken out only on this occasion.

In Souvannavong's day, the *teekhee* match had been a highly ritualized affair between two teams: on one side had been Royal Lao Government authorities, clad in red, and on the other a group of commoners, dressed as they were able. The match was never much of a nail-biter: of three games, the "people" were always required to win exactly two. If they won only one game, or all three, it signified misfortune for the entire nation. And while a victory for the authorities would have been interpreted as an exploitation of the people, a balanced victory of the people assured peace and prosperity. Consigned to their inevitable loss, players on the royal team were rarely very enthusiastic. There were also fewer of them than the commoners—their numbers were limited by the availability of official uniforms, always in scarce supply.

These days, the hockey game remained much the same as it had been before the revolution. Basically, the two sides used heavy bamboo clubs to try and whack the sacred ball into the opposition's goal. But if the activity itself hadn't changed much, its political significance had all but disappeared. In the wake of the dissolution of the monarchy, the match had become a simple sporting event between two teams from different quarters of Vientiane. And in perhaps the clearest sign yet of the New Economic Mechanism reforms, the two teams were now sponsored by the private sector. This year, the match was a contest between Nescafé and Beer Lao. I caught a glimpse of Sisavath Keobounpanh, the prime minister, calmly presiding over the match from his perch inside a shaded viewing tent. Whichever side prevailed this year, his government wasn't going anywhere.

When I returned to That Luang that evening, the monument had been fully illuminated. Like a beacon in the distance, the Grand Stupa guided my path as I approached the plaza on foot. Tens of thousands had congregated for the evening's candlelit procession, or *bientiene*, around the stupa.

At the west gate, I waited for Souksan, who'd suggested at the office the day before that we meet up. I wasn't surprised when he didn't show up; Souksan's name was Happy, not Reliable. I purchased my offering—a small bundle of orchids, sticks of incense, and miniature orange candles—and entered the temple alone. As soon as I stepped inside, I was swept along by the circling crowd. At the head of the procession walked That Luang's resident monks and novices, led by the supreme patriarch. The crowd was dense, the procession slow. A pair of policemen, armed with whistles, attempted in vain to control the flow while I tried my best to avoid setting those walking in front of me on fire.

Through the loudspeakers I could hear the prompts that preceded most prayers, uttered by the lay people and religious officials alike: *Namo tassa, bhagavato, arahato, sammasambuddhassa*. This phrase was repeated three times—just as the candlelit procession would circle the stupa exactly three times. After I had completed my own circuit, I chose a spot at the base of That Luang and knelt to present my offerings. Following the lead of those around me, I planted two burning incense sticks firmly in the ground, melted the bottoms of the candles and stuck them to the base of the stupa, and placed the flowers behind them.

After bowing three times, hands clasped together in the traditional *nop*, I prepared to make my own silent wish. What would I ask for? Long life? Financial success? A better love life? As I began to consider what mattered most, the din of the crowd circling behind me faded away. I focused on the glow of the candles and the soft sound of the monks' prayers. A calm fell over me and I felt quite at peace. And then it hit me. I knew that eventually I would have to leave Laos, likely heading back to the harried pace of life in the West, where quiet moments like this could be hard to come by. So in the end, my wish was pretty simple. I asked only that the beauty of this moment, and the sense of peace it afforded, would remain with me throughout my days.

Once I left the stupa—through the eastern gate this time, just to be sure—I waded through the crowds back to my motorbike, parked in a makeshift lot near the spot where I'd given my offerings that morning.

The November cool disappeared in the crowd, swallowed up by the mass of warm, excited bodies. I bumped into a young boy who had been silenced for at least a moment by the wonderment of the evening. He clasped his mother's hand and gazed upward, first to my strange foreign face, then quickly to the sky above. My eyes followed his to the sight of the brilliant full moon. As if on cue, a display of fireworks—a homage of flowers of fire to the Buddha—lit up the sky over That Luang.

As gasps of excitement and cries of joy erupted, I remembered the description of the festival Souvannavong had offered so many years before: "The procession is followed by music, singing, dancing, and love that continues and finishes very late at night, as the full moon projects on the limpid sky the slender and majestic silhouette of That Luang."

Not even war and revolution could change the powerful hold that the Great Stupa had over the Lao people and their nation.

Sugar Daddy

If you want to help someone, don't do it unless it dignifies him.
Lao Proverb.

It felt like Christmas Day at the NTA.

One morning in December, I arrived at work to find Mon, Souk-san, and Seng huddled together in a corner of the UNDP project office. Shredded cardboard boxes were everywhere. Mountains of packing material had been strewn about with abandon. I waded through the plastic wrapping and twine to the corner where they had gathered, to find out just what was going on. It turned out that a new computer, monitor, and printer had just arrived; an unsolicited gift from the UNDP.

My friends were gathered around the new equipment, intently scrutinizing the directions in the English-language printer instruction manual. This particular printer was the largest I'd ever seen—larger, in fact, than the monitor and computer put together. It did it all: double-sided printing, color printing, collating, and binding. It practically wrote the document for you.

But this morning, all Seng wanted to do was print a single black and white page. No graphics. No color. No binding. No problem! Or so Seng and I thought. In fact, the printer took more than five minutes to warm up, another five to re-position and paginate, and two minutes simply to feed a sheet of paper through the tangled web of gadgetry deep inside. Finally, something popped out of one of the many holes on top. It was a blank sheet of paper. "Great printer!" Seng joked. He would have been better off using the "old" one we already had—a gift from the UNDP last Christmas. Or even the trusty old manual typewriter we kept upstairs, just in case.

As Seng consulted the manual again, I looked around and noticed that almost everything was labeled with a small UNDP sticker. From the computers and printers to the desks and chairs, right down to the smallest tape dispenser and staple remover, everything had been marked. Nothing in the room had actually been purchased by the government; it had all been donated by the UNDP. Today's new gift came with Microsoft Internet Explorer, even though Internet access at the office was to remain a dream deferred throughout my time in Vientiane.

The fact was that, even if we'd been able to use these new toys, we didn't need them. Indeed, none of my colleagues could remember requesting the new equipment. The UNDP had simply decided to dump a few thousand dollars of gear on the NTA. Whether or not it would be of use was immaterial.

But at the end of a century marked by unrelenting foreign intervention and intractable poverty, the Lao had learned the cardinal rule of international development: never kick a gift-horse in the mouth. The NTA staff wasn't about to send this stuff back, so we set about figuring out how to use it. . . .

———————

That afternoon, in the changing room at the Lao Hotel Plaza gym, I finally met Bob.

Bob was the country representative for a UN aid program, and had lived in Laos for more than six years. Six years! That made him practically a native. I had been searching for the man ever since the day I'd moved into my house, when I'd discovered a pile of *New*

Yorker magazines gathering dust in the corner of my living room. In a city in which the Welsh owner of Laos' only English-language bookstore, Raintrees, seemed to consider Harlequin paperbacks to be high literature (not even John Grisham qualified at Raintrees), this was quite a find. I spent many a night under the stars on my balcony, swatting away mosquitoes as I devoured short stories by John Updike and non-fiction pieces on genocide in Rwanda and administrative intrigue at the Metropolitan Museum of Art in New York. It was Bob's name that graced the address labels on these *New Yorkers*, and for months I'd been determined to find the man behind the magazines.

On my way into the gym, I had noticed Bob's name on the members' sign-in list. This list was a veritable *Who's Who* of Vientiane society. On any given day, you might find the signature of Pino, the ebullient owner of L'Opera Italian restaurant, the best Western place in town. He liked to work off that delicious *tiramisu* on the rowing machine. If the head of the Asian Development Bank's representative office in Vientiane was on the list, he was probably using the treadmill. And if you saw the name of the foreign minister, it likely meant he was in for a massage—on the house, of course.

I found Bob in the men's room and, as I changed out of my work clothes, I introduced myself and explained the magazines. It turned out that Bob had known my landlady's family for years. Every month, when he finished with his *New Yorkers*—received through the UN internal postal system—he passed them along to his friends.

Such a warm gesture contrasted sharply with Bob's demeanor. He rarely smiled, and spoke with the gruff manner one might expect from a guy who had been raised in New York City. Even the angles of his face were severe. His shaved head was indicative of the austerity inherent in his approach to life; nearing sixty, Bob was in better shape than anyone else at the gym. Lean and muscular, his physique put me and my 23 years to shame. During endless sessions on the gym's rickety exercise bike, he wore a thick headband to prevent the torrent of sweat from running off the top of his bald head and into his eyes.

Bob was also a fountain of cynicism about Laos and its future: "Is anything getting better in this country?" he asked me as we took turns lifting weights. "I don't see it, do you?"

In Laos, I saw a country that was slowly succeeding in raising the standard of living of its people, while at the same time struggling to preserve what set it apart from the rest of the world. Bob saw a falling currency, rising prices, crumbling roads—and, above all, a development community that was doing more harm than good. When I dared to suggest the possibility of UNDP funding a small campaign at my office to discourage drug use by tourists, he scoffed: "So you want to get at the trough as well, huh?"

The "trough" of which Bob liked to speak was the seemingly endless source of money that funded UN operations in the developing world. It was this trough that kept everyone associated with the world of development in business: not only the international consultants, the highly paid UN "volunteers" and local support staff, but also the restaurateurs, nightclub owners, and real-estate agents who relied on them to survive.

A news report about the refugee crisis in Kosovo appeared on the TV in the gym, and Bob began to laugh. "You know why we didn't get in there sooner? Because this war benefits everyone— the media, the aid agencies, everyone. And it just means more work for the UN." When the reporter mentioned Bob's own UN agency and its emergency relief activities in the war-torn region, he emitted a jaded cheer.

Bob was about to retire from the UN, and it struck me that it wasn't a moment too soon. He had been drained of all enthusiasm for his job, having lost sight of the lofty goals that had once driven him to work overtime. After nearly a decade in the trenches, he had come to view the development community as little more than a self-perpetuating money machine interested primarily in its own survival. That morning, his agency's headquarters in New York had faxed him a budget for the upcoming year. According to the proposal, his food distribution program would hand out only a fraction of the rice in Laos that it had during the current year—but with three times the staff, a new four-wheel-drive vehicle, and more computer equipment in Vientiane.

"My boss wants us to spend 18,000 dollars on computers over the next year, and buy a new vehicle. We only have two staff, and we have two cars already! And how can we possibly spend 18,000 on computer equipment when you can get a top-of-the-line PC here for a thousand bucks?"

At the same time that they were increasing funding for admin offices in Vientiane, many UN agencies in Laos were cutting costs out in the field: "I just had a big argument with my boss," Bob told me. "She wanted to pay the guys who actually carry the rice less next year. So basically she wanted us to cut spending on the little guy while we treat ourselves nice up here."

Bob's steady stream of woes pointed to what he saw as the real goal of the development community in Laos—keeping itself in business: "Just make sure you spend all your budget this year, so you can ask for an increase next year," he said. "Who cares if you don't need the money?"

A large portion of foreign aid money, it was true, failed to reach the Lao for whom it was intended. The sharp increase in the number of cars on the roads in Vientiane in just the short time I was there was a testament to the rampant diversion of aid money into the deep pockets of government officials all over town. Just as motorbikes had all but replaced bicycles as the preferred mode of transport for Vientiane residents, hulking Mitsubishi Pajeros and Land Rovers were now clogging the streets as well. Considering that the government had imposed a 100 percent tax on all imported vehicles, and that almost all financial transactions were conducted in US dollars cash, buying a new car was no small feat. The equivalent in America would be walking into a dealership, plunking down 100,000 in cash, and driving off with a shiny new four-wheel-drive. It was hard to imagine, but in Laos this happened all the time. In a country that was one of the ten poorest in the world, you couldn't help but wonder where all this money was coming from. When I first arrived at the NTA, the UNDP tourism development project had been stalled for months due to a single request: the staff wanted to blow the budget on a new Mercedes.

But even when aid money was misspent, no one seemed to care. "The Japanese are the worst," said Bob. "They know what's going on, they know where the money's going, but they say nothing."

Japan was Laos' largest foreign aid donor, funding an array of projects, including the new international airport terminal, improved roads and bridges in the south, and upgraded educational and medical facilities throughout the country. The snappy Official Development Aid logo seemed to pop up wherever you looked. "Evidently the ambassador was really mad when he saw an aid project vehicle driving around Bangkok one weekend. But he did nothing."

The Japanese aid agency also failed to act when a public park it had built on the banks of the Mekong was torn up during the city's road construction extravaganza. The park disappeared overnight, and Vientiane was left without a single public recreation space. Nevertheless, on an official visit in January—the first by a Japanese premier to Laos in 33 years—Prime Minister Keizo Obuchi would pledge an additional 8 million dollars in assistance.

"We cleaned out the files at the office yesterday," Bob continued. "It was the most depressing reading. Files from the 1980s read just like reports today—the same problems, the same promises. We've been doing the same thing here for ten years, and the government hasn't done a fucking thing. Except spend our money. And now they want to piss away more money in this country." Bob shook his head in disbelief.

Why do international aid agencies, foreign governments, and NGOs continue to clamor to get in the door in Laos? First, it is relatively easy to get funding. Laos has signed all the right international treaties, and while it may not abide by many of them, the government has sensibly sought to develop a very accommodating foreign policy. In addition, the UN classifies the country as an LDC, a "Least Developed Country," which opens the floodgates to vast amounts of foreign aid money. It allows Laos to qualify for aid now denied countries like Vietnam and Thailand, which have moved out of the LDC classification. As popular aid recipients leave the dreaded world of underdevelopment, the aid community must find new places to spend its money.

A second and far more important reason was that for the average development worker, Laos was a rather nice place to work: "Hey, everyone smiles at you," Bob said, "and the government says okay to basically everything you ask for—at first, anyway."

It may not have had the most exciting nightlife around, but it was a far cry from some other LDCs, where foreigners lived under fear of assault and were spat upon in the streets. In sum, it was easy to get stuck in Laos.

"Some of these [development workers] are married, and they have really specialized skills. Back home, there's not much use for an irrigated rice expert who speaks Lao," Bob told me. "Even me, I don't know what I'm doing next year, so I'll stick around for a while after I retire."

The development community had a tremendous vested interest in staying put, and it would create work for itself if necessary.

At the NTA, Seng, who continued to work weekends to support his wife and son, had his own ideas about why foreign governments kept on giving to Laos. He recognized little difference between the international development effort and a for-profit enterprise: "They have a strategy in the developed countries, and a strategy in developing countries like Laos," he told me after returning from a Japanese-government-funded study tour on tourism in Tokyo. "But the goal is the same: to make money!"

To Seng, the donation of a fleet of new public buses to Vientiane by the Japanese, and the construction of a new Honda car factory in Thailand were two sides of the same coin. The buses were free, to be sure, but all replacement parts would have to be imported from Japan. Even the simplest of repairs would require the help of Japanese contractors. In fact, whenever the Japanese funded aid projects to build roads, bridges, and airport terminals in Laos, the contracts always went to Japanese companies.

The Japanese weren't the only ones, of course; France and the US were also notorious for such "tied-aid" practices. Seng and his colleagues at the NTA were no fools; they knew what was going on. If they didn't complain, it wasn't because they were unaware: "We cannot say anything because we have no money." Remember the cardinal rule: never kick a gift-horse in the mouth.

The Lao government had no money, but it did have one major hold over development workers in Laos: the visa.

Ah, the dreaded visa. The power of a tiny red stamp to force a *falang* to run from one ministry to the next, his tail between his legs, trying desperately to obtain the correct letter of approval for his visa extension. The power to place a man's career on hold, to destroy his plans for marriage, to make a fifth-grade student at the

Vientiane International School cry, wondering if she'll be able to return next year to rejoin her friends and classmates.

One afternoon not long after I'd arrived in Vientiane, I stopped by the UNDP headquarters to introduce myself to the staff responsible for the tourism development project at the NTA. The office was a sprawling, air-conditioned compound shaded by palm trees. A fleet of gleaming white sedans, each emblazoned with the sky-blue UN logo, surrounded the complex. While I waited in a meeting room for the tourism development program officer to arrive, the receptionist provided me with a menu of assorted drinks from which to choose; flattered, I decided on an iced coffee.

During our meeting, the very first thing the program officer showed me was a flow chart that had been produced by the UNDP "Governance and Public Administration Reform" project. (Doesn't *that* sound like fun!) The document outlined the steps a UN worker had to go through in order to get a visa. In this "red tape" case study, there were 16 little boxes winding their way through a maze of ministries and approval signatures. The box at the finish line read, "Sometimes there is a problem with issuing a visa." Now there was an understatement.

"They treat the agencies so poorly," Bob told me. "I mean, last year, they refused to renew the visa of the aid co-ordinator at the US Embassy, who was bringing in millions of dollars every year. Completely gratuitous, just to show who's boss."

The government used the power of the visa to keep expats on their knees and in line. And since most aid workers simply weren't willing to give up their cooks, guards, drivers, and maids, their dinners at L'Opera and daily lunch specials at the Canadian-owned Healthy and Fresh Bakery, they didn't complain. After all, if their visas weren't renewed, many would have nowhere else to go.

Back at the NTA, we were beginning to wonder if a gift from the UNDP was worth all the trouble. All the manuals in the world wouldn't get the new printer to work. And even if we did discover the trick, we probably wouldn't be able to use it for long. "They give us these big machines, but we have no money to use them," Seng told me. "When the ink is finished, we'll have no money to buy a new cartridge!"

The NTA staff may have questioned the worth of certain gifts, but they never explored the larger mystery at hand: why should Laos get any foreign aid at all? When I posed this question to Seng, I was met with a baffled look of confusion. The development frenzy had created a culture of desert that pervaded the society, from the highest levels of the Party leadership down to the man on the street. Many Lao seemed convinced that they deserved this money, that they had somehow acquired a right to it due to Laos' status as one of the world's poorest countries. Hands held out, they simply waited for more. In the development community as well, no one was asking why Laos should be the recipient of so much munificence. Aid workers skipped this fundamental query and settled for the more immediately manageable ones: how much to give, and to whom.

As for me, I was in a unique position to ask these questions. My situation at the NTA was unlike any other. Unaffiliated with the UNDP or anyone else, I arrived with no promises of money or "technical assistance." All the NTA got was what they saw: a guy who showed up, did what he could to help, and hoped that something came of it. Heck, I couldn't even provide textbooks. If the government decided to cancel my visa, so be it. I'd simply up and leave. I would be sad to go, of course, but for me the consequences would have been minimal. Without the responsibility of a wife or family, I had the luxury of thinking primarily about myself. I had little money but more freedom than I was likely to ever have again. It was to preserve this freedom and the objectivity it allowed that I turned down opportunities at aid organizations for more work. I was lucky to be free, and I knew it.

The day before I left Laos for my own Christmas holiday, the new printer still wasn't working. As it gathered dust, the staff used it as just another piece of furniture. Forgotten documents piled up on top. But the UNDP label, affixed prominently to the front, reminded us all who had been responsible for this marvelous gift.

For the Birds

One intelligent man is not necessarily more right than a band of fools.
Lao Proverb.

One Thursday afternoon in February, I left the office in a particularly good mood. I had completed a project at the office, it was a beautiful day outside, and I was heading home to a three-day weekend.

Friday was International Women's Day, one in a seemingly endless stream of international holidays sponsored by the UN and celebrated in Laos. There was International Children's Day; Teacher's Day; and Older Person's Day. Not to mention World Food Day and, though no one could remember the last time one had occurred in Laos, World Natural Disaster Reduction Day. In Vientiane alone there were more than enough unnatural disasters to cope with. Each time one of these holidays came around, the government would dutifully hang a banner just outside the Presidential Palace, proclaiming just what International Day it was. There seemed to be one for each day of the year.

International Women's Day was officially a holiday for women only, but in Laos, everyone took it off. At the NTA, this made perfect sense, for my male colleagues were incapable of functioning without their female counterparts. And the men certainly didn't want to miss Friday's party, when their wives, sisters, and daughters would prepare an elaborate and delicious meal—and then do the washing up.

Just as I made my way out the door, my restless young friend and colleague Thanh appeared out of nowhere and grabbed me by the arm. "What will you do tomorrow?" he demanded, as a sly smile spread across his face. Thanh always seemed to have grand plans for the weekend. Whenever he went out on the town with his friends to drink, he would don his prized black leather jacket and race through the streets on a powerful Suzuki motorcycle. His machine made my Honda Dream look like a tricycle.

"I'm not sure," I answered warily.

"Then you go to the picnic!" Thanh exclaimed.

"What picnic?"

Thanh cheerfully explained that, in celebration of Women's Day, the NTA staff would be having a picnic lunch at Nong Nok, a small lake about 65 kilometers north of Vientiane. To my surprise, Thanh's suggestion struck me as a perfect way to spend my day off. I'd been to visit the lake with some friends only a week before, and had been thoroughly enchanted.

Nong Nok, or Bird Pond, was actually a seasonally flooded meadow covering an area of sixty hectares during the wet season. It was known as Bird Pond because a great variety of birds, including Chinese Pond Heron, Black Crowned Night Heron, and Common Kingfisher, had made it their home. In the late dry season, more than 1,200 Whistling Teal roosted in the wetland. Such an intense concentration of bird life was rare in Laos. In Vientiane, just about the only birds I ever saw were those sold at temples, kept in wooden cages no larger than their wingspans. For good luck, worshippers would buy the birds and set them free. This new-found freedom didn't last long; the birds were immediately re-captured for re-sale.

At Nong Nok, nearby villagers used the lake for commercial fish breeding. Every year, fry were released into the lake during the wet season. Then, during the dry season, they were caught and sold to nearby communities and in Vientiane. The villagers worked hard to maintain the wetland's delicate ecological balance: regular guards ensured that the birds weren't killed and the fish weren't poached.

When I first visited the lake, I'd been lucky enough to enjoy the most marvelous of picnics, prepared by the local villagers. My friends and I had settled down among the trees, shaded from the hot sun, while dishes of fresh vegetables, rice noodles, sticky rice, and peanut sauce were placed on a large banana leaf on the ground. The village headman appeared and offered each of us a small glass of rice whiskey. Women from the village soon joined us with fish freshly caught from the lake, which they grilled on an open fire nearby. Hundreds of birds roosted peacefully on the single tree that sat in the middle of Bird Pond. A flock of brilliant white egrets occasionally rose into the sky, forming a graceful arc over the lake. A gentle breeze whispered over the entire affair, and we were disappointed when it was time to leave. I told Thanh I'd be glad to come along for the NTA picnic.

"Okay! See you tomorrow morning. Seven o'clock a.m.," he said.

Seven o'clock seemed a bit early for a picnic lunch, so on Friday morning I turned up at the NTA late—and was still the first one there. One thing I had yet to learn about life in Laos was just when to arrive for an appointment. Arriving on time was out of the question, of course; one of the many joys of Laos was that everything ran behind schedule. But just how late to arrive was a mystery. On this particular morning, we didn't end up leaving until 9:00.

I didn't mind the late start, as it gave me time to enjoy Vientiane in the early morning, before the motorbikes took to the streets and the steady trickle of cars began to make their way down Lan Xang Avenue past the office. I strolled over to the Morning Market and bought a fresh baguette. Breakfast in hand, I returned to a small shop just beside the NTA and ordered a hot coffee served in a short glass. Like the iced variety, Lao coffee usually comes with a healthy serving of condensed milk, and is so thick that you have to practically eat the stuff to get it down; so strong that after a cup you wonder if you'll ever fall asleep again—and so sweet that it's followed by a chaser of weak Chinese tea. But it is a truly delicious experience. My first sip was a jolting reminder that the day had begun.

Long after I'd finished the coffee, my colleagues began to show up. As the sun continued its ascent over Vientiane, we prepared for departure. Soon enough, a group of us piled into the van, Thanh popped his latest bootleg cassette of Western music in the stereo, and we were on the road, the wheels pounding the potholes in perfect rhythm with Will Smith's "Gettin' Jiggy With It."

"What does 'jiggy' mean, Mr. Brett?" Thanh asked.

"Whatever you like," I responded, confident for once in the complete veracity of my response to an English vocabulary question.

When we arrived at Nong Nok, I immediately sensed that something was amiss. This wasn't the same place I had visited only a week before. In the spot where I'd taken a short nap after our picnic, I saw a garbage truck. Where there had been a small field of grazing cattle, a parking lot had been laid. And right where we had eaten that delicious food, the trees had been felled and the area razed to clear the way for a stage with microphones, speakers, and a set of drums. Near the lake, there were booths selling sugar cane juice and grilled chicken to a steady stream of revelers, mostly Vientiane urbanites out for a day in the country. This was no cozy office picnic. I was the last to know, but the NTA was in fact hosting a two-day festival to celebrate Visit Laos Year, International Women's Day, and the development of the Nong Nok wetland into a new "eco-tourism" site.

Today, the village headman was busy making the rounds with General Cheng, beaming as he shared whiskey with his guests. Panh, the man at the NTA who'd been put in charge of the development of Nong Nok, tagged along behind them.

Panh directed the Planning Unit, which meant that he spent his time traveling to far-flung areas, drawing up plans for tourist facilities that never got built. He was also the NTA's official logo man; for today's event, he had designed a special graphic featuring the outline of a bird. He had high hopes that one day a set of Lao-style bird-watching huts would be constructed at Nong Nok.

Panh had earned a degree in architecture in Paris, and when he spoke English, it was with a heavy tinge of Francophone disdain.

He used the refrain "of course!" in the same way so many French like to use "*Bien sûr!*"—to dismiss an unwelcome query. Today, as always, Panh was dressed snappily in a pair of spotless, starched and pressed white slacks, a colorful Thai silk shirt, and polished black leather shoes. There wasn't a hair out of place on his head. Except, that is, for that one unsettling strand of hair that sprouted from his chin. A sign of wisdom, perhaps? But of course!

I became wary whenever Panh pulled me aside at the office to discuss his plans for eco-tourism. Here was a guy who kept a pet monkey in a cage behind his house in Vientiane. The monkey spent his days endlessly scampering back and forth, grasping and occasionally gnawing at the chicken wire. "Do you think this is the best way to protect Laos' natural heritage?" I once asked him during a visit to his home.

"Of course!" Panh replied. "He is happy here."

Once the guests at the Nong Nok festival had settled down for lunch, they set about creating small piles of rubbish near the lake. Some strolled over to the water to observe the focal point of the day's event, Bird Pond. "There aren't many birds, are there?" one complained.

A week before, the lake had been filled with birds, but today only a few were to be seen. Where had they all gone? "What a disappointment," one picnicker sighed before heading back to the festival site for another Beer Lao. His attention was drawn to the band, which was already testing out the sound system.

"Hello. Hello. *Neung, song, saam.* Hello. One, two, three."

Finding myself all alone at the lake, I decided to take a walk along the path that led around to the other side. Making my way through the trail of discarded tissue paper and plastic bags, I soon came face to face with a cow, terribly skinny, like most of his bovine brethren in Laos, yet strong. Along with the rest of his family, he was lazily chewing his cud. But he seemed unsettled, not sure whether to go on eating or flee from the racket emanating from the stage. The amplified sound echoed across the pond, and was almost inescapable. But not quite.

As I made my way further along the trail, I found that refuge did exist. At the end of the lake, up in a tree that was sheltered from the noise, there they sat: the celebrated Little Egret and Whistling Teal, waiting patiently for the eco-tourism festival to end and the unwelcome visitors to go home.

Back at the festival site, the NTA roadshow was underway. Performers in traditional costume graced the stage. A female soloist, dressed in a red and gold *sin*, sang a love song as male dancers encircled her. A male soloist then performed his own love song, surrounded by a group of dancing women. Both the male and female dancers were strikingly beautiful, and, but for the traditional costumes, largely indistinguishable. According to Thanh, most of the men in this troupe were gay. These guys offered "two in one," Thanh liked to joke. The love songs were followed by the obligatory children's song, performed by a pair of kids perhaps ten years old— though the girl was made up as if she had been twenty, and nearly tipped over as she wobbled across the stage in her heels.

The show's finale was the Visit Laos Year theme song. Composed by Ounkham of the Ministry of Information and Culture, with whom I had partied in Sainyabuli, this was a theme song for a campaign supposedly designed to attract foreign tourists to Laos. And don't get me wrong, it was a great song. But it was entirely in Lao. "*Sieng khene, den dok champa, ben sannyalak bpee tongtiow Lao,*" the performers sang. "The sound of the *khene*, the land of frangipani, these are the symbols of Visit Laos Year." By the time the performers reached the second refrain, the crowd—which, by the way, did not include a single foreign tourist—had already begun to dwindle. Only a few guests who weren't NTA staff remained. Two or three men, passed out after one too many beers, lay on the ground near piles of trash. In celebration of International Women's Day, their wives and daughters scurried about cleaning up the mess. The birds had long since flown this coop, but the band played on, trying its hand at a few Lao imitations of Thai imitations of American pop songs: "Come on in to the Hotel California," the lead singer mumbled.

As the sun beat down, the NTA staff waited patiently for General Cheng to finish laughing it up with his buddies. My colleagues lounged about on straw mats, munching on salted watermelon seeds and spitting them out to pass the time. As seeds flew past my face, I, for one, was going mildly insane. I was stuck. I couldn't go anywhere, for I was dependent on the NTA van for the ride back. If I took another walk, I might miss the departure and end up sleeping with the birds. And I couldn't complain openly, for I knew that among my colleagues such personal expressions of frustration in public were unacceptable. I risked losing face. Then again, if I didn't say anything, I risked losing my mind.

After four hours of bad music and drunken revelry, even my colleagues' seemingly unlimited well of tolerance for the absurd was showing signs of depletion. I exchanged many a knowing glance with Mon and Seng. Privately, in hushed voices, my friends agreed: it was time to go. But no one would say so out loud. Not a single staff member would openly acknowledge his desire to leave before the chairman. Finally—as if Buddha himself had answered our silent prayers—our boss rose from the ashes of Nong Nok and signaled his intention to return home. As he bid his farewells and expressed his gratitude to the village headman, his driver, Oudom, made a beeline for the parking lot. In a matter of seconds, our trash was cleared away, the straw mats were rolled up, and the NTA crew was back in the van. Thanh popped Will Smith back into the tape deck, and, before I knew it, we were on our bumpy way back to Vientiane.

––––––––––

Over the weekend, as I recovered from the abortive eco-tourism celebration, I mulled over what had happened that afternoon. Why had the staff been so reluctant to leave early? After all, the chairman had his own transportation—he didn't need the NTA van. Some staff had their own motorbikes, and could have gone home at any time. On Monday, Seng helped me to understand. Let's say the staff had in fact cleared out early. What if, when he arrived at work on Monday morning, the chairman had asked one of his secretaries, "By the way, why did you all leave the festival so early on Friday?" An appropriate response might have been, "Oh, because we were all very tired, and we agreed it was time to go. So, together, we decided to leave." But, after shifting in his boots for a few moments, his assistant would more likely have come up with, "So-and-So pressured us all to leave, so we finally gave in to his demands." This was what worried Seng and the others: in the official version of events, there always had to be someone to blame.

At the office, anyone who openly expressed a personal opinion usually stood alone. He had little chance of receiving support from colleagues, even those he considered close friends. Seng gave me an example: a few years ago, the chairman had decided that, in order to increase efficiency and to better manage technical problems, it would be best to put all the office computers in a single room. The new computer room would be manned by two or three staff who would carry out all word processing requests from all sections of the office. Privately, everyone agreed that this was a ridiculous idea. Imagine the chaos that would result if, any time someone wanted a document typed up, he had to submit a request. The office would quickly fall apart.

At a general staff meeting, Seng voiced his disapproval of the proposed reorganization. But no one came to his defense. If it was the chairman's idea, then it had to be good. So the plan went ahead, and after only three days, centralized efficiency had degenerated into pure silliness. No one could get anything done. The plan was aborted, and the computers were re-distributed to the section offices. Overnight, everyone's public opinion of the plan suddenly changed—it seemed it hadn't been such a good idea after all. But Seng didn't feel vindicated, as nothing was said of his original opposition to the scheme.

Seng now kept quiet at staff meetings. "My parents always tell me, 'Don't waste time,'" he said. "Sometimes it's better to keep silent, to keep your job. If you criticize the government, they put you in prison, and you might never come out. You can lose time in prison, many years."

Why didn't at least some Lao stand up and reject the chaos that surrounded them? Why did so few Lao demand change? Seng's answer was simple: "It's just the Lao character. We don't protest."

For an American upstart just out of college, his answer was, in a word, unsatisfactory. "We are different from the Chinese, the Koreans, and the Thais. It's in our spirit." It was an explanation I could understand, but not fully accept. And besides, it didn't tell the whole story.

Laos was certainly a laid-back place to live. But beneath the surface, a deeply ingrained culture of fear pervaded government and society. To comment publicly on an issue, to express an opinion, or even to acknowledge a problem that everyone already knew existed, was to be avoided at all cost. People may have been relaxed, but they were afraid. And not only of the big guys who flew down Lan Xang Avenue behind the tinted windows of their Mercedes sedans, sirens blaring. Or of the policemen who blew their whistles and stopped traffic to let the officials through. They were also afraid of one another. There was little trust, and even among friends it was too risky to speak your mind.

You just never knew—even the birds might be listening.

The Lost Generation

At precisely five o'clock each evening, just as the sun was beginning its lazy descent over Vientiane, a black Toyota sedan would pull up in front of the Lao Hotel Plaza. A handsome Lao man in his late twenties—dressed to kill in a black silk shirt, black pants, and black loafers—would step out of the back seat and trot up the front steps to the main entrance. Just as he reached the front door, it would swing open, as if by magic, and he would sail through, leaving a bewildered doorman in his wake. This was Paul, a friend of mine and a regular at the Lao Hotel Plaza gym. Paul hadn't yet learned to drive, so each day he caught a ride to the gym in his family's chauffeured car. Paul was a name he had picked up while studying and working abroad. These days, only his parents called him by his given name.

In the early 1990s, Paul had graduated from Vientiane High School, in the same colonial building that once housed the prestigious Lycée Vientiane. It had been decades since the communists had taken over, but the crumbling edifice remained a bastion of the Vientiane elite; if you were a child of the upper class, you went to Vientiane High School. Paul did well there, and he was granted a scholarship to study construction and engineering in Moscow—at the time, still the most prestigious of placements. After leaving the Soviet Union, he continued his studies in Bangkok before taking a job with an Austrian architecture firm in Vienna. Paul whiled away many an hour in Vienna's cafés, sipping coffee, eating rich Sacher tortes, and smoking filtered Gauloises. It was a far cry from Vientiane. He loved the freedom, the fashion, the style.

"But one thing, you know," Paul told me, "the Austrian people are not friendly. They never smile. One time I was sitting at a bar, and I smiled at a woman across the room, a stranger. She was so surprised that she came to me and said, 'Thank you so much. I have lived in Vienna my whole life and no stranger has ever smiled at me. Thank you.' Most people, if you smile at them on the street, they think you're crazy."

Despite the icy stares and social isolation—you couldn't ask for a more stark contrast to life in Vientiane—Paul had liked living in Vienna. But after only one year, his parents insisted that he return to Laos; he was needed at home. Now back in Vientiane, he was living at home and working for the family business, a consulting firm employed by private investors and development aid agencies alike for advice on construction projects. His father had recently signed a lucrative long-term contract for multiple aid projects with the Japanese government, and there was much work to be done. The oldest of three sons, Paul felt obligated to use the skills he had acquired abroad to help the firm. He was, however, bored out of his mind.

Even by American standards, Paul's family was very wealthy, and his life in Vientiane was nothing if not comfortable. Chauffeured cars, mobile phones, designer imports—he had it all. But living at home meant that Paul had lost all of the independence he had come to know and to cherish while abroad. "I want to stand on my legs," he told me in his idiosyncratic English. (What else would you stand on? I wondered silently.) He felt just like a high school student again, a helpless teenager dependent on his parents to survive.

All the trappings of wealth in the world could not silence Paul's chorus of complaints about Vientiane: there was no nightlife, no culture, no romance. As an escape from the doldrums of his daily routine, he would often call a former lover in Thailand. To conceal the relationship from his parents, he always used his cellphone. Whether the object of his affection was male or female remained unclear, as Paul hadn't yet mastered the all-important distinction between the English pronouns "he" and "she." In Lao, simpler than English as always—although not as clear—the single pronoun *lao* is used to refer to both men and women. Then again, perhaps Paul's mistake was intentional, and I elected to preserve the ambiguity.

One evening after his daily sauna at the Lao Plaza (he rarely did much else at the gym), Paul reminded me that it was Valentine's Day. I wasn't aware of it—indeed, I had no reason to remember. I may have enjoyed the freedom for which Paul yearned, but, romantically speaking, it had done me precious little good. I remained as single as I'd been for years. In celebration of the pathetic state of our respective love lives, we decided to go out to dinner. Before we left, Paul checked himself in the mirror one last time, dabbing a bit of cologne behind his ears and styling his hair with a healthy application of gel. The image of the two of us in the mirror made for a striking contrast. Paul was almost painfully stylish, not a single hair out of place and dressed in the latest Bangkok chic. I, on the other hand, hadn't bothered to shave, and it had been months since I'd purchased a new item of clothing.

We ate at Namphu restaurant, at the Fountain Circle, just a few minutes walk from the Lao Plaza. The Namphu was one of the oldest and most expensive restaurants in town, and, given my precarious financial situation, I'd been there only once before. By expensive, I mean to say that an entrée ran you about five dollars, but for me even this was quite an extravagance. Paul, on the other hand, was a regular. His new Seiko, bought on a recent trip to Bangkok, glistened in the soft lighting. He laid his miniature cellphone on the table just to the right of his setting, as if it were another eating utensil. It rang every ten minutes or so throughout our meal, usually a call from a family member wanting to do a little business, or a friend wondering what his plans were for the evening.

Paul lit a cigarette—he now smoked only Marlboro Lights—and began, not for the first time, to recount his latest troubles of the heart. He often pined for ex-lovers in Russia, Thailand, and Austria. Although he was Lao himself, he found romance in his native country a mysterious and frustrating endeavor. "I don't like Lao style," he claimed.

What exactly was Lao style? I asked.

"You know, the face, the body, the character—Lao style. It is very difficult for me to find someone in Vientiane."

My friend tended towards the dramatic whenever the topic of romance came up. "You know, love is poison," he told me. Paul's English lexicon had been strongly influenced by MTV Southeast Asia, particularly the ubiquitous boy bands that plagued the airwaves. His statements often sounded like a refrain from the latest Boyzone or N'Sync hit. "I want to live for today," he liked to say. "I need to follow my heart." When I suggested that I was also struggling with the mysteries of "Lao style" romance, he would tell me that it was simply because "You don't know how to love." If ever I tried to change the subject from our love lives to other, more substantive matters, Paul invariably demurred. Once during our meal at the Namphu I asked him what he thought of the Lao economy. "I don't care about the Lao economy," he said with disgust, and lit another Marlboro.

After we'd finished eating, I asked Paul where he was heading.

"Home," he replied. "My mother worries."

I also worried about Paul. All dressed up with nowhere to go, he dreamed of a life in the big city even as his own life was confined to the narrow corridor between his home and the Lao Plaza gym. His life in Vientiane was indeed a cushioned, chauffeured existence, but it left him feeling unbearably empty. He longed to break free of his doting mother and demanding father, but felt constrained by the obligation he felt to his family.

Paul was a member of what I called Laos' Lost Generation. This group of upper-class twenty-somethings hailed from wealthy families, and most had been granted the opportunity to study in the West. But despite—or perhaps as a result of—their tremendous fortune, Paul's peers were struggling to make it in Vientiane. Many felt listless and without purpose; in essence, they had everything and nothing at the same time. Their concerns were far removed from those of the average Lao, it's true, but they were no less painful.

The manager of the Namphu, Sone, stood behind the bar and fixed me a gin and tonic. It was rare indeed that I'd treat myself to such an extravagance, but Sone's G and Ts were the best around. He always had the mix just right, and the atmosphere made a drink there worth most any price. A well-worn recording of Stan Getz and Astrud Gilberto filled the dining room as I sipped my drink and slowly got to know the man behind the bar.

Sone's mother had opened the Namphu more than a decade before, when it had been just about the only restaurant in Vientiane that catered to expats. Back in Paul's class at Vientiane High, Sone hadn't been known as the brightest of students. He had, however, been lucky enough to study in Australia following graduation. Upon his return to Laos, his mother had designated him the Namphu's manager; it was up to him to make sure the red wine flowed freely and the renowned blue-cheese hamburgers were always fresh.

Sone was the perfect host; a jolly fellow, always ready to greet his customers with a smile and an outstretched hand. His belly already protruded quite a distance beyond his waistline; it struck me that perhaps he had enjoyed a few too many of those famous burgers himself over the years. In fact, Paul and others who had been his classmates at Vientiane High often mentioned that Sone had put on weight in recent years. His healthy appetite notwithstanding, business at the Namphu wasn't great. But with a surname like his, Sone didn't really have to worry. He was an Inthavong, and thus heir to at least part of one of the largest family fortunes in Laos.

The Inthavong family business—which included three hotels, three apartment buildings, an office complex, a joint-venture hydroelectric dam, and a construction company—was said to be worth more than 500 million dollars. Sone's grandfather, Somboun Inthavong, had been born in 1907 in Luang Prabang. As a young man, he worked as a construction apprentice in the royal palace. There, he cultivated the practical skills and official connections that would come in handy later in his career. In 1935 he left Luang Prabang to serve as the chief of the Royal Lao Government's Housing Department in Vientiane. Before he retired from the civil service in 1940, Somboun had set up a trading company that supplied consumer products, office equipment, and other imported goods to the local market and to the government.

Somboun had been a savvy businessman. Even as the country had descended into civil war in the 1960s, he maintained close friendships with key figures in each of Laos' divergent political factions. He was buddies with the centrist Prince Souvanna Phouma, the right-wing Phoui Xananikone, and the communist Phoumi Vongvichit. After his retirement, he founded the country's first construction company and undertook his own property development projects in Vientiane, including apartment buildings, office complexes, and markets. During the Indochina War, he was awarded government contracts to build a military camp and an apartment building for US officers in Vientiane. His buildings were leased to American and French officials, and the value of his properties rose to more than 25 million dollars.

Due to Somboun's broad political connections, the communist victory in 1975 hardly put a dent in the Inthavong family business. If anything, it was a boon; the revolution conveniently eliminated most of Somboun's competition. After 1975, he was granted state contracts to renovate and construct buildings in Vientiane such as the Presidential Palace, the Morning Market, and the Ministry of Education. After the government abandoned socialism in the late 1980s, Somboun began once again to lease his properties to private enterprises. Remember the US officers' apartment building? The Novotel Hotel group paid 90 million dollars for a twenty-year lease.

In the wake of Somboun's death in 1994, the Inthavong family was struggling to build upon his tremendous legacy of sustained success. It wasn't easy. Somboun had 14 children from two wives: nine sons and five daughters. All of them had been sent to study in France, Switzerland, Germany, Australia, or the US; only four had returned to Laos. Those who lived in Vientiane still had plenty of cash to throw around, but the business seemed to be falling apart.

As marriages collapsed, children feuded, and cousins fought, the Inthavong name suffered. Many in the younger generation seemed aimless, unwilling, or unable to properly manage family properties. One of Somboun's major post-war projects had been a five-story building just opposite the Namphu on the Fountain Circle that had once housed a French language and culture center. For years, his children had been bickering over the future of the building, and no one could agree on who had the right to develop the site. In the meantime, it just sat there, sad and empty, a blot on the downtown landscape.

Perhaps most emblematic of the Inthavong family's fall from grace was the decaying Phonexay Hotel, a bit further out of town. A few weeks before, I had driven up to the hotel to have a look inside. The Phonexay was an imposing, cavernous structure. At one time you might even have called it grand. But it had been years since tourists had even considered staying there. These days, the only guests were laborers from India, Pakistan, and Sri Lanka; around town, it was known as the "Indian Hotel." These South Asians, temporary workers in Thailand, stayed in Vientiane for only a few days at a time, just long enough to renew their visas at the Thai consulate. While they waited, they lounged about the hotel's foyer, joking with one another and playing cards. In the afternoons, a few inevitably drifted across the street to Nazim's Indian restaurant for a cup of milk tea. Perhaps the dank, dark, air-conditioned interior and melancholy Indian tunes playing at Nazim's—which rarely attracted any non-Indian customers (a great pity, as the food was excellent)—reminded them of home. But by evening, most were back in the foyer, playing cards.

When I stopped by, a good-humored young Lao man was sitting quietly behind the reception desk. He seemed genuinely surprised to see a *falang* in his establishment, and immediately set about dissuading me from renting a room.

When I made it clear that I simply wanted to have a look, he took a key from behind the desk and, with an apologetic expression, led me up an unlit stairwell to the second floor. We made our way down a long, dark hallway and past a carpeted conference room that hadn't been used in ages. At the end of the hallway, the receptionist unlocked the door to a bedroom and let me inside. The room was filthy. Suspicious streaks of red and brown marked the wall just above the bed. The sheets looked as if they might devour anyone who dared lie down for the night.

I thanked the receptionist and made a quick exit. As I was leaving the building, though, I noticed the vast concrete pillars on either side of the main entrance. They gave the place an air of majesty, I thought—in spite of myself, I still believed the Phonexay had potential. But the Inthavong family hadn't lifted a finger to maintain the building, never mind renovate it to welcome the increasing numbers of tourists visiting Laos. What had happened?

"I am trying," said Sone as he tallied up the bill for the only other customer at the Namphu. He was the family member who had the most responsibility for the Phonexay, and he had plans to give the exterior a badly needed new coat of paint. But I sensed that Sone's enthusiasm was on the wane. "In Laos," he explained, "it is very difficult."

Where was Sone headed? I wondered. Would he spend the rest of his life behind the bar at the Namphu?

Sone would often speak with fondness of his years as a student in Australia. And like many of his friends, he couldn't understand why I had decided to leave the US for Vientiane. What good could I possibly find among the crumbling buildings and unpaved roads of this small country? Why come all the way here when there was so much opportunity waiting for me *there*? No matter how many times I tried to explain, most of my Lost Generation friends failed to see what I could possibly gain from leaving life in the West. Having experienced it for themselves, they knew what it had to offer: everything they couldn't find in Vientiane.

When it came time for me to leave Laos months later, the Phonexay would remain untouched, a crumbling monument to a family's decline and a generation's malaise.

———

Sophie was no stranger to the Inthavong family; in fact, she had once come quite close to marrying Sone's brother. She lived at her family's house in Vientiane, a villa typical of those built during the capital's wartime boom. The living and dining areas were combined in one spacious room, decorated with large, colorful oil canvases that depicted scenes of everyday life in Laos. I had come to meet Sophie for lunch, and as I entered the room, the indignant poetics of the late American rapper, Tupac Shakur, blasted from the stereo.

Sophie emerged from the kitchen dressed elegantly in black slacks, a simple white blouse, and black designer glasses. She greeted me with a kiss on each cheek, and we sat down to enjoy the light meal she'd prepared: cheese omelets, mixed salad, and fresh baguettes from the market nearby. We washed this typical French repast down with a bottle of red wine. Was I still in Laos?

Sophie had grown up in Vientiane, but had left Laos with her mother back in 1974, before entering high school. The Royal Lao Government had not yet fallen to the communists, but Sophie's mother had seen the writing on the wall. She wasn't royalty, but her family did belong to Vientiane's merchant aristocracy, and her husband had done business in the US. The way political events were unfolding, the future looked bleak. Sophie and her mother left for India to join her aunt, who was working in the Lao Embassy in Delhi. When the revolution took place, they all moved to Paris. The only member of Sophie's family to remain in Vientiane was an uncle who was able to hold onto one of the family's houses—two were immediately confiscated by the new regime—until Sophie's return, more than twenty years later.

When it came time for high school, Sophie left France for the States, where she lived with an aunt. She attended a public school in Los Angeles, and the American accent she'd acquired there remained with her even today. Her speech was punctuated with a heavy dose of "likes," "oh, my Gods" and other typical California-risms. After graduation, she enrolled at the University of California at Berkeley to study political science, but ultimately completed her studies at a small community college nearby in order to save money. She had been living in an apartment with two roommates, driving her own car, about to begin the next chapter in her new American life when, one day, her mother called from Paris.

"It's time," she said, and Sophie knew just what she meant.

For years, Sophie and her mother had been discussing the possibility of returning to Laos. As official "traitors" to the regime, they were understandably wary. But by 1995, after having heard reports from other émigrés who had successfully gone back, they had decided that it was safe. Sophie dropped everything in LA and flew to Vientiane. She and her mother moved back into the house her uncle had been holding onto for so many years, and Sophie set about looking for a job. During the first few months, she felt strangely uncomfortable in her own home. Her relatives welcomed her back, of course, but they remained suspicious of the motives for her return. After all, Sophie and her mother had escaped, while they had stuck it out. Why had they bothered to come back now? Even in the mid-1990s, most Lao remained wary of returnees, even family members. After so many years away, Sophie wondered if she had anything in common with her relatives any longer. She felt alone, and isolated.

Indeed, Sophie was not a traditional Lao girl. Her manner of speaking, the way she dressed—her entire approach to life—was more the result of her years abroad than her Lao upbringing. She had aspirations that were unbecoming for a young woman in Laos. She even spoke of founding her own consulting firm, through which she would work to attract foreign direct investment to Laos. In considering such business endeavors, she saw extraordinary opportunities not only for herself, but also for the future development of her country.

But much of Sophie's time was spent trying to come to terms with what it meant to be a Lao carrying a foreign passport in Laos—in the culture of her birth, but not entirely of it.

Just as Sophie was struggling with questions of her identity, her mother was trying to marry her off. As a child, her mother had been good friends with one of Grandpa Inthavong's sons. One night, the younger Inthavong and his wife invited Sophie to dinner. She was enjoying a good conversation about French literature and philosophy when Mrs. Inthavong suddenly brought up the topic of her son. He had completed his studies in Russia, she said, and at 29 was ready for marriage. Both were appropriately well-bred, and hailed from two families of similarly high status. They would be a perfect match! But Sophie already knew about his reputation around town as a playboy, and she wanted nothing to do with him.

She had little desire to be among the gaggle of hopeful young women who surrounded him in every nightclub he frequented.

"He is a bit turbulent," his mother allowed, "but we think he has promise." And then there was always the money. "You can have everything you want," she told Sophie. "We can even get you two houses: one to live in, another to rent out." As Mrs. Inthavong continued to extol his virtues, the prodigal son walked in, just in time for dessert. Upon entering the room, he transformed from the joker Sophie had always known to a polite, well-spoken, and respectful son. Swept away by his charm, Sophie agreed to a few dates and, before she knew it, they were "a couple." Soon enough, the mothers began to plan the wedding. After all, this match had less to do with love than it did with business and social status. It was in the best interest of both families for their children to marry within Vientiane's upper class. Sophie could already imagine her life as the wife of an Inthavong, the pressure of always having to impress Vientiane society by wearing the right color *sin* at parties and enough new gold jewelry at weddings. She soon determined that this playboy and his family weren't for her.

When she put an end to the relationship, he didn't go quietly. If he ever saw Sophie in a nightclub, he would promptly dump the girl with whom he'd arrived and join her. Once, while she was having a business dinner in a Vientiane restaurant, he approached her table, kissed her on the lips, and announced, "This is my wife." After she exploded and demanded an apology, he finally got the message. But Sophie wasn't accustomed to this sort of behavior; she expected to be treated as an independent woman, free to make her own decisions about her future. She found it hard to understand why so many girls in Vientiane continued to throw themselves at this guy's feet, hoping desperately for a marriage proposal, while he treated them like dirt. Unlike these women, Sophie had seen the possibilities.

Life in the world beyond Vientiane had taught Sophie that even an heir to the Inthavong fortune was nothing special. She knew there were far better men out there—in Vientiane, they were just especially hard to find. But how long could she hope to resist the pressure to please her mother and to impress the neighbors? She began to wonder if it wouldn't be better to leave Laos and head back to the States after all. Would she ever be able to find happiness in the country of her birth?

It may seem strange that I cared so much about these people and their lives. To be sure, in a country where one in five children dies in infancy and adult life expectancy is just more than fifty years, their struggles were minor.

What did these rich, spoiled, twenty-somethings have to complain about? They'd been granted opportunities to see the world that most of their fellow countrymen could never hope to obtain. Above all, I suppose, I was intrigued by members of Laos' Lost Generation because they were my peers. And while we were close in age, we found ourselves in strikingly different situations. I had left the West behind by choice. I was living far away from my family, working for a communist government in a developing country, making just enough money to get by—whenever we went out to dinner, I was inevitably the poorest one at the table—and absolutely loving it.

On the other hand, my friends were living only a few paces from where they had studied as teenagers. They found that the good fortune of their upper-class background only served to stifle their independence and personal growth. They had plenty of money, but nowhere to spend it. Plenty of new ideas, but no way to implement them. Many, like Paul, had felt obligated to come back to Laos. Among those like Sophie who had freely chosen to return, many had yet to find what they were looking for. Their lives were on hold. Having been exposed to life in the West, they felt left behind in Vientiane, and quietly pined for something more.

Across the River

At the NTA, much of my colleagues' time was spent figuring out what on earth to do about the Visit Laos Year 1999–2000 campaign. Frantically organizing celebrations in each of the provincial capitals, drafting speeches by deputy prime ministers, designing logos and dreaming up catchy mottos, the staff were consumed by the campaign. Much of my time, however, was spent trying to figure out why on earth we were even having a Visit Laos Year. The roads in the capital were impassable; the UN and most foreign embassies had condemned Lao Aviation as unsafe; and a full-scale military conflict with the Hmong was brewing in the Northeast. The Party was by no means certain that it even wanted foreign tourists roaming around. All this led me to think that it was perhaps not the best time for the campaign.

A few years back, the Party had decided that the NTA should organize a promotional campaign for 1999. But given the enormity of the task and the absence of funding, the NTA soon ran out of time to prepare. When 1998 rolled around and it became clear that the country wasn't ready, the Party fudged the issue: rather than canceling Visit Laos Year 1999—which would have required the awkward reversal of an official decision—it decided to re-name the campaign Visit Laos Year 1999–2000. This afforded some breathing space, and some welcome ambiguity.

When I arrived in Vientiane, no one was quite sure when the campaign was supposed to begin. Was it January 1999? Or perhaps the Lao New Year in April? As it scrambled to prepare, the NTA did little to alleviate the confusion. Every few weeks, someone in the Marketing and Promotion Unit would come up with a new slogan as we prepared for Visit Laos Year (or was it Years?): "Laos—Your New Love;" "Laos: Jewel of the Mekong;" and "Fabu-Laos!"

In Bangkok, the Tourism Authority of Thailand, along with some highly paid Western consultants and a budget that dwarfed that of the entire Lao government, had long before come up with its own cohesive tourism promotion campaign: "Amazing Thailand." That's *Amazing* Thailand, mind you, as in "Amazing Gateway," the "Amazing Doi Ting Tour," and "Amazing Chiang Rai's Hilltribe Shangrila Adventure." And don't forget the country's "Amazing Cultural Heritage," "Amazing Natural Heritage," and "Amazing Arts and Lifestyle." Not to mention fun-filled activities like the "Amazing Mini Light and Sound Presentation Chiang Rai."

In short, the Amazing Thailand campaign was inescapable. Whenever I crossed the Friendship Bridge over the Mekong, the first thing that greeted me was an enormous billboard that read, "*Amazing Thailand Grand Sale—50–80% Off!*" The entire country was on sale.

Living in Vientiane, I often thought of the Kingdom of Thailand as one big shopping mall. It was the Promised Land of Kentucky Fried Chicken and McDonald's. If ever an expat in Vientiane needed a fast food fix, all he had to do was to make a run for the border and cross the Mekong. In Thailand, particularly during the Asian economic crisis, nothing was sacred. Everything was for sale, from the country's natural heritage to its cultural identity, its ethnic minorities to its young women. And that was the most amazing thing of all.

Thailand's influence in Laos was overwhelming. Thai finger-prints were all over the spheres of commerce, fashion, finance, and popular culture. A simple stroll through the Morning Market in Vientiane revealed the degree to which the daily life of the average Lao was suffused with Thai influence. Nearly every product was an import from across the river. Toothpaste, milk, clothing, even sugar and salt—it was all foreign. As the Lao economy slid deeper into recession, the government exhorted its citizens to buy Lao and reject Thai imports in order to boost domestic production. It was a lost cause. "Of course I want to promote Lao products," my colleague and friend Chanh told me over lunch at his house one day. "But the Thai quality is just much better."

When Chanh graduated from high school in Vientiane in 1985, he had been at the very top of his class. The government offered him a scholarship to study at the university level in one of the usual Cold War suspects: the Soviet Union, Czechoslovakia, Vietnam. Most of his classmates would have jumped at the chance. They weren't interested in the academics, but rather in the possibility of making a little extra money to send back home. (Even today there are Lao merchants in Moscow and St. Petersburg, stuck in a post-Soviet, not-quite-capitalist culture dominated by the mafia.) But Chanh wanted something different. He wanted to go someplace no one from his school had ever been. He wanted to live someplace warm. And, realizing that Russian influence was on the wane, he wanted to learn a language that might one day be useful. So Chanh chose Cuba.

He lived in Havana for five years, studying economics at the National University, and never once leaving the country. He spoke Spanish fluently, and the resulting effect on his accent was clear: I loved to listen to his festive pronunciation of English words, which brought to mind the steamy streets and sensual nights of Havana. Chanh's accent wasn't the only aspect of his character that had a Latin influence. His moves on the dance floor at the nightclubs in Vientiane we would visit together would often devolve into a salsa of sorts. A highlight of his time in Cuba was a meeting with Fidel Castro, who came to visit the National University and to chat with the international students for a few brief, exhilarating moments.

Chanh had never joked with Laos' president, though one of his best friends was the man's only daughter, a colleague of ours at the NTA. A statue of Che Guevera sat on Chanh's desk at the office. "I'm not a communist," he once assured me. "He is just an inspiration."

Che probably wouldn't have approved of the array of electronic products in Chanh's bedroom in Vientiane. He owned a stereo, television, and laptop computer, each of which he'd purchased in Thailand. Chanh had been able to acquire these prized items due to one of the major perks of working for the NTA: whenever he traveled abroad on trips approved by the Ministry of Foreign Affairs, he was permitted to bring one purchase into the country tax-free. Ordinary Lao citizens re-entering the country from Thailand, on the other hand, had to pay a 100% percent import tax on consumer goods. It was no surprise that the NTA staff put a premium on access to UN-funded "study tours" and other international travel opportunities.

Chanh once returned from a tourism development seminar in Thailand with a new CD player. At the airport in Vientiane, he was stopped by a Customs official and forbidden from taking his new toy into the country; he had forgotten his all-important Foreign Ministry approval forms. Chanh left the machine at the airport and spent the day going through a series of bureaucratic hoops in order to get his precious new purchase into the country tax-free. He now enjoyed waking up in the morning to Elton John's greatest hits— or at least a passable Thai imitation.

Certainly the most pervasive influence of Thai culture in Laos was on the airwaves. As the languages of Thailand and Laos were so similar, most Lao had no problem understanding Thai radio or TV. If I ever glanced into a living room while walking through the streets of Vientiane, at any time of the day, I would invariably catch a glimpse of the family gathered around the TV, glued to a Thai soap opera or game show. People rarely watched the state-run channel, which was a dreary affair. Newscasters sat in front of a cardboard cut-out depicting one Vientiane landmark or another, and read news reports about the successes of the revolution—everything from the improved living conditions of remote villagers to increased productivity at a chicken farm near Pakse. They provided commentary on endless government meetings with delegations from friendly nations like Cuba and Vietnam. The sight of aging Party cadres shuffling in and out of yet another seminar was enough to send anyone channel surfing.

Once you changed the station, you'd encounter something quite different. Thai TV offered a steady stream of crass commercialism. One game show I saw from time to time was nothing more than a tacky, hour-long advertisement. Standing in front of large billboards advertising soap, perfume, and yogurt, contestants competed to take home the very products that supported the show. Thailand's soap operas weren't any better, depicting a world inhabited by bitchy girlfriends, scheming stepmothers, and oafish hunks, and permeated by graphic gun violence. This stuff put even the least subtle of America's daytime TV to shame—but the Lao ate it up.

If they ever listened to the radio, most of my Lao friends tuned into the FM station based in Nong Khai just over the border. Accessing Thai radio hadn't always been so easy. Until the mid-1980s, radio entertainment had been limited to patriotic songs about the glory of the revolution. These songs, written and produced by the Ministry of Information and Culture, had been designed to encourage a non-existent Lao "proletariat" to keep on working even when times were tough. But by the late-1990s, anyone with a radio could receive Thai programming, and contemporary Lao songwriting had been rendered a dying art. Whenever I asked a friend if he could name a famous Lao singer who was still alive, I drew little more than a blank stare and a nervous laugh in response.

Teenagers in Vientiane, like teenagers everywhere, were searching for models to imitate as they came of age, and they took their cues from across the river. They followed Thai fashions slavishly, careening through the streets on their motorbikes and shouting Bangkok slang to one another. In the Master barber shop on Dongpalan Street, where I'd get a pretty good haircut for less than a dollar every few weeks or so, the wall was plastered with posters of Thai teenage models sporting the latest hairstyles. No matter what the masterful barbers did to my hair, I felt distinctly unhip.

I knew how much my identity as a young American had been shaped and molded by a uniquely American popular culture. But what if the popular culture in my own country had been entirely foreign? What if, on the TV, all the commercials had been in another language? And on the shelves in the local supermarket, all the products had been imported? What if my favorite stars had all been foreigners? Soon enough, I figured, this foreign culture would replace mine.

And I would make it my own.

Despite their love affair with Thai products, TV, and music, my Lao friends rarely had a kind word to say about their neighbors. "You know, Mr. Brett," Chanh told me one day, "in Thailand, if you give someone 500 baht [about 13 dollars] and tell them to kill someone, they'll do it. Just like that. But not here in Laos. It's not possible."

"How about in twenty years, when the Lao economy has developed?" I asked. "Might people change?"

"No, the Lao are just different."

I had heard this story about the notorious 500-baht contracts countless times before. In fact, it came up whenever I raised the subject of Thailand in conversation with a Lao. Perhaps it was based on an actual incident, but I had my doubts. Regardless of its truth, the story fulfilled a basic need for those who told it. The endless comparison between the innocent Lao and their sinful, sullied neighbors struck me as a thinly veiled attempt by the Lao to differentiate themselves from Thailand. Their languages were similar, their ethnicity in some regions almost identical. But even as they lapped up Thai culture, the Lao took pains to draw distinctions.

In English class one day, I asked what my students thought about the problem of school shootings in America. The tragic Columbine massacre had appeared in the Vientiane papers just that week, and all of them had heard about it. Would this ever happen in Vientiane?

"Never. We cannot buy guns," Kham, the Paradise nightclub's star performer and my connection to Amarillo, answered with a smirk.

"But what if you could? Would Lao people kill each other then?"

"No," Kham answered quickly. "We are not like the Thais. Different character. Thais talk sweetly, but underneath they will trick you."

Under pressure, my students conceded that young Lao men might be susceptible to gun violence—but only because of the negative influence of Thai popular culture. Just look at what they watch on TV every night! When they looked at Thailand, the Lao did see a land of opportunity. The furious pace at which Thailand's economy had grown since the end of the Vietnam War had long put them to shame. But now, they also saw a land of many a lost opportunity. Overrun with tourists, blighted by pollution, violence, prostitution, environmental devastation, and AIDS, Thailand was everything the Lao people abhorred. Most Lao I knew had an acute sense of what they did not want for the future of their country. The real problem was figuring out just what they did want—and how they could get it.

If the Lao perceived Thailand as a modern day Sodom, a pit of sex and sin, for the Thais, Laos was a kind of Eden. It was the last frontier. Having ravaged their own environment, rendered their capital morally bankrupt and its roads hopelessly congested, Thai day-trippers flocked to Laos for a glimpse of what might have been. They came to experience what life in Thailand had once been like, before the post-war program of rapid and unplanned economic development had begun. In Laos, Thais discovered Thailand before the fall.

But if the Thais idealized Laos, they had no real respect for their smaller neighbor. Most Thai visitors regarded Vientiane as little more than a frontier town, a dusty backwater capital of the Wild East. Thai men and women traipsed through the country with abandon wearing tight blue jeans, leather cowboy boots, and—clipped to their belts, where in a different time and place you might have found a revolver—mobile phones. They raced through the open rice fields and down the dusty roads in their four-wheel-drives as if the entire country was their own backyard. Already, Thailand used at least three-quarters of the hydro-electric power produced in Laos, and would consume most of the water generated by all of the dams and power stations that were in the works. At the end of the day, the Thais viewed Laos as just another province of Thailand.

When a foreign power had such a strong hold on Laos' economy and its popular culture, what became of Lao national identity? The notion of a strong and independent Lao identity had always been precarious. Laos had not even been a unified country when the French had arrived in Indochina. Even after independence, the king, essentially appointed by France, had represented only a certain segment of the population; ethnic minorities existed largely outside the realm of government control. It was only since the revolution that the government had insisted on a certain degree of linguistic and cultural continuity throughout the country, with limited success. But the influx of Thai music, images, and ideas, in the wake of Laos' recent liberalization, had led to renewed concerns about just what it meant to be "Lao." It was similar to the dilemma facing citizens in countries like Austria and Canada, who struggled with the inescapable influence of their own powerful neighbors, Germany and the US.

The Party sensed this collective national identity crisis, and every once in a while, it attempted to crack down on Thai influence. In a state-sponsored children's singing competition in Vientiane, for example, no Thai songs were allowed. The organizers only permitted performances in Lao, English, Chinese, or Vietnamese—"My Heart Will Go On" was acceptable, but the latest Thai hits were not.

But it wasn't only the government that was bothered by the predominance of Thai music in Vientiane. Paul, among the most disaffected of Laos' Lost Generation, was struggling with the issue as well. In the Lao Hotel Plaza sauna one evening, as we discussed Thai pop songs, he became so worked up I thought he'd lose his breath. As the temperature increased, he began to let off some serious steam.

Paul told me of his experience as a visiting university student in Bangkok a few years back. One night, all the international students at the school had gathered for a welcoming celebration in the dining hall. Each student had been asked to sing a song from his or her homeland. As the others had taken turns proudly belting out folk songs, national anthems, and pop hits from their home countries, Paul had only squirmed in his seat. He'd been stumped. "I could not think of one Lao song," he told me. "Only Thai songs. I felt so shy."

Paul's discomfort was indicative of the wildly contradictory feelings many Lao had for their neighbors. "I hate it. Every night, at the pubs in Vientiane, only Thai songs," he complained. "No

Western songs. In Bangkok, you can hear Western songs every night. But here, only Thai songs!" What had begun as an expression of nationalist outrage at Thai cultural imperialism had ended up a pathetic lament about the absence of *Western* songs at Vientiane's nightclubs. Although he was unable even to recall his own national anthem, Paul seemed unfazed by his ignorance of Lao music.

Sometimes, Laos' struggle with national identity spilled over into international politics. A few months before I left for good, an enormous controversy erupted over the alleged comments made by a young Thai pop singer, Nicole Theriault. Nicole—no one could pronounce her last name—enjoyed tremendous popularity in Laos, and rarely a day went by when I didn't hear one of her catchy tunes around town. Although Nicole was from Bangkok, she sold thousands of tapes in Laos and in Northeastern Thailand, where the population is predominantly ethnic Lao. Nicole's youthful good looks had a lot to do with her popularity. Physically, she was the best of both worlds: a *luk kheung*, literally "half child," the daughter of a Thai woman and a white American man. Almost all models, singers, and TV stars in Thailand were *luk kheung*; having a white parent had become a prerequisite for success in the Thai entertainment business. When I asked friends in Vientiane why they liked Nicole so much, they would inevitably refer to her "beautiful white skin," unconsciously revealing the insecurity that lay beneath the surface of the ensuing controversy.

One evening in early March, Nicole appeared on the popular Thai TV variety show, "At Ten." The star talked with the host about the usual topics, but at one point, according to some viewers in Laos, the conversation took an abrupt turn for the worse when Nicole was asked which foreign countries she might like to visit. Allegedly, she responded that Laos was among the places she would never want to visit—it was undeveloped, crowded, dusty, and, above all, Lao women were dark-skinned and dirty. During the next week, news of the interview spread through the streets of Vientiane, and the capital's rumor mill began to turn. Not only had Nicole called Laos dirty, people said, she had called Lao women "dogs."

The reaction of the Lao government to the incident was un-characteristically swift. Even though they could provide no evidence that Nicole had ever said anything negative about Laos, the Lao Women's Union lodged an official complaint with the Thai government. The Union stopped short of demanding an apology, but the idea was clear: Nicole's statement was an affront to all the people of Laos, who would not stand for such derogatory comments from any of Thailand's public figures. The Thai Ministry of Foreign Affairs was keen to nip this controversy in the bud, and it tried to clear up matters by requesting that the producers of the show release a videotape of the episode in question. The relationship between Thailand and Laos was perpetually troubled—recall the border dispute in Sainyabuli province that had exploded into war only a few years before—and another dispute was the last thing the Thais needed.

The TV producers maintained that Nicole had never made any derogatory comments about Laos, and gladly provided the video-tape to the news media. According to the producer, Laos hadn't even come up during the interview, and the videotape backed up their assertion. But the Lao Women's Union rejected the evidence, arguing that the tape could have been doctored.

For her part, Nicole argued that she had never made any negative statements about Laos or its people. In fact, she had been to visit the country the year before, and had had a great time.

"I was dismayed and dumbstruck," Nicole told the Thai media. "I was very shaken."

Despite the fact that all evidence pointed to Nicole's innocence, the controversy would not go away. It even came up at high-level meetings between Thai and Lao government representatives. A month after the interview, the state-run *Vientiane Times* carried a photo displaying one of Nicole's CDs—on the cover of which her face figured prominently—lying in pile of garbage as a man crushed the CD with his foot. Such an image was a great insult, as in Thai and Lao culture alike the head and feet were to be kept as far away from one another as possible. The Lao government continued to insist that Nicole had publicly insulted the Lao people. According to the *Vientiane Times*, "Ms. Manivone Luangsombath, a senior official of the Lao Women's Union, told the Thai newspaper *The*

Nation that it was very unfortunate that an educated and talented woman like Nicole would say such a thing. 'I saw and heard it with my own eyes and ears.'"

Such propaganda seemed to be having its intended effect. A few days after the story broke, I was waiting in line after work to pick up some photographs I'd dropped off for development the day before. Despite this impressive next-day service, the shop's major attraction was its photocopy machine, around which was huddled a group of jittery high-school boys, chattering excitedly as they awaited their printing request: hundreds of copies of a drawing one of them had produced in class that morning. By the next day, the posters had been pasted in public places all over town. In the crude image, Nicole was depicted in a compromising position, dressed only in her underwear, smoking a cigarette and injecting a needle into her arm. A dog sniffed at her crotch as two conservatively dressed Lao women pointed at her and snickered in the distance. "Nicole is a dog," the poster read, in English. The debate had turned nasty, and the singer was quickly being demonized. No one in Vientiane would dare be seen with one of her CDs, let alone buy one. Playing Nicole's songs in public was unpatriotic; in bars, whenever one of her hits came on the radio, someone would quickly change the station. Overnight, Nicole had become a symbol of all that the Lao hated about Thailand.

The truth of the allegation was largely immaterial. The controversy served only to demonstrate the fragile state of Thai-Lao relations, and the extraordinary sensitivity of the Lao to expressions of Thai superiority. Of course, the Lao had reason to be bitter: ethnic Lao were almost always portrayed on Thai TV as less civilized than their Thai brethren, usually appearing in the background as maids, gardeners, or other service workers. And this wasn't the first time a popular Thai singer had been accused of insulting Lao women. The last time, when a male star had publicly derided Laos and its people, there had been a nationwide campaign to burn the singer's tapes. The Lao had come to expect racism from the Thais, so it was easy for them to believe that Nicole actually had made the comments.

If the Lao were predisposed to accepting Nicole's guilt, their leaders only encouraged them. In fact, as the controversy unfolded,

I suspected that the Lao government was using the issue to distract its citizens from the intractable economic and political troubles facing the nation. In a country where there was no free press and little reliable information, it was easy enough to convince people of one conclusion despite evidence that pointed to quite another. People were used to relying on hearsay and rumor, rather than concrete proof. The government seemed to have no problem with these teenage boys' expression of free speech, and their posters were left untouched.

Thong, a Thai friend who worked in the marketing department at the Lao Hotel Plaza, was unimpressed by the entire affair. When Nicole had been to visit Laos, she had stayed at the hotel, and Thong had been assigned to take care of her throughout her time in Vientiane. One night, they had gone out to a nightclub with a group of Thais and Lao, and Thong recalled that Nicole had in fact made a point of emphasizing how much she liked Laos and its people. Thong suspected foul play on the part of the Lao government. "You see this brainwashing?" he asked me. "Just look at this thing with Nicole! I met her, and I know she couldn't have said it. She liked Laos, told me about the shyness of Lao women."

"So you think the government just made it up?" I asked.

"Hey, you didn't hear it from me," said Thong.

———

For the Lao, molding an independent identity in the shadow of one of Southeast Asia's most successful economies was a great challenge. With more ethnic Lao living in Northeastern Thailand than in Laos itself, the task was more a matter of defining who they were not as it was of defining who they were. For while my friends remained intensely proud of their own heritage, they had little to offer as an alternative to Thai popular culture. There simply was no Lao equivalent to a sensation like Nicole.

In fact, some of what was distinct about the landlocked country had already been absorbed into the Thai kingdom. The process had begun with the first invasion of Vientiane in 1778, when the sacred Emerald Buddha was taken by the Siamese to Bangkok, where it remains. But it continued even today. Before I left Vientiane, a domestic Thai airline had already begun offering direct flights from Bangkok to Luang Prabang, bypassing Vientiane completely. Package tours in Northeastern Thailand now included a short day-trip across the border. And the Tourism Authority of Thailand had even begun to advertise Luang Prabang as one of Thailand's own tourist attractions.

Laos had become just another part of Amazing Thailand.

Alone

The first time I met her was at a party, but I'd seen her before that Saturday night, many times. Vientiane is a small place, after all, and I had noticed her around town, at the restaurants and pubs. She spent a lot of her time around foreigners, men and women, which immediately set her apart from most other Lao women her age. I knew from observing her, even from afar, that Kee was unusual. She was lively and unabashed in her speech and gestures, never bothering to cover her mouth, for example, when she laughed. Her appearance was boyish: closely cropped, spiky hair; blue jeans and a faded T-shirt. It was nearly impossible to imagine her in the *sin* and silk blouse that most women in Vientiane wore. Demure she was not. And Kee spoke English—not perfectly, by any means, but well enough to engage in the playful banter that seemed to dominate her interactions with the foreigners she knew. By spending so much time around foreign men, I knew that Kee had made a choice. And for a Lao woman in her early twenties, that choice could be dangerous.

This party had been in the planning stages for some time. People had been talking it up, anticipating what promised to be a fun night at the home of two expats I knew well: Sarah and Melanie. Sarah was a few years older than I, a primary school teacher from Holland who had been hired by the Dutch community in Vientiane to teach their children. We had been friends since my first days in Vientiane, before her boyfriend from home had joined her. After he arrived in Laos and moved in with Sarah, we had inevitably grown apart, but I'd made an effort to keep in touch, and we still had dinner occasionally. Sarah and her boyfriend lived together for a while, but things didn't work out—for one thing, he couldn't find a job—and he left the country after a few months. Sarah soon picked up and moved in with Melanie, an Australian of about the same age, who taught English at a private language school. Melanie was larger-than-life, always dressed in wonderful, bright clothing. Her tie-dyed shirts and bell-bottoms were straight out of the 1970s. She had a prominent nose-ring, and traces of glitter often graced her face. Melanie tended to speak in riddles, and I was never quite sure how seriously to take her. She and Sarah smoked constantly, and they liked a good vodka tonic.

What I loved most of all about Sarah and Melanie was their deep affection for Laos, and their enthusiasm about life in Vientiane. They were exuberant about the culture, the local traditions, and the people they knew. Entirely absent from any conversation with these two were the sullen lamentations about life in Laos that marked discussions with many other expats in town. Sarah in particular was taken with Laos—and remained so even after her house had been broken into—and would speak about her life there with such excitement that I wondered if she'd ever return to Holland. Like me, she felt lucky to have been granted the opportunity to live and work in Vientiane, and was determined to make the most of it.

Sarah and Melanie had poured a lot of effort into this particular party, going so far as to print up invitations and craft a theme for the evening: "Come as you are *not*." The idea was for people to dress as differently as possible from the way they ordinarily did.

In essence, they encouraged guests to adopt entirely new personas for the evening. I'm usually not one for costumes, but I gave in to Melanie's unrelenting pressure, and on the afternoon of the party I set about putting something together.

I knew exactly where to head: just off Thadeua Road, near the banks of the main canal that ran through the center of town, where a series of impromptu tents had been set up. The proprietor of one offered to repair old shoes; another fixed watches; and a third—armed with large sheets of transparent plastic, an electric iron, and a clamp—provided lamination services. In the fourth tent, which served as a sort of Lao Salvation Army, you could find shirts, jackets, and shoes that, while they had been discarded, were in perfectly good condition. To the great amusement of the elderly woman who sat underneath the parachute that served as her umbrella and awning, I began trying on the old clothing, most of which was far too small. While creativity in dressing is hardly my forte, with some help I eventually came up with an outfit that looked ridiculous enough: a fluorescent orange and pink T-shirt, a blue jean-jacket from which the sleeves had been torn, and a pair of old Converse sneakers. With enough grease in my hair, I managed to look like a psychedelic James Dean, which, all things considered, wasn't bad. In any case, it wasn't me.

Late that evening, I walked over to Melanie and Sarah's place, just a few blocks—or temples, really—from mine. As I passed through the grounds of Wat Ong Teu, I greeted the novices who were lounging about outside their dormitory. They seemed unfazed by my absurd get-up. Just another crazy *falang* out for a stroll. As I approached my friends' house, I could hear the familiar strains of Cuban jazz drifting out into the warm night air. I immediately recognized the album: the *Buena Vista Social Club*, which was fast becoming something of a soundtrack to my life in Vientiane. During the previous weeks and months, whenever I'd been to a friend's home for dinner or a party, I had inevitably heard the heavy brass and joyous rhythms of the Havana masters. Whenever I did, I always thought of Chanh, who must have danced to this music in Cuba.

You see, there was only one CD shop in Vientiane that sold non-Lao (or Thai) music, and every young Westerner I knew shopped there. The tall, tanned, fit and friendly Frenchman who owned the shop along with his Lao wife, traveled to Bangkok occasionally to buy Western music, ranging from jazz to hip-hop, classical to rock. He'd make copies of the CDs at an undisclosed location in Vientiane, and then sell them at his shop for a few dollars. His selection was excellent—no Britney Spears or boy bands here—and you couldn't beat the price. It was limited though, and before long, everyone in Vientiane had the same music. If I ever heard any new tunes around town, I'd know that the Frenchman had recently returned from Bangkok, and it was time to pay him a visit.

When I arrived at the party, the festivities were well under way. All the usual suspects were present. Sarah and Melanie were resplendent in sequins and pearls, high heels and mascara. In the dining room, converted to a dance floor, Jon, a lawyer from Oregon who now worked on environmental issues in Laos and Vietnam, was in a tutu. Michel was there as well, dancing up a storm in his loose, organic style. And then there was the inimitable Danny, a large, bearded red-head and computer specialist from New Zealand, outfitted in black combat boots and fixing himself a drink or three in the kitchen.

But expats weren't the only ones at the party. The best thing about gatherings like these was that they always attracted a good mixture of foreigners and their Lao students, colleagues, and friends. These two groups, despite vast differences in culture, language, and life experience, interacted with effortless comfort and ease. Of course, the Lao were often amused and even perplexed by the strange traditions of their foreign friends (at this party, only a few had taken the hosts up on their suggestion to wear a costume) and there was some inevitable segregation. But, for the most part, the atmosphere was one of free and equal exchange. As far apart as these people might have been—I often wondered what on earth a young man from Croydon or Tasmania had in common with a guy from the suburbs of Vientiane—they respected one another and got along well. On the other hand, this interaction only went so far. Romantic relationships across the cultural divide were extremely rare; only a handful of young expats had taken the plunge with a Lao man or woman. Of those who did, most failed, and quickly.

That night, I was in the mood to dance, and I soon joined the growing crowd on the makeshift dance floor. Sarah had replaced the *Buena Vista Social Club* with Earth, Wind, and Fire, and already there wasn't much space to move. I danced all the time in Vientiane, but mostly at wedding receptions and old-fashioned nightclubs. The *lamvong*, which demanded delicacy and restraint, just wasn't the same as this disco. Lost among the guests at Sarah and Melanie's, a few feet from the towering speakers they'd rented for the evening, I felt a freedom I hadn't felt in some time. Released from the constraints of traditional Lao custom, I let loose.

I'm not sure when I first saw Kee that night. At some point, though, I found myself dancing opposite her. I was immediately taken by her full lips and broad, warm smile. In a tight grey T-shirt and camouflage military trousers, she had managed to wear a costume and look good at the same time. I leaned forward, brushing her smooth cheek with mine as I shouted an introduction in her ear. She did the same. Soon enough, her hands were around my waist, and our bodies were close. I knew that people were watching—the next day, word would spread quickly—but perhaps the combination of the alcohol and the heat led me to ignore the attention.

After a few songs, I suggested we go outside for some air. As we sat on the front steps, near the herd of motorbikes parked out front, Kee told me a bit about her life. She worked at a bar downtown, but lived with her family in a small village a few kilometers outside Vientiane. She had yet to save up enough money to buy a motorbike, and was stuck with only a bicycle. As she spoke, I couldn't help but notice the sweat that accentuated the spikes in her hair. It glistened in the light. I placed my hand on the back of her neck, and felt the sweat against my skin. When I offered her a ride home on the Honda Dream, still parked at my house, she accepted without hesitation.

Before I knew it, we were stumbling toward my house, hand-in-hand, carefully avoiding the gaping holes in the pavement that led to the drains below, relics of the sewerage system the French had installed a century before. I've no idea what time it was by then, but it must have been late, as the streets were deserted. The rush of motorbikes that hit downtown at about one o'clock, when the city's nightclubs shut their doors and the teenagers made their way home, had already come and gone. We probably made more noise than we should have, and a neighborhood dog barked its disapproval. As we passed through the temple grounds, I wouldn't be surprised if we inadvertently roused the novices from their slumber. If not the novices, then the neighbors. Informal militias throughout Laos, along with neighborhood committees, were responsible for maintaining public order and reporting instances of moral turpitude to the Interior Ministry. Every so often, I would run into an armed militia volunteer strolling about the neighborhood, making sure everything was in order. Someone was always watching and listening.

Safely inside the house and behind closed doors, leaning against the wall in my living room, we kissed for the first time. It was a clumsy affair, I'm sure. But it was nice. Her lips tasted good. So did her neck, slightly salty from the sweat. The supposed ride home was quickly forgotten.

While Kee was in the shower, I went upstairs to my bedroom. I turned on the two powerful ceiling fans in an attempt to cut down on the heat, and also to create some background noise. I could hear most everything my neighbors did. A baby's scream, the lively conversation at a dinner party—I heard it all. Just a few nights before, I'd woken up to a heated argument between the Vietnamese couple next door. Eventually the words had softened, and I thought they had come to a resolution. Later, though, I could hear the quiet sound of tears. In this weather, I couldn't close the windows, so I relied on the fans to keep the neighbors out of my life.

As I lay in bed, waiting for Kee to come upstairs, I thought about the neighbors. I also thought about how Kee was feeling, what she was thinking. I probably thought as well about what the morning would bring. But when Kee finally crawled into bed with me, I stopped thinking.

———

It was early afternoon by the time I stirred, and Kee was still asleep. I gazed at her body for some time, dwelling on each of the features I liked the most, before she finally woke up. She seemed exhausted, as if she hadn't had a good sleep in months. Unfortunately, though, we couldn't lie there forever, and Kee quickly got going. After all, her parents would be wondering. Refusing a ride, she left for the bar where she worked, and where she had left her bicycle. On her way out the door, she wondered aloud if she would see me again. "I'm sure you will," I answered, and waved good-bye.

But the truth was, I wasn't sure at all. It had been wonderful, but the more I thought about Kee, the more I began to worry. Who was this girl, after all? I didn't know her age. I wasn't even sure of her name. Above all, I couldn't separate any potential relationship with her from the fact that I was a foreigner, and she a Lao. In cities across Asia, I'd seen white men and Asian women together, and they had often made me feel uneasy. The cultural disparity and power imbalance was striking. I couldn't escape what many people on both sides of the cultural divide thought about couples like these: that the men only cared about the sex, and the women just wanted the money—and perhaps even a ticket to the West. Of course, this was not always, or even usually, the case, but the perception was widely held. I had never had a relationship with an Asian woman, and I'm sure this was partly due to my discomfort with the whole idea. Back in the States, people spoke derisively of men with an "Asian fetish." It seems silly to me now to have felt so strongly about it, but I was determined not to end up a mere stereotype.

After I showered and dressed, I tried to go about my usual routine. I spent a few hours at the office working on a brochure with Seng. He joined me for lunch at the noodle shop next door to the office. After work, I went to the gym, and then met Michel at the Liao Ning dumpling shop for a quick dinner. But I couldn't really concentrate on much, and I was preoccupied throughout the day. My mind was elsewhere, and I went to sleep thinking about Kee.

The next morning, when I stumbled downstairs to take a shower, I was still half asleep. But as I passed the living room, I noticed that something wasn't quite right. Usually, the morning sun streamed through the glass doors that opened onto the living room. But that morning, the room was entirely dark. After a moment, I realized that the outer metal gate had been pulled shut. I never closed this gate unless I went away for more than a few days. Perhaps, I thought, the landlady had closed it as a security measure. I hadn't put on my glasses yet, so I couldn't see very well. But as I moved toward the front of the living room, I did notice some pink coloring on the inner glass doors. Upon closer inspection, I saw that these pink spots were in fact words. The large, clumsy letters had been scrawled in pink lipstick on the outside of the door on the right. I opened it so that I could properly read the following words:

"Do you remember me? I am Kee. Call me. 212 345. Do not forget me! Kee."

She must have come over in the middle of the night, left her message, and then pulled the gate shut to hide it. Had she knocked? Had I been asleep at the time? Had anyone seen her? After the initial surprise, my first thought was that the words had to be erased as soon as possible. I could hear the couple next door getting ready to leave for work, and the last thing I needed was for them to discover a message scrawled in hot pink lipstick on their neighbor's door. In nothing but my towel, wrapped tightly around my waist, I went to the kitchen for a bucket of water, soap and a sponge, and quickly washed the lipstick away. Looking back on it now, I am surprised by how uncomfortable Kee's message made me feel. I might just as well have been overjoyed at her words. I might even have taken a photograph. Instead, I was in such a hurry to get rid of the words that I didn't even write down her number.

I doubt this was an oversight. I was frightened. I was afraid to get too close. After all, what did Kee and I have in common? How would a relationship between us ever last? What would we talk about? I couldn't bring myself to limit my thoughts to the short term, to simply view things casually. I knew that there really was no such a thing as a "casual" relationship in Laos. It simply wasn't done. Things were changing, yes, but Laos remained an extremely traditional society, and women weren't expected to become involved with men outside of marriage. So when I thought of a relationship with Kee, I thought immediately of the other foreign men I'd met in Vientiane who had married Lao women and were now struggling with the cultural clash. Not to mention the administrative nightmare of securing a visa so their wives could actually visit their homes and families back in the West.

But most frightening of all was the thought that I might fall for Kee. Then where would I be? Images of her on the back of my motorbike, visiting me every night after work, sleeping at my house, and eventually moving in—all of these appeared in my mind as clearly as if they had already occurred. In many ways, of course, they struck me as wonderful, beautiful, as exactly what I wanted in my life. I was lonely, living by myself in a large house, far from home. I hadn't been in a serious relationship in years. But my thoughts always returned to the moment when I would have to leave. I had returned to work there for another year, but I wouldn't be in Laos forever.

So, without even giving it a chance, I decided not to pursue a relationship with Kee. This decision took some self restraint, to be sure. I liked her a lot, and I needed someone. But restraint had never been a problem for me. At its root, this decision was all about my cowardice. I just couldn't bring myself to fall for Kee. So I left it. In any case, I convinced myself, I didn't have her number. I couldn't call her. Rather than confronting my feelings for Kee, I ran away from them. Or, at least, I tried.

———————

About a week later, some time after midnight, I was lying in bed, trying to fall asleep. It wasn't easy, given the heat and the thoughts that wouldn't leave me. All of a sudden, I heard a loud banging on the glass doors downstairs. I knew immediately who it was. The banging persisted, followed by the rattling of the metal gate outside.

At the foot of the stairs, I stopped at the doorway of the living room and peered out through the glass doors. Sure enough, there she was, pacing back and forth outside. She was wearing a Walkman, and holding a can of beer. Before she had a chance to make her presence known again, I hurried over and opened the front door. The music in her Walkman, Nicole's latest, was so loud I could hear it through her headphones. She began to shout, so I quickly pulled her inside, and then shut and locked the door.

Kee smelled of beer and smoke. When I removed her headphones and asked her what she was doing, she laughed loudly. She was drunk. "You didn't call," she said.

"Um, I lost the number," I replied feebly.

"You lie." She laughed again, took another sip of her Heineken.

"So what are you doing here?"

"You lie!"

"Why aren't you at home?"

She didn't answer, but instead shut off the Walkman, plopped down on the sofa, and put her feet up on the coffee table. I went back to the kitchen and poured some bottled water. I had been in Laos long enough to know that, even at two in the morning, I couldn't invite someone in without offering them at least a glass of water. When I came back and sat down, Kee began to talk. She told me more about her family, the difficulty of finding work, how she hated living at home along with three siblings and her parents. She hinted that she and her father didn't get along well. I sensed that she wasn't talking about the occasional verbal disagreement, that the situation was far more serious.

"My father, he doesn't like me," she said.

"I'm sorry—" I began, but she cut me off before I could continue. "No, don't."

She talked as well about the man whom she'd been involved with for some time. He was German, and quite a bit older—in his thirties, perhaps. I might even have known him, and as she talked, a list of possible suspects ran through my head. She had essentially moved in with him, but due to his job he was away from Vientiane for months at a time. It struck me that her romance with the German had destroyed whatever relationship she had with her family. Moving in with an older foreign man could not have been a good move. The German didn't treat her well, she said, didn't care much for what she thought or how she felt. "But you, you let me feel . . ." she began, and then broke off.

We sat quietly for a few minutes, gazing out through the glass in the front door. I had no idea what to say. Why had she decided to tell me all of this?

A stray cat ambled up to the house, hunting for food. Suddenly, Kee turned to me. "Can I be your girlfriend?" she asked.

I thought for only a moment before responding, "I don't think so." I was prepared to go through with her what had been on my mind over the last week; to provide some sort of rationalization for my feelings, some explanation of my behavior. But Kee didn't ask for any of that. Perhaps she already knew my reasons. She just smiled, nodded, and took another sip of beer.

"Can I stay here tonight?" she asked.

There was no way she was going to make it very far on her bicycle, and I was too tired to drive her, so I said yes. But I did insist that she stay in the guest room. After she took a shower, I led her upstairs across the hall from where I slept. She crawled under the covers and closed her eyes. I kissed her on the cheek, said good-night, and shut the door behind me. Exhausted, I collapsed on my bed and, for the first time in days, fell asleep without any trouble.

When I woke up, just before dawn, Kee was lying next to me, staring directly into my eyes. I wasn't surprised, of course. I'd been hoping she would come over. We said nothing, but held each other for some time. Eventually, when the sun had just begun to rise, she decided it was time to go. I tasted her lips for the last time, and she crawled out of bed, leaving me alone to drift off to sleep again.

When I finally left for work, the Heineken was still sitting on the coffee table downstairs. The can was almost empty, but not quite. I took a sip of the warm beer, and then poured what was left of it down the drain.

———————

There's an old Lao folk tale Desa told me about during one of our last conversations, at his home in Vientiane. It was a story Desa's father liked to recount to his children long ago, and one that he had translated into French and published in an old issue of the *Bulletin des Amis du Royaume Lao*. Desa's father was a master of channeling the tales that had grown out of Laos' great oral story-telling tradition through the more traditional Western medium of the written word. The story is called "The Two Sparrows," and it goes something like this:

It was a very hot year, and the trees in the forest were all dried out. The branches would break in even the slightest breeze, and the birds were on the alert for anyone who might set the trees on fire. Two sparrows, a mother and father, sad and resigned, kept watch from their nests.

"If the fire takes the forests," said the mother, "I will die with my children."

"Me too," said the father.

One day, a fire broke out and chased the frightened animals. The two sparrows reaffirmed their pledge, and decided to die with their children. But at the moment when the fire reached the tree where they were perched, the male flew away. The female, faithful and unswerving, threw herself into the furnace with her children. But not before pledging never to talk to another male in all her lives to come.

In another life, the sparrow was re-born the daughter of a great king. But she refused to speak to anyone other than her mother and her servants. When she turned 18, her father proclaimed throughout the land that he would give his daughter's hand in marriage, and the entire kingdom, to anyone who could succeed in reconciling the princess with men. Princes and kings tried, always in vain, to persuade the ravishing young girl to talk. One day, a prince, more handsome than all the others, began to tell the princess a story.

"Once upon a time," he said, "there were two sparrows who loved each other and had many children. One day a fire took the forest. Husband and wife decided together to perish in the fire with their children. But, just when they had to execute their promise, the female took off—"

"It was the male," replied the princess, indignant.

She had spoken.

The court musicians began to play songs of joy, and preparations for the wedding began.

After that morning, I no longer saw Kee around town. I kept an eye out for her at the pubs where once I would have seen her joking with her friends, but she never seemed to be around anymore. I even went to the bar where she'd been working. She wasn't there either. I wasn't sure what I would say to her, but I did want to know that she was all right.

Then, one rainy afternoon a few months later, I happened to stop in at the Xang Café. The Xang was a small coffee shop on Silom Road owned by a young Brit who'd lived in Vientiane for a few years. It was about the only place in Laos that resembled a coffee shop you might find in an American city. Here, you could even get a latté, and granola with fruit. The idea behind the Xang was great, but the execution wasn't, and I rarely went there. Among other things, the owner had a reputation for mistreating his staff, and the employees always struck me as miserable.

As soon as I entered the shop, I saw her. She was standing alone behind the bar, leafing through a magazine. She was dressed conservatively, and didn't seem too comfortable. This was the first time I'd seen her in a dress. When the door closed behind me, Kee looked up, but she didn't smile. She seemed like a different person from the girl I'd met so many months before. I felt as if her spirit had been snuffed out. I was the only customer, and she the only employee, so we couldn't avoid each other. I smiled and sat down at a table in the corner. When she came over, menu in hand, I ordered a cappuccino, and asked her how she was.

"Fine. And you?"

"Oh, fine. It's been a while."

"Yes, it has."

And that was it. She went back to the bar to prepare my coffee, and then served it to me without a word. Soon, she was distracted by another customer. The owner came in and gave her some instructions. As I sipped my drink and pretended to read a week-old issue of the *Bangkok Post*, I wondered about what I had done. Had I made the right decision? Why had I been so scared to get close to her? What would a relationship between us have been like? Now, of course, I would never know.

I finished the cappuccino, left a few thousand kip on the table, and walked out, alone.

Party Time

Living in Vientiane, it was easy to forget that Laos was a communist country. Sure, the Lao People's Revolutionary Party had a stranglehold on political power, and it exercised enormous influence over people's everyday lives. There was no free press, no freedom of speech, and only the slightest rumblings of dissent. In the mid-1990s, in fact, three civil servants had been jailed for forming a group called the Democracy Club; they hadn't been heard from since. Nevertheless, the Party was always careful to remain unassuming in its public displays of power.

Many of the tourists I ran into in Vientiane hadn't the faintest idea that Laos was under communist rule. Their Lonely Planets were chock full of information about the politics, history, and culture of Laos, but they had somehow managed to miss the fact that the country was in fact a socialist republic. So preoccupied were these visitors with securing cheap rooms, good beer, and tasty banana pancakes (not to mention potent ganja), Laos' political situation had simply escaped them. Some would even argue with me, unable to square their knowledge about communism in the Soviet Union and Eastern Europe with what they saw in Vientiane.

"If this place is communist," they would ask, "then where are all the communists? Where's the hammer and sickle? And the secret police?"

In fact, these folks were right to be surprised. It often seemed to me as if the Party was trying its best to hide its ideological foundations. If you looked carefully, of course, you could find hints of the political leanings of the regime. For example, Vientiane's cityscape was dotted with a handful of government-erected billboards that pictured hard-working peasants and engineers, always sure to include equal numbers of men and women, and representatives of each of Laos' main ethnic groups—comrades, all treated equally, coming together to build a better future. These perpetually cheery, two-dimensional characters toiled beneath messages that grandly proclaimed the inevitable progress that would result from dedication to the Party's leadership. Unfortunately, by the time I got to Vientiane, the paint on these billboards had already begun to peel, and the words of inspiration were barely decipherable. This state-sponsored artwork of the social realist school hailed from an era that had passed.

In perhaps the surest sign that such imagery had been relegated to antiquity, these billboards and posters had become collector's items, even inside Laos. In a back issue of the long defunct Lao Aviation in-flight magazine, I came upon a story about a Western expat and her husband who had begun to buy up the art. A photograph featured a striking poster of a Lao People's Army soldier that had been prominently displayed in the salon of the couple's villa in Vientiane. I found it telling that this socialist artwork had been appropriated by two of the city's foreign residents—who until recently would have been barred from even entering the country. But if the paintings weren't of any use to the government anymore, and the people didn't want them, why not sell them to wealthy Westerners?

The Party had good reason to be skittish about flaunting its communist credentials. Laos' leadership had learned the hard way that hard-line communist rule just wasn't going to work in this small Southeast Asian nation. Under the leadership of the father of Lao communism, Kaysone Phomvihane, the Lao PDR's first prime minister and eventually its president, the government embarked on a project of overzealous socialist experimentation after it came to power in 1975. The Party had sharply curtailed the private sector, forced the collectivization of agriculture, and curbed the free practice of religion. In 1976, it had even banned the popular village *boun bang fai*, or rocket festivals, which celebrated the annual harvest. Proclaiming Laos the key "outpost of socialism in Southeast Asia," Kaysone had launched the co-operativization campaign himself in 1978. The end result was severe drought, crop shortage, a resurgence of malaria—and a popular revolt. Those who didn't end up fleeing the country—eventually, a whopping ten per cent of the population—made it clear that the government would have to change course if it intended to stay in power.

In the early 1980s, under Kaysone's pragmatic leadership, the Party abruptly shifted course. Following the lead of its mentors in Hanoi, Vientiane implemented what it called the New Economic Mechanism. This program of reform was accompanied by a steady loosening of control over citizens' daily life, particularly in the sphere of religion. Soon, even Party officials began to wrap themselves in the mantle of traditional Lao culture, smoothing the hard edges of communist rule with comforting Buddhist ritual, to ensure that the people would never again rebel against Party hegemony.

But beyond the support of its citizenry, the Party also had the international community to think about. Key to the success of the New Economic Mechanism, particularly after the collapse of the Soviet Union, was a steady influx of aid from the West. To ensure that Western donors would continue to line up at the border, blank checkbooks in hand, the government had to keep its communist credentials backstage. In stark contrast to its authoritarian neighbor, Burma, an international pariah, Laos had managed to convince the donor community that it was a "kinder, gentler" one-party regime. After Kaysone died in 1992, the government stepped up its effort to make friends with rich powers, East and West. To stay afloat in the alphabet soup of aid agencies and NGOs that flooded Vientiane, the Party carefully replaced its soaring rhetoric about imperialist pigs and capitalist lackeys with soothing words about economic reform, democracy, and human rights. All this would have pleased Kaysone, who was the ultimate pragmatist.

It took more than an hour of concerted searching, wrong turns, and many puzzled looks before I finally arrived at the Kaysone Phomvihane Memorial and Museum. I'd decided to embark on this pilgrimage the day before, while at the office, but none of my colleagues were much help. The memorial struck me as a good tourist attraction in a city that otherwise had very few—not all foreign visitors were unaware of Laos' past, and some were actually very interested—and I figured that I'd better learn something about it. But it hadn't occurred to any of my colleagues that the museum would be of any interest to me or any other foreign tourist, and I couldn't find one who had actually been there. Mon, who had studied in Kiev at the height of Soviet influence in Laos during Kaysone's rule, was perplexed when I told her of my plans for the weekend. She had heard something about the memorial, but the best she could offer was a vague sense of where it might be. She told me to head south out of the city on Route 13 for about six kilometers, and then take a left when I saw an old Shell station. Mon certainly couldn't guarantee that the museum would actually be open when (and if) I arrived. When I suggested that she and her husband and adorable young son might want to come along for a weekend outing, she quite literally laughed in my face.

Undeterred, on a bright Saturday morning, after a good dose of Lao coffee and a fresh baguette smothered in sweetened condensed milk, I strapped on a helmet, got on the Honda Dream, and headed south. It was early enough that the temperature was still cool, and the breeze felt good on my face as I sped past the Patuxai. I whizzed by the UN office and the Lao People's Army Museum, where I was working once or twice a week with a young soldier to put together an English translation of the exhibit. And I drove past the National Assembly and recently erected monument to the nation's war dead, which had been designed to look like a traditional Buddhist stupa.

As soon as I reached the outskirts of the city, my pleasant journey came to a halt when the pavement abruptly ended, and I hit the maelstrom of road construction that recently blown into town. As part of the capital's "development," the government, along with assistance from the World Bank and various other foreign donors, had embarked on an ambitious project to rebuild Vientiane's entire road network. This involved ripping up the existing roads, laying down new pipes for sewerage, and then, at some point far down the road, re-paving. Vientiane's thoroughfares hadn't received much attention since the heady, cash-soaked days of America's war presence, so this was certainly a necessary project. Unfortunately, someone in the city bureaucracy had come up with the ingenious idea of contracting out different pieces of the project to different companies—a Korean contractor here, an Italian one there—all at the same time. As a result, there was no co-ordination at all, and over the months to come there would be days in Vientiane when you couldn't get where you needed to go, because most of the main roads had disappeared. Left in their place were dirt tracks and muddy canals, like a jumbo racetrack in the States. Expats and wealthy Lao responded as you might expect: they purchased ever larger and more powerful four-wheel-drives to navigate the increasingly dodgy urban road network. The rest of us were left behind in the dust. And at the NTA, it made Vientiane an increasingly difficult place to sell as a "relaxing" tourist destination.

It was shock enough when the asphalt disappeared from beneath my wheels. Worse still, in the middle of the road sat a series of enormous concrete cylinders, which were to be set into the ground to replace the nineteenth-century drains. It was a Saturday, of course, so no work was being done, but these cylinders, taller than my motorbike and I, had been left in the middle of the road nevertheless. This made the road something of a slalom course, the cars, motorbikes, and occasional tractors weaving in and out of the cylinders. This race was made even more challenging by the dust that swirled about us. I couldn't see farther than a few feet ahead, and had to rely on the wheels of the motorbike in front as a guide. Just as my frustration—and fear for my life, to be frank—began to overwhelm me, I looked to my right and saw a middle-aged man leading a herd of cows down the road. The cows' hooves were slipping and sliding in the dirt, and as he swatted their backs with a switch of bamboo with one hand, he used the other to hold a piece of cloth over his mouth to keep the dust out. He removed it long enough to look over at me, smile, and shrug, as if to say, "Well, what can you do? Maybe one day we'll have good roads, and all this will have been worth it." Maybe so, I thought, and smiled back.

Unlike many others out on the road that day, I was wearing my helmet with a transparent plastic face shield that worked to keep at least some of the dust out of my eyes. I didn't always wear a helmet in Vientiane, I must admit, but I was glad of it that day. Eventually, through the clouds of dust, I caught a glimpse of a Shell station to my left. I crossed my fingers, hoped for the best, flipped on my blinker (a futile gesture), turned in between two of the pipes in the road, and veered onto a side street that led out of the storm and into a quiet suburban neighborhood. I took a few moments to catch my breath and wipe the dust from my eyelids before I set about trying to find the museum. At the first few shops and houses where I asked for directions, I encountered mostly blank stares. These people did know who Kaysone was, but most had no idea that there was actually a national museum dedicated to him. Many directed me to his gravestone, a stupa located back near the center of town. Some even wondered if I was looking for his hometown, Savannakhet, more than a day's journey away—and certainly more than my Honda could handle.

Eventually, I came upon a small noodle shop in a more isolated area of the neighborhood. Exhausted, I sat down for a Pepsi and began to chat with the owner, who wondered what on earth I was doing out in this area of town. Though I was hesitant to raise the subject of my elusive destination yet again, weary of rejection, I told him. It took the man a few minutes before he realized what I was talking about, but once I made myself clear with extended references to the great leader of the Lao people, the revolutionary hero who had liberated his country from colonialism and oppression, he responded with mild enthusiasm.

"Oh yeah, I know about that museum," he said. "I've never been, of course, but I have heard about it."

Finally, I was getting somewhere. "Do you know where it is?" I asked.

"Sure, it's right there." He pointed directly across the street to a fenced-in forested area and an unmarked, wide-open gate. So here it was, Laos' national memorial and museum dedicated to the founding president of the country, the equivalent of Uncle Ho in Vietnam or Chairman Mao in China—and it didn't even have a sign. Why was Kaysone hiding?

After thanking the shop owner profusely, I downed the last of my Pepsi and ambled up to the open gate. Immediately, a guard emerged from the sentry box hidden behind the fence, and demanded to know what I was doing there.

"Um, to see the museum," I replied, a tad sheepishly.

"The museum? What country are you from?"

"America," I responded, albeit with a certain reluctance. Images of the US bombing campaign in Northern Laos and Kaysone's heroic role in the long struggle for independence came immediately to mind. Much of the museum, I imagined, was dedicated to recounting the dark history of America's involvement here, and the great success that Kaysone had had in leading Laos into the light. There may not have been a sign above the gate, but there was a national flag, and I felt the white sphere in its center, which symbolized the light of communism, burn into my American imperialist self.

"Oh, America, very good!" the guard replied, and his harsh demeanor instantly disappeared. "*Chao ben kon Amelika baw? Dee lai!*" He placed a call from his sentry hut to the museum, to let the receptionist know that a rare visitor had arrived, then proceeded to tell me where I'd find the entrance. He waved as I drove down the long, tree-lined driveway that led to a clearing in the forest. There, I found a collection of one-story, ranch-style brick houses that brought to mind the new suburban neighborhoods that had sprouted up all over America after World War II.

That this place would strike me as a Lao Levittown was no coincidence. The Kaysone memorial and museum, which officially opened in 1994, was located inside the former compound of the US Information Agency, or USIA. It was from the comfort of this suburban paradise at Kilometer Six that the Americans had operated their extensive aid programs and information campaigns during the 1960s and early 70s. Today, it had the unsettling feel of a deserted Anytown, the appealing set for a TV program like "Leave it to Beaver," but without any of the actors. In my mind, I could picture the wholesome American families that had been stationed here in the days leading up to the end of the Vietnam War. Sheltered from the realities of a deteriorating political situation outside, American kids would ride up and down the paved streets on bicycles. When it got too late, their mothers would call them inside, and they'd be welcomed home to the cool relief of their air-conditioned kitchens and a plate of freshly baked chocolate-chip cookies and milk. This was the unreality of American life in Vientiane before the communists took over, and it was carefully preserved up until the very end.

Soon after Kaysone assumed power in December 1975, he and his fellow cadres established their headquarters at the former USIA compound, taking up residence in the homes of their former American enemies. Kaysone lived by himself at Kilometer Six from 1976 until his death in 1992; his family, it seems, lived elsewhere, a slight perversion of the paradisiacal suburbanite lifestyle to which he seemed to aspire. It was from this place that, sequestered behind whitewashed walls, Kaysone orchestrated the failed socialist experiment of his early years in power. Just like the US imperialists before them, the new communist rulers were isolated from the reality of the changing political situation around them.

I was greeted at the entrance to one of the buildings by the receptionist, a young woman neatly dressed in an official green army shirt and *sin*. She directed me first to a meeting room in which a small TV had been placed beneath a portrait of Marx and Engels. The scratchy black-and-white film recounted, in Lao, the basics of Kaysone's life. He had been born Cai Song to a Lao mother and Vietnamese father in Savannakhet in 1920. As a young man he lived in Hanoi, where he studied law, and eventually helped to organize the anti-French resistance movement in the 1940s. Along with 25 other founding members, Kaysone helped to establish Laos' own communist organization, the Lao People's Party, in 1955 in Sam Neua, a small city in the north. Much of the film was dedicated to wartime footage of Kaysone leading enthusiastic communist forces into battle against the Americans. After their victory, he served as prime minister from the founding of Lao PDR in 1975 until his death at age 72 on November 21st, 1992. In a sign of just how much the regime's approach to religion had changed in the nearly twenty years since it had come to power, Buddhist rites were performed during the week-long mourning period following Kaysone's death, and he was cremated in accordance with Buddhist tradition. Given the emphasis in Buddhism on the immateriality of human life, embalming Kaysone in a mausoleum was clearly out of the question. Deprived of a common means of perpetuating the legacy of a fallen communist hero, the new leaders set about creating a museum in his honor—with funding from the Vietnamese government.

A tour of the exhibition itself begins in a hall dedicated to Kaysone's life and that of the nation—the history of Laos and its revolutionary struggle is depicted as a journey paralleling Kaysone's own life story. The exhibit is clearly modeled after the much larger paean to Ho Chi Minh in Hanoi, and even uses similar exhibits like the (albeit rather more crude) diorama displays of important scenes from Kaysone's life, from his humble beginnings and early childhood to his orchestration of the war effort from caves in Northern Laos. The kitschy mock-ups of him deep inside the caves at Vieng Xay reduce what was in fact a genuinely heroic time in his life to a cheap papier-mâché imitation.

In plastic display cases throughout the hall was Kaysone memorabilia: the notebooks he filled while at school, the binoculars he looked at the enemy with, the glasses he used to read with when his eyesight began to fail. Prominently displayed in the center of the hall was one of sixty-odd golden busts of Kaysone that were donated by North Korea—a regime well-versed in the cultivation of cults. These busts have been erected all over the country, at the provincial, district, and even village levels. Whenever I came upon them—in Muang Sing, Luang Nam Tha, Oudomxay, and other out-of-the-way places—these statues always seemed lonely and ignored, summarily shunted off to the side. They struck me as forlorn attempts to convince a people that Kaysone was a man they should not only admire, but worship. It didn't seem to be working.

Kaysone may have been the "Son of the People"—as the title of the government's official 1991 biography put it—but no one seemed to care. I didn't meet a single Lao in the two years I lived there who had ever been to see the museum. At the entrance to the first exhibit hall, I was handed a small golden pin in the shape of Kaysone's silhouette as a souvenir. This gesture was clearly an attempt to further the creation of a "cult of Kaysone," but it only served to remind me of the project's utter futility. Around Vientiane, I did see photographs, pins, and other trinkets that represented the faces of some of Laos' important historical leaders, but Kaysone was never among them. Living room walls bore far more likenesses of Laos' last king, his brother Prince Pethsarath—who was thought to have magical powers—or even King Chulalongkorn of Thailand than any representations of Kaysone. This son of the people had been disowned.

In China, Mao Zedong still makes frequent appearances in households across the country, even though the government has admitted that one third of what he did was wrong. In Vietnam, I was always struck by the degree of reverence even people my age had for Ho Chi Minh. But in Vientiane, I rarely heard anyone so much as mention Kaysone's name. If I were ever to bring him up in conversation, the strongest reaction I could ever elicit was that he was an "important" historical figure. The only people who really seemed to get excited about Kaysone were visitors from abroad. In the museum's guest registration book, a few pages had been left blank for comments. But the only thoughts I could find had been inscribed by representatives of the various foreign communist parties that had made official visits to Laos since the museum's opening in 1994. The book included wishes of health and happiness from comrades in Nepal, Cuba, and even Canada. "The heroic Laotian people," one wrote, "have freed themselves under the able leadership of its important leader, Kaysone."

I signed my name, adding a far simpler message. Just as I closed the book, a fleet of black sedans with tinted windows pulled up to the museum entrance. A group of men emerged from the cars, each dressed in matching suits and sunglasses. As far as I could gather from their lively chatter, these were representatives of China's government in town on an official visit. They were welcomed by a group of young women who had gathered on the museum's steps to greet them, flowers, ribbons—and of course, Kaysone pins—in hand. Before the Chinese entered the exhibition hall, I was whisked away by one of the receptionists and led to the next section of the museum. As we made our way past a slightly overgrown lawn of lush green grass (another suburban American fantasy) to another building nearby, I let my guide know what was on my mind.

"Do *Lao* people ever visit this museum?"

"Not really," she told me. "Only school groups and government officials. You know, it's so far from the center of the city."

Perhaps the Party had decided to place the museum so far from the center of things because they didn't *want* the "people" to come and visit. After all, whatever one thought about his political beliefs and approach to governance, Kaysone had been a strong leader. He had stood up to the French and the Americans, and though he could not have done so without the help of his Vietnamese comrades, he had prevailed. Kaysone had had a vision, and he had achieved it. While he may have presided over a disastrous socialist experiment, he had been pragmatic enough to know when it was time to change course. That alone was more than most Lao people could say for their current leadership.

Kaysone was succeeded by his former deputy prime minister and defense minister, Khamtay Siphandone, the father of one of my colleagues at the NTA. Khamtay seemed more interested in finding ways to benefit personally from the New Economic Mechanism than in promoting real economic growth. He maintained close ties to the country's military, and what passed for economic development often amounted to the timber contracts and trading concessions he secretly negotiated on its behalf. It's true that Vientiane had been transformed in the years since Kaysone's funeral; what had been a sleepy town of bicycles, empty roads, and a strict seven o'clock curfew had become a hectic, neo-capitalist free-for-all. But almost all new wealth was concentrated in the capital, and most of it resulted from the sudden influx of international aid, not any economic boom that Khamtay had orchestrated. One display case at the Kaysone museum was all too revealing, containing as it did, every product 'manufactured' in the Lao PDR: Beer Lao, Pepsi, lumber, cigarettes, and cement.

The only vision for the future that Khamtay seemed to offer came in the image of his new private mansion in Vientiane. His dream house, constructed mostly with materials imported from Thailand, was a glimmering white edifice that towered above all the surrounding homes. A set of tall, thin columns graced the main entrance, and the complex was surrounded by a blank white wall topped with barbed metal spikes. A new sidewalk had been constructed around the perimeter—although the only people I ever saw there were members of the household staff, who washed the outer wall daily. Among the first roads to be completed in the city's reconstruction project were those surrounding the new house, which was situated directly next to the compound in which Khamtay and his family lived, and from which Khamtay rarely emerged. Certainly the largest private home in Laos, the new place was actually meant as a gift to the president's daughter—my colleague at the NTA—and her fiancé. It was always big news at work whenever she returned from a shopping trip to Thailand armed with a new set of drapes, tiles, and other furnishings for her future home.

Khamtay's monstrosity stood in striking contrast to Kaysone's private living quarters at Kilometer Six, which was the highlight of the memorial and museum and the next stop on my tour. Compared with the opulence enjoyed by today's Party cadres, Kaysone's life at Kilometer Six was a modest affair. He lived in a small, one-bedroom house, along with most of his important possessions. Even today, the bookshelves in the living room—which is carpeted, wall-to-wall, with the green shag that was so popular then—were filled with Kaysone's favorite works in Lao, French, English, Russian, and Vietnamese. For a man who once proclaimed, "The best university is the university of the people," Kaysone certainly liked to read. His running shoes and stationary exercise bike stood in the very spot where he left them. His meeting room was located in the house's modest screened-in porch, and according to my guide, the notes on the dry-erase board that you can read today are the very same that were taken on his final working day.

Standing in Kaysone's living room, it became clear why the current regime really might not want its citizens there. A visit might lead some to draw unfavorable comparisons. Perhaps it was better to keep them as politically disinterested in the recent past as they were in the immediate present. What with a glorious king and a magical prince already occupying people's thoughts, who needed another dead leader for people to dream about?

As I've said, it was rare indeed that I encountered any overt symbols of communist rule in Vientiane. So I was surprised to find an enormous red flag bearing the hammer and sickle soaring above the main entrance to the city's post office on Lan Xang Avenue when I went to check my mail one Monday morning. I only went to the post office about once a week, as I rarely received mail during my time in Laos, and it was always something of a treat. The Lao postal service did not actually deliver in Vientiane, so if you wanted an address to which people could send things, you needed to sign up for a mailbox. It was an indication of just how small Vientiane was, that all of this capital city's mailboxes fit into two floors of a small shack in the grounds of the post office, and that a good number of them remained empty. The mail room was reminiscent of the one at my college, a musty room where students would stop off after lunch to check if that eagerly anticipated package or admission letter had arrived. In Vientiane, each box was a simple affair of plywood and hand-painted blue numbers—mine was number 9083—and could only be opened with a key that one obtained at the main desk for a deposit of a few hundred kip. When I first opened mine, I had to clear out the cobwebs and dust.

After I checked my mailbox that Monday morning—as usual, there was nothing inside—I noticed as I drove around town that the hammer and sickle, along with the Lao national flag, was flying all over town—not only on every government ministry, but most private enterprises as well. That night, the city's nightclubs shut down a bit earlier than usual, and the police were out on the streets in full force, flagging down motorbikes and cars on Lan Xang Avenue in the late evening and checking papers even more rigorously than usual. *Les mouches* were up to something.

They were preparing for the forty-fifth anniversary of the founding of the Party, which would be held on March 22nd, 2000. By mid-week, banners were everywhere, gracing even the façade of the Victory nightclub just around the corner from my house, where teenagers gathered every night to drink whiskey and dance to the latest Thai imports. I felt privileged to be living in Laos in 2000, which promised to be quite a year. Not only was it the new millennium and the anniversary of the Party's founding, but it also marked the twenty-fifth anniversary of the founding of the Lao PDR and Kaysone's eightieth birthday. And, lest we forget, it was Visit Laos Year. In short, it was time to Party.

As I'd learned at the Kaysone museum, the Party had been founded in 1955 by a group of Lao representatives of the Indochina Communist Party. The conflict between the Vietnamese-supported communists and the US-backed royalists was quickly evolving into a bitter civil war. Soon, Laos would be the only country in the world where the armed forces on both sides of a civil conflict were entirely financed by foreign powers. The US, from the safety of Kilometer Six, was willing to spend almost anything to prop up the royalist regime and prevent the communists from taking power; from 1955 to 1963, it contributed more aid per capita to Laos than it did to South Vietnam. Beginning in the late 1960s, Laos' leadership engaged in a series of ill-fated coalition experiments, through which the royalists sought to neutralize the communist forces by incorporating them into the Royal Lao Government. But in the face of such strong and unrelenting outside influence from both sides, these coalitions were bound to fail. In the end, the success of the "revolution" had little to do with a popular demand for communism. Kaysone and his forces capitalized on the citizens' desire for a strong and independent nation, free from foreign influence.

By the time the forty-fifth anniversary of the Party's founding rolled around, the revolution was in a rut. During the week of the celebration, Party members spent most of their time stuck in conference halls, listening to endless speeches by cadres about the past, and longing for the next coffee break. According to the *Vientiane Times*, they were busy discussing "the tradition of struggle and deeds of the Party for the cause of national independence in the past, and of national defense and development at present."

The *Vientiane Times* was the English-language mouthpiece of the government, founded in 1994 to serve the growing expat community in Vientiane. It was produced by the government's official news agency, and, although this fact was not well publicized, it employed one or two native English speakers in addition to its staff of local journalists. The one foreigner I knew who worked at the *Times* was an Englishman in his fifties named David, who had played Scrooge brilliantly in the Vientiane Players' annual Christmas production. David wrote under Lao pseudonyms, but you could always tell which articles were his; they were the ones that were actually in English. It was frustrating for a man like David—who not only was well-read but also could write well—to work at the *Times*, where he couldn't write about anything of substance. The paper printed all the news that fit, but none that really mattered. There was no real news, but David did amuse himself by slipping the occasional literary flourish into the dull articles he was forced to compose. When you read a headline like "Lao Cotton Branches Out to Sew its Seeds," you knew that David or another of his non-Lao colleagues had been at work.

While I did read the *Vientiane Times* for news about Laos—after all, there was nothing else out there—I mostly leafed through its pages for comic relief. The headlines drew your attention to important events like "Meeting with Lao-Born People in the USA" and "Lao Ambassador to Slovakia Presents Credentials." Or scintillating international topics like "Lao-Polish Relations." Many articles spoke of the generous international aid Laos received from its foreign friends: "Australia Grants Computer to Luang Prabang Museum." Or "Vietnam Presents Kidney Machine to Laos." A whole kidney machine? Oh, Vietnam, you shouldn't have. Many articles spoke of the country's goals for the future, some that weren't so ambitious: "Taps for Nearly Everyone by 2020," and "A Time for Road Regulations." I wondered when that time would come. Some headlines were hardly enlightening: "Effort Must Continue."

One of my favorite articles, "First Frog Farm in Vientiane," demonstrated the paucity of relevant news in the pages of the *Times*:

While not all societies have formed an appreciation for consuming frogs, here in Vientiane municipality the little croaking creatures have been a staple of the Lao diet for as long as most can remember. Mrs. Deng hopes to continue to obtain funds through loans from the Agriculture Promotion Bank to further

*expand her frog farming business, and she also plans to produce
information booklets and continue giving advice on frog farming
techniques to all those who may be interested in becoming frog
farmers themselves.*

During the anniversary week, the Party cadres were busy participating in meetings about the country's glorious past and bright
future, but according to the *Vientiane Times*, they didn't have much
to talk about. One captivating article, entitled "Party Jubilee," read:
"Party policy is fine. Under the Party leadership, the country enjoys
political stability and social order. The people live in unity, with
their living conditions improving gradually."

Oh, really?

In fact, outside the Party's meeting rooms, things weren't nearly
as rosy as the *Times* would have had us believe. A few weeks before,
I had received a rare message from the US Embassy. It was a Public
Announcement that read: "US citizens traveling in Laos are advised
to avoid travel to the Muang Khoune and Paxai districts in Xieng
Khouang province. The Lao government has restricted travel by foreign tourists to Muang Khoune district in Xieng Khouang province
because of poor road conditions."

But poor roads weren't the problem—we had plenty of those
right there in Vientiane: "The US government also has received
credible reports of violent incidents in that district. Travelers to
certain areas of Xieng Khouang province, now including Muang
Khoune and Paxai districts, run the risk of ambush by insurgents
or bandits."

While the embassy had diplomatically failed to mention it, these
incidents of violence in Xieng Khouang, the province about 110
miles north of the capital that had been so heavily bombed by the
Americans during the war, were not random. In fact, reports in the
international press indicated that Hmong insurgents were staging
organized attacks in the province, and that the government had
begun to respond in kind. The insurgent group was a remnant of
the CIA-backed Hmong forces that had fought the communists
during the war. Already, there were reports of military convoys and
helicopters taking troops north from Vientiane to Xieng Khouang,

and one Hmong village had reportedly already been razed by government forces.

But you wouldn't hear about any of this in the *Vientiane Times*, or from any official source during the anniversary celebration.

The Party treated the insurgency in the northeast in the same way it treated most problems—by ignoring it. As a result, the Party had lost most of its credibility. To commemorate the anniversary, the *Times* interviewed a few people on the streets about how they felt about the Party. Perhaps the most honest account of all was that of one Daovaone, a primary school teacher in Vientiane, who began with the usual positive comments: "I admire our Party for being very active for many years. It has further improved living conditions in Laos step by step. For the future I hope that the Party will do more for the workers, support the poor, and take measures against unemployment." But then she added, "I hope that I will become a Party member one day because members have advantages for work or study."

The *Vientiane Times* surely didn't intend it, but this was the closest the paper came to printing an open criticism of the Party. Daovaone's desire to join the Party turned out not to be much of a ringing endorsement of the revolution—she just wanted the perks and privileges that only membership in the elite club could provide.

Later that week, I learned first-hand about one such perk. I'd heard rumors around town that as part of the anniversary celebration, the government's official drama troupe would be performing at the new Lao National Culture Hall downtown, the grand edifice constructed by the Chinese contractor for which Ming worked. It had been open for a few weeks now, but I had yet to meet anyone other than Ming who'd seen the interior of the building—and I was determined to get inside. None of my colleagues at work knew anything about a performance, but I'd learned not to trust very much they told me. After work that Friday, I stopped by the Culture Hall to see what I could find. At the entrance, beneath the grandiose columns, I encountered a stern policeman standing guard.

"Excuse me, will there be a performance here tonight?" I asked.

"Yes," he replied, surprised that I could speak some Lao.

"What time?"

"Eight o'clock."

"Is it possible for me to come and watch?"

"No."

"So it's just for the officials, then. Only for the *pu nyai*?"

"Yes, only for the *pu nyai*."

So much about life in Laos was reserved for the *pu nyai*, or "big people," the government officials and Party cadres that ran the show. Daovaone's words in the *Vientiane Times* rang true as I considered what it would take for an average Lao citizen to ever get his foot in the door of this hall, a gift to the "people of Laos." In any case, I'd been here long enough to know that, despite his pressed uniform and epaulets, this guard's opinion wasn't the final word. So I went home for a shower and some dinner, resolved to come back and attend the performance.

When I returned at eight o'clock that evening, the entire building was lit up by halogen lamps, which I imagined consumed more electricity in a single night than most neighborhoods in Vientiane did in a week. A crowd of families had gathered in the park out front. The fountain had been switched on, and children were splashing about in the bubbling water. As I watched these kids enjoying the fruits of Laos' improved diplomatic relations with China, my misgivings about the development project disappeared, if only for a moment; this was the only public space of its kind in Vientiane, after all, and the children seemed to be having fun. I couldn't help but wonder, though, for how long the government would be able to keep the place up and running. That much electricity wasn't cheap.

At the entrance, I joined the crowd of ticket-holders pushing to get in the doors, and easily slid past the guard I'd encountered that afternoon. Inside, I was ushered toward the auditorium along with a group of guests by a polite young woman who, if she was surprised to see me there, didn't show it. Just as I was swept into the performance hall, I heard the guard's voice and a slight commotion in the lobby. But before he could catch up with me, I was inside.

By Lao standards, the auditorium was gigantic, certainly the largest indoor facility in the country. It contained 1,500 seats, on two levels, and a vast stage draped with a red curtain. The design was simple, clear white walls and simple red seats, and included no ornamentation at all. As I looked around for a free seat, I realized that I was entirely out of place. It wasn't that I was the only non-Lao in the crowd; this was nothing new. But I was also the only person not in uniform. All around me were men and women dressed in neatly pressed standard-issue military uniforms. I quickly took a seat behind a group of surprised young recruits, who seemed eager to speak to me, but unsure if they'd be permitted. Luckily, I didn't have to try to look inconspicuous for long—the house lights went out soon after I sat down.

"Welcome, soldiers and police officers!" said the announcer.

It turned out that I had snuck into a special commemorative performance by the national drama troupe in honor of the nation's enlisted men and women. I was clearly not supposed to be there.

The curtain went up, and the performance, a piece of revolutionary theater, began. The play told the story of Sithong, a hero who had sacrificed his life for the cause of independence during the struggle against the French in the 1940s. Sithong had been a member of the Lao Issara, or Free Lao, movement, which had formed the first post-World War II government in Laos in 1945. The movement's hopes for independence were dashed when the French re-occupied Laos in 1946 and established the country as a constitutional monarchy within the French Union. The first Royal Lao Government was marked by elite clanism, regionalism, and only nominal central control. The Lao Issara government-in-exile fled to Thailand, and soon after, the First Indochina War broke out.

The play was set during the years when the French were still very much in control, and one of the central characters was a French military officer. The uncommonly tall actor who played the role of the sinister Frenchman did not take a subtle approach: he swaggered about the stage and barked at the other actors in a deep nasal voice. He spoke with the standard-issue foreigners' accent, mangling basic Lao phrases and condescending to those around him; the performance reminded me of the old comedy recording I'd heard during the trip up north I'd taken with Khit and the gang at the NTA a few months before. He spent most of his time making insulting remarks about Lao people—they were "lazy," "stupid," and "impossible" to lead—striking innocent peasant women, and torturing young would-be revolutionaries. After committing each of these dastardly deeds, the "Frenchman" would let out a tremendous evil laugh and stalk off the stage.

Most of the audience found this shtick hilarious, but I did notice a number of people sitting near me who seemed vaguely uncomfortable with the performance. Each time the Frenchman took the stage, these folks would turn their heads, ever so slightly, and glance in my direction. What did the *falang* think of this? Should we really be laughing so hard with him around? On the one hand, they clearly wanted to laugh at the stupidity and arrogance of the Frenchman onstage, but they also seemed embarrassed by the racist tone of the performance.

As for me, I found it all hilarious, and tired to make my reaction clear by laughing loudly each time the Frenchman tripped up or mispronounced a Lao word. This helped to put those around me at ease, although the similarity between my heavy, plodding laugh and the guffaws of the stereotype onstage did make me feel self-conscious.

The audience, on the other hand, didn't seem to take the play seriously at all. The performance was far from polished, and each time an actor made even the slightest mistake, everyone would erupt into raucous laughter. In one critical scene, in which Sithong is threatened at gunpoint by a French soldier, the actor's weapon suddenly split into two pieces and fell to the floor. The audience found this hilarious, and the rest of the scene was drowned out by a chorus of giggles. But the soldiers and police officers didn't laugh only when gaffes were made. In fact, whenever a character was beaten, shot, dragged across the stage, or pushed to his death, everyone would laugh. The cartoonish performance style didn't help; each blow was accompanied by a drum beat and a clash of the cymbals offstage. The performance often seemed like a comic book come to life.

During the climactic battle between the revolutionaries and the French, Sithong tragically dies. But the French ultimately lose, and the play ended with an upbeat victory march. As the proud freedom fighters—including the requisite woman and ethnic minority—marched across the stage, they waved the flag of a newly independent Laos and sang the national anthem:

For all time the Lao people have glorified their Fatherland,
United in heart, spirit, and vigor as one.
Resolutely moving forwards,
Respecting and increasing the dignity of the Lao people
And proclaiming the right to be their own masters.

In order to give the impression of an endless stream of marching soldiers returning home from the front to the welcoming arms of their adoring fellow citizens, the actors would make their way across the stage, dash around the back of the set, and enter the stage once again from the opposite side. Unfortunately, there weren't many actors portraying the revolutionary soldiers, and the stage was enormous, so the well-wishing townsfolk were often left alone on the stage, waving to one another. When the same soldiers who'd exited stage right appeared again at stage left, gasping for breath, many in the audience couldn't help but snicker.

As the soldiers continued to march across the stage, black-and-white footage of the revolution was projected onto a large screen above them. Images of a much younger and more virile President Khamtay and his late boss Kaysone presided over the chaos below. The actors continued to sing the anthem, encouraging the audience to clap and sing along:

The Lao people of all origins are equal
And will no longer allow imperialists and traitors to harm them.
The entire people will safeguard the independence
And the freedom of the Lao nation.
They are resolved to struggle for victory
In order to lead the nation to prosperity.

As soon as the national anthem was sung through once, some in the audience began to head for the doors. Before long, the forlorn revolutionary heroes on stage, now clapping and marching in place, were all alone. By the time the minister of culture climbed up on stage to offer his sincere congratulations to the actors, half the audience was already outside.

I, on the other hand, couldn't get enough of this revolutionary fervor. I had come to Laos in part because it was a communist country. But I'd arrived only to find that the government was doing its best to hide its communist credentials from the outside world. This was the first real celebration of Laos' revolutionary history I'd been exposed to—and it was no coincidence that I was the only foreigner in the auditorium. I stayed until the very end, clapping along to the national anthem and waving enthusiastically to the actors onstage. When the curtain closed, quickly and without cere-mony, and the house lights went up, I found myself alone in the massive hall. Even the minister of culture had gone home.

Unlike me, the rest of the audience had probably heard the story of Sithong—who was in all likelihood a fabrication, or at least a composite—one too many times. The play had clearly not been updated for decades, and it likely struck many in the Culture Hall that night as entirely irrelevant to the concerns of contemporary Laos. With an economy in free-fall, an incipient civil war in the provinces, and the continuing scourge of land-mines left over from the revolution, it seemed right to question why the Party was spending so much time and money on this anniversary celebration. What did they have to celebrate? To be sure, the cavemen who remained in power could rightfully point to the glorious history in which they had participated. But if people were going to celebrate the Party's past, they needed to know their country had a future.

Outside the hall, trucks waited to take the young soldiers and police officers away. The men and women were packed tightly in and driven off, perhaps to fight the insurgents in Xieng Khouang. They had been drafted into fighting for a regime that couldn't even provide them with seats, and that had nothing more than tired old propaganda to inspire them. The revolutionary struggle was surely glorious at one time, but the sheen had long since worn off. The *pu nyai* were having their fun, but that's about it.

I watched the trucks drive off, and behind me the lights that had illuminated the Culture Hall all evening were shut off. As I walked home, I thought of the president's daughter and her shopping sprees, her father and his new White House, and General Cheng and the clear-cutting of Laos' forests.

What would Sithong have thought of all of this?

Thank You Very Much

Open wide your eyes and ears, but know how to
remain discrete and to respect secrets.
Lao Proverb.

The chocolate cake at Just for Fun was the best in all of Laos. That may sound like an exaggeration, but it is a claim I feel I can make with some authority; I've tried every chocolate cake for sale in the country. The dried coconut curry and drunken noodles at this little Thai restaurant were, of course, extraordinary as well. But I really looked forward to the chocolate cake, of which I partook only on special occasions.

And so it was that I found myself at Just for Fun on a Thursday evening in March enjoying a cup of coffee and cake with Ming. I was leaving Laos soon, and this would be one of our last dinners together. Although it was already nine o'clock, and the restaurant was about to close, we savored our dessert as we sat outside, talking about what the future might hold. Neither of us were sure where we'd be in a year, and what our experiences in Laos would mean for the rest of our lives. Who knew what might happen?

All of a sudden, our ruminations were interrupted by a tremendous explosion. The sound was deafening. Our table shook, my coffee spilled. The big bang had come from down the street, near the Fountain Circle. At first, I thought it might have been an old car, or some falling scaffolding. But it was far too loud for that.

After a few minutes, a steady stream of residents and tourists alike began to move toward the apparent source of the explosion. Ming and I quickly paid the bill, left our half-eaten cake on the table, and joined the crowd. Children in pajamas, women in towels—virtually everyone in the neighborhood had emerged from their homes. They were all walking in the direction of a restaurant named Kop Chai Deu, or "Thank You Very Much."

Kop Chai Deu was a small outdoor drinking garden just off the Fountain Circle, opposite the Namphu restaurant. Opened only a few months before, it was the sort of innovative establishment the Lao tourism industry desperately needed. The owner, Chanti Deunsavanh, was a well-known Lao writer who had recently been awarded the Association of Southeast Asian Nations literature prize. The backdrop to the restaurant was the façade of an old French villa, lit with soft floodlights. Rather than renovating the villa itself, the owner had decided to highlight the beauty of its crumbling façade by opening up the restaurant in the garden. The Kop Chai Deu quickly became a popular hangout for tourists, young expats, and the occasional Lao customer as well. The food wasn't great—the menu was limited to simple items like fried rice and grilled meat—but the Beer Lao was cold and the atmosphere unbeatable.

That Thursday night, however, the atmosphere was deeply unsettling. While policemen were already in place, shooing onlookers away, I was able to get close enough to see that a large hole had been blown through the side of the villa. Shards of glass were scattered around the garden. I could hear a few cries emanating from the site, but there was no ambulance to be seen. For the aftermath of what seemed to have been a great explosion, it seemed oddly quiet. Ming and I said good-night and I drove home, wondering what could possibly have gone wrong.

When I drove by Kop Chai Deu the next morning, all traces of the incident had been erased. The hole in the villa façade had been patched up, the glass swept away. By dusk, a new batch of tourists was already enjoying the beer garden.

As for the government, which it seems had forced the restaurant to re-open, it simply chose not to acknowledge that anything had happened. The national news service refused to address the subject for days. Across the border in Thailand, the event had already made the nightly news, and even the international press had taken notice. But from official Laos, there was not a sound.

Of course, by now the entire city knew. The rumors had begun to fly almost as soon as the glass and debris had settled the night before. It had been a grenade, some said. No, said others, it was a gas explosion. No, it was just a broken transformer. Maybe it had something to do with the water pipes? Nine people had died. No, only two. No, six people had been injured, and none had died. Only foreigners had been injured. No, hang on, a Lao waiter had been hurt. At the office later in the week, Seng even told me that a Japanese tourist had been split in two, his body parts strewn about the restaurant.

When the government finally acknowledged that an explosion had in fact taken place, it claimed that it had been the result of a gas leak at the restaurant. The government tried its best to keep all reliable information about the incident out of Vientiane. For days, delivery of the *Bangkok Post* and *The Nation* was interrupted. An Australian Broadcasting Corporation reporter and cameraman who had been at Kop Chai Deu at the time of the explosion—and who had been able to film the aftermath—were detained for four hours. The police confiscated their camera and videotape.

When we were once again granted access to the Thai newspapers, they weren't much help. The reporting was based almost entirely on rumors, obtained from all sorts of "informed" and "highly placed" sources in Vientiane.

Everyone had something to say—from the vice president of the Lao Writers' Association, who thought the attack was the result of a business dispute, to a Western diplomat who saw the blast as "a direct challenge to the powers-that-be" in Vientiane.

I pieced together an account of the evening by talking to friends who had been at the restaurant at the time of the explosion. On the evening of March 30th, two men had been driving their motorbikes along Setthathirath Road past Kop Chai Deu. Just after nine o'clock, one lobbed an explosive device over the fence and into the garden. The object first landed on the canvas awning above the grill, then fell to the seating area below, where it exploded in the middle of a group of customers.

At that point, chaos ensued. *Tuk-tuks*, which as usual were parked at the Fountain Circle nearby, substituted for ambulances and were summoned to drive the wounded to the hospital. Some drivers demanded fares of up to two dollars to make the five-minute drive.

At the hospital, the staff was entirely unprepared, and victims with no medical experience performed operations on themselves. Luckily, Australian Embassy officials arrived at the scene and convinced government authorities to re-open the Friendship Bridge to Thailand—which was only open during the day—so that the seriously wounded could be taken to a hospital in Nong Khai.

In the end, at least 13 people, including at least six foreigners, were injured. Tourists from the UK, Germany, Australia, and Denmark were among the victims. At least three foreigners were hospitalized in Thailand due to shrapnel wounds. A waiter at the restaurant was the most seriously injured.

To this day, why the attack occurred remains unclear. After the gas explosion theory was ruled out—the restaurant had only a charcoal grill—the government began to characterize the incident as a terrorist attack. The official daily, *Pasason*, reported that the Party Central Committee had "asked the general public to co-operate with police in the investigation to safeguard the peaceful life of the capital's residents and to foil terrorism."

Some officials claimed that the terrorists intended to sabotage the Visit Laos Year campaign by discrediting Vientiane's ability to provide a secure environment for tourists just when the government was banking on the sector as an important source of revenue. An implied connection was drawn between the bombing and the continuing unrest out in the provinces. The wave of irrepressible insurgent movements had washed up in the nation's capital.

But no one I talked to really believed that the incident had been the work of terrorists. Many thought it had something to do with an emerging rift within the Party, a division along multiple fault lines that threatened the current regime's hold on power. Younger Party members against their elders. Reformers versus hard-line socialists. Southerners against northerners. And those who were allied with Vietnam against those, like the ascendant foreign minister, Somsavat Lengsavad, who were close to China. Perhaps the struggle to shape the country's future was spilling out into the streets.

I wasn't immune to conspiracy theories; almost as soon as I heard about the bomb, I thought of the mysterious Saigon restaurant explosion in *The Quiet American*.

Then again, maybe all of this was just the result of a personal vendetta against the owner of the Kop Chai Deu. Did he really deserve to succeed as an entrepreneur, even after winning the prestigious ASEAN literature prize?

To me, the most plausible explanation was one that no one around town had given much thought to. I figured that the two men on motorbikes weren't men at all, but teenage boys, gang members high on amphetamines, who had nothing better to do that Thursday evening than to throw an old grenade they had found into a restaurant crowded with *falang* tourists.

One could understand why the government wasn't eager for people to explore this story. The timing, after all, couldn't have been worse. The Party had just completed its grand anniversary celebration. The National Assembly had just convened to discuss the criminal code and measures to increase social stability. And reliable reports of Vietnamese troop movements in Xieng Khouang province—designed to help the Lao security forces suppress the rebels, the Vietnamese presence had risen to at least 10,000 troops—were appearing in the international press. Now someone was causing trouble right in the capital, where the government's power was strongest. For the first time since the communists had taken power in 1975, bringing a welcome end to decades of civil war, Vientiane seemed to be getting less, not more, secure.

Whatever the real explanation for the Kop Chai Deu bombing, it was nothing but bad news for the Party. Vientiane's peaceful existence had been shattered, and whatever faith its residents had ever had in the government had been severely diminished. The city would never be the same again. And a new era in Laos' history had begun.

Forgetting

Leaving Laos wasn't easy. I had arrived in Vientiane with no language ability, no experience living in a developing country, and no local contacts. But somehow I had been able to craft a life for myself that I truly loved. For the first time, I had found a place to live, made the most of an often impossible job, and found some good friends—all from scratch. My house, sitting just around the corner from the Mekong, was far larger and more graceful than anything I could afford in the West. My job had been filled with frustrations, but the occasional productive day had made me feel as if I was contributing something worthwhile to the country. And the extraordinary individuals I had met, from places as far away as China and France to as close as the house next door, had enhanced my life in ways I'd never imagined possible. Conversations with Ming at the Liao Ning and Mon at the noodle shop next to the NTA, with my next-door neighbor Bing over iced coffee, and

Michel over *confis de canard*, were at the center of my daily life in Vientiane. Never again would I be able to structure my life so exclusively around friendship; free from the constraints of a demanding job or the responsibility of a family, I could spend as much time as I liked thinking about and learning from other people's experiences—and my own.

Nevertheless, by the time the spring of 2000 rolled around, I knew it was time to leave. For one thing, the Visit Laos Year campaign was coming to an end. While I'm quite sure the campaign itself had very little to do with it (and certainly I had contributed nothing), the number of international visitors to Laos had exploded during the period I lived in Vientiane. Among backpackers in Southeast Asia, Laos had become a destination they couldn't miss. Newly refurbished colonial-era hotels and restaurants in Vientiane and Luang Prabang attracted high-end travelers like the American tour group that flew by private jet around Southeast Asia and touched down in Laos twice while I was at the NTA. Government policy had certainly influenced this change: in the fall of 1998, a visitor to Laos had to go through an arduous visa application process; by the spring of 2000, that same tourist could simply buy a visa on arrival at most entry points. Laos would never be Thailand or Vietnam—thank goodness—but almost overnight, it had become the fastest-growing tourist destination in Southeast Asia.

To say that the Lao government had fully embraced the idea of international tourism would be misleading, but it had recognized the benefits of opening up to foreigners and their dollars. I had worked with my friends and colleagues at the NTA not only to promote Laos and to provide tourists with some advice about what to do once they arrived, but also to consider the potential problems of tourism development, including increased recreational drug use, environmental destruction, and serious cultural disruption. None of these issues had been resolved, by any means, but I did feel comfortable that, perhaps with the power of General Cheng behind it, the NTA was in a strong position to influence the course that tourism development in Laos would take in the years to come. In any case, the money from Princeton had run out, and the NTA wasn't about to start paying me.

Then again, jobs in Vientiane weren't hard to find. I would have been able to secure a position with an NGO or international organization or, as a last resort, as an English teacher at a language school. If I had really wanted to stay, I could have found a way. But that was just it: if I had stayed, I wasn't sure I'd ever leave. I could imagine myself living in Vientiane for years, applying to renew my visa every few months and holding my breath as I awaited a new lease on my paradisiacal lifestyle. I feared ending up like Joe, another quiet, bitter American who had renounced his ties to the US but had yet to find a home for himself in Asia. The ease with which I'd slipped into a comfortable routine in Vientiane frightened me, for it wasn't clear where it would lead. Among other things, I'd been entirely unsuccessful in love, repelled rather than stimulated by the difficulties of pursuing relationships with Lao women.

But the main reason I felt I had to leave was more simple: everyone else was always leaving. While I'd lived there, most of my closest friends had left. Michel had moved on to teach French in Korea; Gong had returned to China. Sure, it was fun to meet the occasional visiting consultant, to learn from the mishaps of the likes of Kawabata and Nigel as they floated from one poor country to the next. But this was no substitute for the real friendships I'd established, and it was difficult to watch as the men and women I had come to know disappeared. As for my Lao friends, if they hadn't found a way out already, most were trying desperately to leave. I couldn't live in a place that people were always trying to escape from.

In the months after I left Vientiane, I followed the news from Laos as closely as I could, and it struck me that I'd made the right decision. On a Monday evening about a month after the Kop Chai Deu bombing, another explosion took place near the Evening Market. On the rare occasions when I had actually cooked a meal in Vientiane, it had been to the Evening Market that I'd ventured for ingredients. Fresh fruits, vegetables, hand-made egg noodles, and small plastic bags of peanut sauce—these were what I thought of when I heard mention of the market. But now, far different images came to mind. Again, the details of this incident were unclear. Some reported seeing a person on a motorcycle lob a grenade toward the open-air market. Others mentioned a violent confrontation between the owner of a bar across the street and a group of unruly customers. When the owner had asked the drunks to leave, they had refused. He had then emerged from the bar carrying a grenade, which had exploded in his hand, killing him and injuring two others. The Ministry of Foreign Affairs maintained that a new army recruit who lived near the market had accidentally dropped a small training bomb, setting it off and killing him. He had just returned home from military training.

As I observed Laos from afar, I read in horror as the explosions kept coming. By July, there had been at least five blasts in Vientiane. In addition to the Kop Chai Deu and the Evening Market, bombs had exploded at the central bus station, at a downtown hotel, and on a bus. No one claimed responsibility for any of the incidents. Then, on July 3rd, about sixty rebels armed with assault rifles and grenade launchers crossed into Southern Laos from Thailand. They attacked the border officials, taking hostages before being gunned down by government forces. At least five of the rebels were killed, and 28 were captured after retreating into Thailand. According to Thai reports, the raiders were linked to Crown Prince Soulivong Savang, heir to the Lao throne, who at the time was working to build support in the West for an overthrow of the communist government. The insurgents, a group of inexperienced fighters including an elderly taxi driver, had been promised money and property in a liberated Laos.

At the end of July, seven people were injured when a bomb went off at the post office in Vientiane. The explosion took place at eleven o'clock in the morning, just about the time when I myself would have strolled over from the NTA to check my mail. In January, an explosion at the Friendship Bridge injured a group of bystanders, and in February a small explosion occurred next to a market in Luang Prabang. Again, no one claimed responsibility for these incidents.

In the face of all of this chaos, Laos' top rulers retreated from view. It was left to lower officials to come up with explanations, and some tried to dismiss the incidents—the first of their kind in 25 years—as nothing to be concerned about. The foreign minister told the international press that the bombs could have been caused by business disputes or personal vendettas. "All countries have both bad and good people," he said. "Why are these bombs a matter of surprise to Western reporters?"

Newspapers in Laos did not report on the government's investigations into the bombings.

The Lao government vehemently denied any internal rift. But the Party was clearly losing control. The social contract that had held Laos together since the communists had taken power—in return for the re-establishment of order and a modicum of prosperity, the people would keep quiet and let the cavemen stay in power for as long as they pleased—was unraveling. Due to the government's mishandling of the Asian financial crisis, Laos' economy was heading south while the rest of Southeast Asia was recovering.

Western reporters liked to describe Vientiane as the "sleepy capital" of a "tiny communist nation" with "serene smiles and placid ways." Laos did at times seem like a happy place where nothing ever went wrong. But beneath the surface, deep and inescapable tensions had begun to emerge. When men and women like Seng were not receiving their government salaries and had to work weekends to supplement their devastated savings; when government offices relied on the largesse of foreign donors just to keep their printers stocked with paper; when well-educated twentysomethings like Paul saw no future for themselves in their own country; and when teenagers in Laos' urban areas looked to amphetamines as an escape from the boredom of their lives—when all of this was happening, it was to be expected that the government would face some sort of opposition. And since no dissent or dialogue of any kind was permitted in Laos, these frustrations were channeled into violence.

While I was living in Laos, one group of courageous citizens had made a non-violent attempt to force political change in Vientiane. In October 1999, on the very day that I'd been enjoying the boat races as part of *Boun Awk Phansaa*, at least fifty students and teachers at the National University had held a peaceful protest outside the Presidential Palace. I had been just a few minutes away, but heard nothing about it until days later. In an open letter I found on the website of a US-based anti-communist group, the protesters called for respect for human rights, the release of political prisoners, a multi-party political system, and elections for a new National Assembly. This brave call would be their last. While refusing to acknowledge that anything had happened, the government unceremoniously carted the protesters off to prison. At last count, at least five remained in detention without trial.

In the end, the most important weapon the government had was Laos' political vacuum: it was the only game in town. Unlike in Burma, there was no organized opposition. There had never been a student movement, as there had been in China. In Laos, there was no alternative to the Party. Even the disaffected royalists across the world in France and the US had little to offer their compatriots in Laos other than reminiscences about glorious days gone by. There was no guarantee that any of them could do a better job of governing Laos than the communists.

The people of Laos were stuck.

As time passed, I became less fastidious about checking up on the situation in Laos. I could feel the country slipping away, my experience there receding into memory. I enrolled in law school in the US, and began to engage, however reluctantly, in an attempt to understand the intricacies of tort law and the rule against perpetuities. Laos may have been falling apart, but the country rarely made it into the headlines in the West.

I had to work hard to find out what was happening in Vientiane, and my contacts in Laos didn't always feel free to speak openly about the situation there. The Lao government did its best to keep tabs on Internet usage, and was known to intercept e-mail communication. The government controlled all domestic Internet servers, and occasionally blocked access to sites that were critical of the Party; in October 2000, the National Internet Control Committee passed Internet-related regulations, making "disturbing the peace and happiness of the community" a crime.

My Lao language skills began to fade, and soon I found myself struggling to recall the names of places that not long before had been entirely familiar. I found no one with whom I could even share my experiences in Laos, let alone practice speaking the language. To meet someone who had even visited the country was rare; to find someone who had lived there was impossible. Most of my classmates had no reaction when I mentioned that I'd lived in Laos. For American students who had spent the previous two years reaping the benefits of an overheated economy and steeped in the petty political scandals that had dominated American public life, a life in Laos must have seemed irrelevant and uninteresting. What bearing could it possibly have had on their lives and their future aspirations? Surrounded by disinterest, I found it difficult to draw connections between my time in Laos and the life I was leading in Cambridge. A wall had been erected between the two experiences, and only occasionally and with much effort would I succeed in climbing over it. I couldn't think of Laos casually; to really remember my life there required an almost complete immersion in the images and senses of the place. Given all the work I had to do, and the new life I wanted to forge for myself, I simply couldn't afford such excursions.

During a break from school, I took a trip to Paris, where Michel was now living. I looked forward to exploring the city, from the ancient gravestones of Père-la-Chaise to the cafés of Montmartre, and enjoying some good wine. But most of all, I looked forward to the opportunity to talk with Michel about Laos. We met at a small café near the Bastille, a funky little place run by a lesbian couple who served up a rather suspect, but in the end not unenjoyable *plat du jour*. As usual, Michel was brimming with enthusiasm. He talked excitedly about the new life he was building with his wife, whom he had met in Korea. He told me all about a jazz festival that was in town and the exhibits I needed to see before I left. When it came to Laos, however, Michel had little to say. In the time since he'd returned to France, he had made no effort to connect to the large Lao community in Paris, and had forgotten most of what he had known of the language. While I wanted to talk about Laos, Michel seemed to want to avoid it.

"Do you ever talk with anyone about Laos?" I asked him.

"No, not really," he replied.

"But don't you ever think about it?"

"Well, sometimes. But not much, Brett. In fact, I *can't* think about it. *Je n'ai pas le droit d'y penser.* I don't have the right to think about it."

Michel felt that he didn't have the luxury to think about his life in Laos. He couldn't allow his mind to travel back to a time before he had even met his wife. His life in Paris was complete—and completely separate from his life in Laos. He simply preferred not to scale the wall that kept the two experiences apart. It just wasn't worth it.

I know what Michel means. I often feel as though I don't have the right to think about Laos, that there's no space in my life today for memories of it. I wonder if the two experiences will ever be reconciled. But I know that my time in Laos was far more than a two-year break. It remains an integral part of my life today, here and now, and the person I have become. The way I think about the world. And my place in it. So I try to remember. As I sit at my desk in Cambridge, I try to recapture the details of my life in Laos. . . .

But it's hard, even, to imagine I was ever there. It seems so far away, sometimes. So far from this life.

About the Author

Brett Dakin grew up in London, and has lived in New York, Washington, D.C., Tokyo, Vientiane, Vienna, and Sarajevo. He has worked for the Japanese parliament, the US Department of State, the United Nations, and the Human Rights Chamber for Bosnia and Herzegovina.

His writing has appeared in the *International Herald Tribune, The Washington Post,* the *Harvard Human Rights Journal, The Christian Science Monitor,* the *Journal of Oriental Studies,* and the *International Journal of Comparative Sociology.* Brett is co-author of the *Insight Guide to Laos & Cambodia,* and was Laos correspondent for *Traveller* magazine.

He now lives in Cambridge, Massachusetts, where he is a student at Harvard Law School.